I0458402

Someone Like Me

SHEILA MAE

Copyright © 2025 Sheila Mae

Paperback: 978-1-968519-06-3
Hardback: 978-1-968519-07-0
Ebook: 978-1-968519-52-0

All rights reserved. No part of this publication may be reproduced, distributed, or transmitted in any form or by any electronic or mechanical means, without the prior written permission of the publisher, except in the case of brief quotations embodied in critical reviews and certain other noncommercial uses permitted by copyright law.

This is a work of fiction. All of the characters, names, incidents, organizations, and dialogue in this novel are either the products of the author's imagination or are used fictitiously.

Scripture quotations are taken from the Holy Bible, New International Version®, NIV®. Copyright © 1973, 1978, 1984, 2011 by Biblica, Inc.™ Used by permission of Zondervan. All rights reserved worldwide.

Ordering Information:

Books to Life Marketing Ltd
128 City Road, London, EC1V 2NX, UK

Printed in the United States of America

Acknowledgements / Dedication

First and foremost, I want to acknowledge and thank my heavenly father for blessing me with his guide to creating his novel.

Secondly, I want to thank my mother for allowing me to write about her upbringing and her life. I had a lot of questions and she simply answered them. This is dedicated to you mama!

Last but not least, I want to thank all the lovely people who believed in me and supported me in the journey of writing my first novel. Thanks, y'all!!!

PART ONE

1

*D*OWN IN THE Bayou, colored folk could only afford but so much, let alone a nice funeral. Still, when they heard that the good Lord had called one of his children home, they came to pay their respects. More so it was like an event. There just wasn't too much of anything going on down there. It was either, just getting by, living from pay check to pay check, or easy living as folks say. Now when you hear folks say easy living, they don't mean having money saved up for a rainy day. What it means is that they just don't care; for today will take care of today and tomorrow…well, let's just see what happens.

Everyone pretty much stayed to themselves. Folks mind their own business, so it seemed on the surface if you're not from down there. However, once you've lived there for a minute… Lord have mercy. You'll see that the Bayou was off the chain. Because down there, you have some folks that are ignorant, and they know that they're ignorant, and that's okay. But when you got some folks that are ignorant, and they don't know that they're ignorant…watch out!

Now every town had that one person who knew how to put on airs, so to speak. You know…thinking that they're all of that and then some. Well, the Bayou had this one "gentleman," and I use that word loosely. His name was Mr. Robert Lee Page. This man was a tall, slim build, dark skin, fried hair, smooth-talking brother who called himself a black Cuban. He was well-liked by just about everyone, and a real favorite among the ladies. On the weekends, you could see him cruising through town in his white-wall tire, candy-apple red Cadillac. The Cadillac, aka Caddy for short, was constantly full of young beautiful girls. To be on a shrimp boat worker's salary, somehow, he was always dressed to kill, and wore fine jewelry to boot. Pockets were always loaded with money. He showered them ladies with gifts of one thing or another, if you know what I mean.

Anyway, this one particular young girl named Pearl Rousseau, who was half Native American and half Negro/French, met Robert Lee at a dance one night. Her physical beauty swept him right off his feet. She had long, straight, jet-black hair and her complexion was of red clay. Her cheek bones were high, and her nose was so little you could barely see it. She had an hourglass figure. To the men, the eye catcher was her round, plump butt. Some men would say that she had a pair of onions back there. Others would say that her butt was so big you could set a teacup on it. With all the men talking about her physical beauty, Robert Lee knew one thing, and that was that she was the one for him. She was a keeper sho'nuff. He had to have her for his own. He didn't want any of the other fellows showing him up with her on their arms. So, within a few weeks of courting, they got married. The following year, a beautiful daughter named Lilly Mae was born.

Lilly Mae was a lovely little replica of her mother growing up in the Bayou. She had everything a little girl could want for. She lived in the prettiest house in the neighborhood. She had her own bedroom, which was full of toys. And her closet overflowed with pretty outfits. She was never hungry because their refrigerator was always packed with food. And to top it all off, both parents were living underneath the same roof. Everything was just lovely in the Page household; or was it…

In the first few years of Lilly Mae's life, she had a very bubbly attitude and was always happy. However, as the years went by she became an introvert. In addition, for some reason, she was always tired. A lot of times during her fifth-grade year while she attended class, her teacher had to call on her several times to wake up, to pay attention to the day's lesson. She slept in class so often her classmates gave her the nickname Sleepy Head. Some of the kids made a rhyme out of her new nickname, and taunted her during their lunch break. They would gather around her and shout, "Sleepy head, pee-pee head; you don't get no sleep at night, creepy head." The tiredness and taunting from her schoolmates went on for some years. But when she started puberty, she became very outgoing, alert and full of energy.

Because she was the only child Robert Lee had, he showered her with her heart's desire. He even gave her enough lunch money to treat herself, and others to some pop at the local corner store near the school. Whenever she wanted to go shopping for new clothes, he would always take her.

One day, the family went to a clothing store to shop for Lilly Mae's upcoming high school program. She saw a pretty dress hanging from the rack and grabbed it.

"Oh daddy I love this pretty, orange dress. Can I have it?"

"That's fine. Go ahead and get it."

"But you don't even know how much it is," Pearl said.

Ignoring his wife, they continued to walk through the store. Lilly Mae came upon another beautiful dress.

"Daddy please, may I have this one also? It's so beautiful. If you get this for me now I will *never* ask you for anything else *ever* again," she said with sorrowful eyes.

"Go ahead and get it. There's nothing too good for my little girl."

Jumping for joy she kissed him on his cheek.

"Thank you so much daddy!

In silence, Pearl became jealous because she remembered how he used to treat her that way. But for some-odd reason or another he stopped.

Pearl would ask him, "Baby, do you think you could take me shopping for a new outfit?"

His reply would always be with a grunt.

"Woman, your job is to take care of this house and not be out shopping."

Some say Lilly Mae was a daddy's little girl. To him, her school years went by really fast. It seemed like yesterday that she was just a little bitty thing bouncing around on his knees. He was very proud of her graduating from high school with a GPA of 3.8, and scoring high enough on her SAT to get accepted at Louisiana State University. She was very excited about finally being on her own, and living on campus with a roommate from her high school. At first, her father didn't approve; thinking that she was way too young to be away from home. However, after the crying and carrying on about him telling her no, he decided to let her live on campus. But there was a catch-22 with his decision. He told her that she could live on campus only if she came home every weekend. You'd think that a girl her age would be upset about this, but she wasn't. Actually, she looked forward to it because she knew that she would be treated like royalty from him.

As her college years flew by, life for her mother got worse. It had gotten to the point where Pearl felt like she really didn't even exist in the house when her daughter came home. Her life was uneventful until one afternoon, when she went to wake up her husband from a nap for lunch. She saw that he was completely still; eyes looking at the ceiling without blinking. Her husband was dead as a door knob. The doctor couldn't explain what had happened to him. It was noted on his death slip "Deceased by Natural Causes." Rumor had it Pearl hired an old voodoo lady from down in the swamps to cast some type of death spell on her husband. Mrs. Pearl heard about this ridiculous rumor and decided not to entertain it. She had other, more important things to deal with, like planning her husband's funeral.

Pearl did what any good wife would have done: gave her husband a very nice funeral. At the church, huge bouquets of flowers were everywhere. She had his casket specially made from cherry wood and lined with white silk. The color enhanced his favorite gray and pink pinstripe suit he had on with a white, silk shirt and handkerchief to match in his lapel. The fresh perm he had in his hair was slicked back. He had on his favorite thick, gold necklace with two matching diamond pinky rings for the packed church to see.

It was wall to wall standing. Everybody was dressed in their Sunday best. With all them folks up in there, it got hot as hell. People had them cheap-looking hand held fans with a picture of a blue eye supposing to be Jesus looking up to the sky; going in every direction trying to stay cool.

Pearl and Lilly Mae arrived outside the church and parked in their designated space. They were surprised to see so many people attending the funeral. A lot of folks were standing outside waiting to get in. As they walked up the steps, several church members gave their condolences. Once they got inside to the little greeting area, they saw two young male ushers standing at the main entrance. One was passing out the program for the funeral, and the other was escorting people to available seats. Pearl noticed that the escorting usher was rushing folks, and she knew the reason why.

From attending the church a few times in the past, she knew that folks in this particular church loved to schedule one event on top of the other. Knowing this upset her a little, and she be damned if she was going to allow them to do her and her daughter that way.

This is my husband's funeral, and I dare not be rushed, she thought. So, when the usher greeted them and began to walk fast to their front-row seat, Pearl grabbed Lilly Mae's arm and told her to walk in step with her.

As they slowly walked down the aisle, people stared at them and whispered among each other. Even so, they weren't bothered by the least. Once to their seat they sat down, and kept their heads high to the sky. No emotions were displayed. They just sat there watching the circus of women crying before Robert Lee. One woman walked up to the casket, took one look at the man and fell out. An usher ran to her and gave her some air with his fan. After a few seconds of that, she came back to life so to speak. Helping her to her feet, the youthful man escorted her poor soul outside. Pearl and Lilly Mae didn't even flinch. They just sat there holding each other's hands for support. The Pastor, who was an elderly gentleman with a nice looking three-piece black suit on, walked up to the podium and said, "Let us pray."

2

THE REPAST WAS held in the basement of the church. The decor matched her husband's suit. It looked really nice. The tables had pink and gray tablecloths on them, with beautiful white and pink flowers as a center piece. Damn near everyone was in that basement. Reason being not for the deceased and his widowed wife; it was for the free food. People stood in line for the home-cooked meal and pop. There was fried chicken, pigs' feet, chitterlings, potato salad, macaroni and cheese, collard greens, kale, crawfish, catfish, shrimp gumbo and then some.

Sitting in the far left-hand corner of the room on an old couch, Pearl and Lilly Mae watched them folks eat up the food. Occasionally, someone would come by and express their sorrow for their loss. Others just looked from afar and kept it moving. Tired of sitting, Pearl tried to get up from the couch.

"Help me up, baby. I got to go to the bathroom."

Lilly Mae stood to assist her mother.

"Are you going to be alright?"

"Yes, I'll be fine," Pearl responded without even looking at her.

With her bad left hip, she limped to the bathroom on the other side of the room. Lilly Mae wondered where her mother got the strength to keep going. Feeling a little uncomfortable, she sat back down.

Mrs. Vivian Johnson, who was Lilly Mae's best friend since childhood, approached her with two plates of food.

"Here you go, baby."

Lilly Mae pushed it away.

"No, I can't eat right now."

Mrs. Johnson pushed the plate back to her.

"Go on, now. You have to eat."

"No, really, I'm not hungry."

Mrs. Johnson sat down and looked at Lilly Mae's stomach, and then back to her.

"You may not be, but somebody else is."

Smiling, Lilly Mae took the food and began to eat. Happy that her friend was eating, Vivian took in a big spoon of potato salad and began to talk.

"Girl, don't let these people get to you; they don't mean nothing to y'all. They just here to get some free food, that's all." She pointed at the people. "Look at them laughing and stuffing their face at the same time. They don't care."

Lilly Mae looked at all the people around the room, and sadly put her head down.

"I know they're talking about us."

Vivian stopped chewing. She never did like her best friend's timid demeanor. Putting her plate on the couch, Vivian stood up with a belly just as big as Lilly Mae's.

"So what. Look, you can't stop people from gossiping. The only thing that matters is that y'all get through this."

Vivian's truthful remarks caused Lilly Mae to cry softly. Sucking her teeth, she sat back down and hugged her.

"Please don't cry. You know how I get when I see you cry."

She handed her a napkin from off her plate.

"I'm sorry. I just get so mad when you act all timid and shit."

With eyes stretching from here to kingdom come, she realized that she just used a bad word in the Lord's house. Quickly, she put her hands over her mouth.

"Oh, shit...did I just cuss in God's house?"

Exasperated, she threw her hands in the air.

"Oh, crap. I just said it again!"

She began to pray out loud.

"O Lord, please don't strike me down for using bad language in your house. Forgive me please, Amen."

Taking a deep breath, she continued.

"Lilly, all I'm saying is that I'm here for you, okay."

"Yes, you're right. I have to stay strong for Mama's sake anyway," She managed to say between sobbing and wiping her tears away.

Vivian gently lifted Lilly Mae's face up and said with all sincerity, "And for you and your baby."

Giving her a half smile she turned, and looked at all the people again, and realized that most of them she didn't know. She couldn't even tell you the relationship that some of them had with her father. *Are these the people who caused my daddy to die without a penny to his name? Are they glad that he's dead because they owed him money?*

"I just don't know what we're going to do with all the bills he left us with," she mumbled.

In shock, Vivian's mouth dropped open. *What the hell? Bills? I thought they were well to do.*

She regrouped her thoughts.

"Well, what did he leave y'all with?"

"Girl, all he left us was alone. I mean the little insurance money we did get went towards this funeral," she said.

"What!"

Vivian's outburst caused the people in the room to turn toward them. When they saw that nothing was going on, they went back to eating and chatting.

With a lower voice, she asked, "He didn't leave y'all *nothing? Nothing at all?* I thought he was making a lot of money."

Lilly Mae pointed to some of the women eating and laughing with each other.

"You see them women over there? We don't know them fools."

From her remark, Vivian got the full picture of what her dad was really about.

"What are y'all going to do about the house?"

"I don't know. Stay in it until they put us out, I guess."

Vivian stared at her like lights hitting a deer. *Where is the fucking logic to that?*

"Then what's going to happen? I mean, where will y'all go?"

Getting tired of what seemed like 21 questions Lilly Mae frowned and said with an attitude, "I don't know. Go to a boarding house or something. Mama will think of something."

Seeing that her friend was getting upset, she decided to stop with the questions and offer some type of resolution.

"Well, if it comes down to that, let me know. I...well my husband knows a man who knows the woman who runs a boarding house over on Wallis Street."

From across the room Vivian heard her name being called by her husband and smiled.

"Speaking of husband, here he comes now." Waving to him she yelled, "Over here, honey!"

She saw her tall husband making his way through the crowd. Being about 6'5", Mr. Bugalue Johnson saw his pregnant wife sitting on a couch next to a lady. He had to say "Excuse me" several times for people to move out of his way. Finally making his way over, he bent down and gave her a kiss on the cheek.

"Hey, baby, sorry I'm late. I just can't get used to some of these no-name roads."

Vivian smiled at the tall, dark and handsome love of her life.

She met him on campus while attending her second year at Syracuse University. But before the fall semester of her third year began, her mother told her that she could no longer afford the out of state tuition, nor the travel to and from school during the breaks. So she had to go back home and transfer her credits to Louisiana State University. In spite of the distance, Bugalue, who was from New York City, stayed in contact, and on occasions went to visit her.

After graduating with a degree in Business Management, Bugalue applied for several jobs all over New York, Connecticut and New Jersey.

But there weren't any jobs for a young man that was fresh-out-of-college, with no experience under his belt. After discussing his situation with Vivian, and with her telling him that she was now two months pregnant, it was agreed that they would make a life together down in the Bayou. With her securing an excellent job through her mother just after graduation, she told him that she would hold the bills and rent down until he found a job.

Once Bugalue got settled into his new location, he did some research into the job market. Not really liking the information he obtained, he decided to go into business for himself. After successfully completing a real estate course at the local college, his next move was to get a small-business loan, which was approved. Thus, BJ&V Real Estate was born.

Within a few short months, his business was doing very well, and Vivian received a 10% raise after her probationary period was over. So, with that, they decided to get married and buy their own home before the baby was due.

Yep, life was looking pretty good for them. That was until the market slowed down. For some reason, no one was selling or buying, and he hid this little problem from his wife. He didn't want her to have any worries with the new baby coming and all. So for income he took on odd jobs; some that kept him away for days.

Vivian introduced her husband to Lilly Mae with a note of sarcasm in her voice.

"Honey, you remember Lilly Mae, my girlfriend from LSU. The one who could never find the time to hang out with us when you came to visit me? The one who didn't attend *our* wedding for whatever reason?

Hearing her name, he recognized it from somewhere...*but where?* Then it hit him like a Mack truck.

He remembered sitting in a Pub across the street from LSU, having drinks with his frat boys, when this pretty, petite, fine thing came rolling in with a few of her sorority sisters. They all had on their pink and green sweaters with the letters AKA (Alpha Kappa Alpha) on the front, big as day. Their attitudes were uppity as all outdoors. They thought they were all of that.

The petite AKA with the pretty eyes caught Bugalue's attention. He had to have a taste of that sweet, tender-looking, light-skinned thing. So he put his game face on. However, before making his move, he looked at his watch to see how much playtime he had before Vivian was finish packing for the long break with him up in NYC.

He nudged one of his boys.

"Yo, watch me make a move on light eyes."

His boys edged him on as he gave himself a look over.

"Yo, check it. Is my shit tight or what?"

One of the brothers jumped from the bar stool, and with a paper napkin wiped down the OMEGA SI PSI shield that was dead center on his hoodie. Bugalue stepped back and profiled.

"How you like me now?"

The Qs barked like dogs while beating the air with their fists. The girls looked over at them and smiled. To Bugalue, their smile was his cue to make a move.

He approached light eyes with that New York swagger kind of manner. His game was tight. He had her laughing and smiling in no time. Offering her a drink, he pulled out a big wad of bills to show that he wasn't no cheap dude, and that impressed her very much so. After talking and drinking for a few minutes…Bam! Bugalue was hitting the skins in the back seat of his car. Ten toes up and ten toes down with no protection. They never bothered to discuss personal stuff like—are you seeing anyone? How old are you? What's your last name? What's your major—none of that. It was pure, mad, animalistic sex. After they finished, they exchanged numbers and promised to keep in contact with each other. And indeed, they did.

During Lilly Mae's last year of attending LSU, Bugalue was still calling her up whenever he was in town to visit Vivian. They would meet up at some cheap fleabag motel to have sex. Afterward, they rolled out. Lilly Mae didn't have a problem with their arrangement at all until this one episode.

While sitting at the bar drinking a Coke at the very pub she and her lover first met, Vivian and Bugalue walked in. They were all hugged up on each other laughing and playing around. They had just returned from a basketball game. Lilly Mae knew this because he had called her earlier and told her that he wanted to see her later that night after the game. She told him that she would be waiting at the pub across from the school. When she spotted him with her best friend at a distance, with the quickness she rolled out the back door without being seen by them. She wasn't upset about him being with her best friend. She just felt like he disrespected her for bringing Vivian in her presence. Truth be told, he totally forgot about meeting her at the pub.

The next day he called Lilly Mae's dorm several times to see what was up with her. And every time she answered the phone, and heard his voice, she simply hung up. Tired of her childish ways, he said fuck it. It is what it is. Now here she sat before him with a big stomach like his wife, barely cognizing her because she had put on so much weight with her pregnancy.

Feeling a little uncomfortable, he spoke.

"How you doing, I mean besides the unfortunate loss of your father." Nervous as hell, he pulled out a white handkerchief from his pants pocket and wiped the sweat off his forehead.

"I'm making it. How you doing?" she replied nonchalantly.

A sigh of relief came over him when she didn't say anything about them knowing each other.

"Fine, fine, I can't complain. Umm, baby, we need to be going. I have some people coming by the house to take care of some business for me."

"Look, honey, we both are pregnant. We were so sick on grad day. I don't ever want to go through that again."

Remembering throwing up in her cap because she was so sick, Lilly Mae started to snicker.

Bugalue tried to speed things up a bit.

"Baby, can we go now?"

"Okay. You know, you don't look too good. Are you alright?"

Saying nothing he turned his head away from her.

"Well, let me know if y'all need a place to stay, Lilly, and I'll..."

Abruptly, he turned back around and cut her off.

"Place to stay...? What are you talking about?

Gently taking her husband's hand, she began to rub it.

"Lilly Mae and her mother might be losing their house. They're going to need a place to stay."

With understanding, he breathed a sigh of relief.

"Oh, *need* a place to stay, not meaning to stay with us."

"I mean, if it comes to that, so be it. I can't have them on the street. They like family to me."

"Did you tell them about my buddy Joe Carter, who knows the lady that runs the boarding house over on Wallis Street?"

"I'm way ahead of you on that. Let's go."

She grabbed a potato chip off Lilly Mae's plate and popped it in her mouth. "Call me, okay."

Vivian gave her best friend a kiss on the cheek and walked away. "Y'all take care."

Walking behind his wife, Bugalue kept looking back at her. He observed her biting into a piece of chicken as she rubbed her plump belly. *Could that be...? Am I the...? No, it can't be... Can it?*

Vivian saw Mrs. Pearl coming out of the bathroom and waved to her. With a big smile, she greeted her and they gave each other a hug.

"Mama Pearl, you take care."

Mrs. Pearl was like a second mother to Vivian. That's how close Lilly Mae and Vivian were. Some folks thought that they were actual sisters, because when you saw one, you saw the other. If one was in a fight, they both were in a fight. When they were little, they took a small pocket knife and cut each other's thumbs. Rubbing each other's blood together solidified that they were stick partners for life.

"Alright, baby. Tell your mother I said thanks for the flowers."

While hugging Vivian, Pearl observed Mr. Johnson, who she had seen several times around town with his wife, looking back at what seemed to be her daughter.

Limping to the couch, Pearl struggled to sit down. After waiting a few minutes, she asked her daughter, "Baby why was Vivian's husband looking at you like that?"

Sucking her teeth and folding her arms across her swollen breast she responded.

"And what makes you think he was looking at me?"

Surprised at her daughter's nasty demeanor, Pearl rolled her eyes.

"Well, excuse the hell out of me for asking."

They both sat there with tension between them. Nevertheless, knowing that no matter how much they got on each other's nerves, their love for one another would never change. Lilly Mae suddenly stood up.

"Mama, I'm ready to leave."

Pearl looked up at her daughter. *Lord, I swear. She knows how hard it is for me to sit down, let alone get up.*

3

*T*HE CHURCH WAS only about fifteen minutes away from the Page residence. As they pulled up into their driveway, they saw a white man in a blue police uniform leaving their house. They stared at the officer as he got into his squad car and pulled off. After he passed them, they got out and started walking toward the house. They stopped at the bottom of the steps when they saw a pink slip taped to the front door. There was no need to read it because they already knew what it was. Walking up the steps Lilly Mae looked at her mother.

"Another note for the collection…"

Pearl fumbled through her purse looking for her keys.

"Don't these people know that your father's funeral was today?" Lilly Mae snatched the note down as Pearl opened the door.

"Those white folks don't care. They just want their money." The Page house was a picture-perfect home. Their house was a very nice size filled with nice furniture, compared to other folk's home on their side of the railroad track. One thing that really stood out in their living room was a beautiful crystal vase with fresh flowers on the coffee table.

Pearl took off her hat and threw it on the sitting chair. Tired, she slowly plopped down on the sofa. Lilly Mae walked over to a tall, wooden stand that had an Asian designed music box sitting on top. When she opened the lid, it played beautiful oriental music. Her father brought it for her sixteenth birthday. After starring at the pink slip in her hand, she placed it under the box along with the other stacks of overdue bills. Some had the same color as the one they received today. Closing the box, she went over to her mother and sat down at her feet. Removing her mother's shoes, she began to rub her swollen feet. Looking up at her, she smiled.

"Better?"

"Yes child, much better." Pearl sighed with relief.

"Mama, what we going to do now that he's gone?"

Pearl leaned her back against the couch, and closed her eyes.

"We pray, child. Something's going to come through. We just pray."

Lilly Mae got up and sat next to her mother. Complete silence filled the room. Eventually, she laid her head down on her mother's lap, and closed her eyes. While humming a spiritual song, Pearl began to rub the top of her daughter's head. Slowly, they dosed off to sleep.

4

*P*EACEFUL HOURS PASSED by. Lilly Mae was stretched out on the living room couch. She heard a faint knocking at the door, but refused to acknowledge it. She wanted to continue her peaceful sleep. When she repositioned herself for comfort, deep sleep immediately overwhelmed her.

Knock-knock-knock.

This time she didn't know if it was a dream or reality. Her mind was back to her being eight years old asleep in her bed.

Knock-knock-knock.

Startled, she woke up and stared at the door. The knock became louder.

Bang! Bang! Bang!

Panic took over her little body. Terrified, she sat up in the dark room, and pulled the covers up to her face.

"No, not again…"

Slowly, the door opened. There stood before her a silhouette of her father. With his head tilted back, he guzzled down a small bottle of dark whiskey. After he finished its contents, he placed the empty bottle in his rear pocket. He wiped the bitter sweet spirits from his lips with his sleeve.

"Baby girl, you sleep?" he asked with a slur.

Drunk as a skunk, he staggered into her room.

"Baby girl, I say you sleep?"

"Please daddy no," in a whisper, she begged.

In fear, she screamed as her father approached her while unbuckling his belt. Lilly Mae heard herself screaming, and woke up from her dream. Disoriented, she fell onto the floor with a hard thump. The knock was heard again. But this time she knew that it was coming from the front door.

"What the..." Confused, she looked around the room. "What's going on?"

"I'm coming! Stop knocking on my door like that!" she heard her mother yelling from the kitchen.

Pearl entered the living room, and saw her daughter on the floor.

"What the heck... Why are you on the floor?"

"My goodness, I slept out here the whole night?" she asked.

Knock-knock-knock.

Pearl continued toward the door.

"Yes, you did. You were tired, so I didn't want to disturb you."

"But daddy never lets..."

Putting her hand up, Pearl stopped her before she could finish.

"That don't matter no more. And why are you still on the floor, child? The couch ain't good enough for you? Get up."

"I fell off the couch. I was having this bad dream and..."

Bang! Bang! Bang!

"I'm coming, gotdammit!"

Shocked at her mother's foul language, Lilly Mae yelled, "You cussed!"

Pearl didn't respond and answered the door.

"Can I help you gentlemen?"

Standing on her front pouch were four big, white men in dungarees. "Who is it, Mama?" Lilly Mae asked as she got up off the floor. The Sheriff, who was a pleasant-looking white man, with deep blue eyes, got out of his squad car. He removed his hat as he walked up the steps and cleared his throat before speaking.

"Good morning, Mrs. Pearl."

Pearl recognized the young man speaking to her, because she used to babysit him when he was a little boy. Through the screen door, she greeted him.

"Morning, Sheriff Brevard. What can I do for you this early in the morning?"

Lilly Mae came to the front door to peek at what was going on. But Pearl blocked most of her view. The Sheriff saw a small portion of Lilly Mae's face, and was immediately drawn to her beauty.

Sometimes when Lilly Mae came home from college, on the down low, she and Sheriff Brevard spent intimate time together. They had liked each other since they were little. On several occasions, Pearl caught them doing the nasty in the hall closet. To save himself from getting a spanking, after Pearl told his mother, he would cry out that Lilly Mae made him do it. And of course, his mother believed him. When Lilly Mae said that he was lying, Pearl skinned that poor girl legs up.

"Top of the morning, to you Ms. Lilly Mae," Sheriff Brevard said as he tipped his hat towards her. But she didn't speak. Stepping out on the front porch Pearl addressed him again.

"Sheriff Brevard, what's going on? Why are you here with these men?" A big fat white man with a serious tan walked up to her.

"What's going on? I'll tell you what's going on! You're being evicted. That's what's going on," he said in a heavy Creole accent.

The Sheriff stepped in.

"Now, Jacques, let me handle this."

Jacques, who was always irritated by the Sheriff's calmness in dealing with colored folks, threw his hands up in the air.

"Well, handle it, then. We got several jobs to do today," he said as he walked back over to where the rest of the men were, and folded his arms.

Baffled, she whispered, "Evicted...?"

"Yes ma'am. Mrs. Pearl the bankers said they done mailed you several letters about being behind on your mortgage. They say they never got a reply, no payment, nothing."

Still not quite understanding what was going on, she started to explain.

"Well, my husband just passed away, and I know he paid the mortgage last month. He told me he did. And I never had a reason, not to believe my husband. Can you just give me a little more time to get this month's money together?"

Out of nowhere all four men burst out laughing. Pulling a white piece of paper from his shirt pocket, Jacques walked back up to her, and put the paper right in her face.

"Last month...? Lady, do you see this here? It says that your mortgage hasn't been paid for the last *three* months."

In shock, Pearl grabbed her heart, and stumbled backwards.

Jacques turned and walked back to the men.

"Oh, what the hell am I showing her this for? Probably can't read, no less write."

"Jacques, didn't I tell you to let me handle this?" Sheriff Brevard said.

Hands in the air, Jacques backed off.

"Okay, okay. Handle it then."

The Sheriff continued in a professional manner.

"Mrs. Pearl, we left you a note on the front door yesterday."

Angrily, Lilly Mae stepped out onto the porch, and got up in his face.

"Well we didn't read it!"

"Well whose fault is that?!" Jacques fired back. "Lamar, is we going to stand out here all day talking to these niggers?"

After looking at both ladies for a few seconds, the Sheriff put his head down. He really didn't want to say it, but had no choice.

"Orders are orders."

No sooner than the words were out of his mouth, Jacques put the men into action.

"That's right, okay let's do this! Y'all go in there and take *everything* out. You know the routine. Put the stuff at the edge of this here curb."

The men walked passed Pearl and Lilly Mae without a care in the world. It would take them less than an hour and a half to have the house cleaned out, boarded and locked up. Sheriff Brevard and Jacques walked down the steps.

"Jacques, I swear I'm going to tell Mama on you with the way you talk to these colored folks."

Blowing his younger brother off with his hand, Jacques stood wide leg in the middle of the street. Proudly, he watched his men do what they did best. Sheriff Brevard leaned against his cruiser and waited for them to finish. Pearl, who couldn't believe what was happening, walked to the steps and sat down.

"Mama what are you doing?!"

"Orders are orders," Pearl said, just as calm as the wind.

The men were removing their stuff so fast Lilly Mae couldn't believe her eyes. Glass shattered from inside the house.

"Stupid fool! Watch what you're doing!" Lilly Mae yelled as she ran into the house.

"Hey, you can't go back in there! Pete!" Sheriff Brevard yelled.

Pete was sitting in the cruiser, drinking coffee and eating donuts. When he heard his name called, he jumped out his skin, so to speak; spilling hot coffee all over his uniform. He flew out the car and ran to his partner.

"Yes sir...yes sir I'm here."

"Get her out of there!"

He ran past Pearl, falling up the steps as he went.

"Get up and get her out of there *now*!"

"Yes sir, I'm on it; I'm on it right now!" he said as he quickly got back to his feet.

The Sheriff walked over to Mrs. Pearl. Gently, he put his hand on her slumped over shoulders.

"Ma'am, is there anything I can do for you?"

Pearl didn't respond. Mentally, she was in another world.

"Is there someone I can call for you?"

No answer.

As the men were steadily taking stuff out the house, Lilly Mae was yelling from the top of her lungs. Suddenly, Officer Pete kicked the screen door open with Lilly Mae in his arms. He was carrying her out the house like they just gotten married; only she was kicking and yelling up a storm.

"Get your hands off me, you, cracker!"

Officer Pete tried to reason with her but to no avail.

"Miss please calm down."

"Calm down! My father just passed away, and you do this to us!" Sheriff Brevard saw them coming and hurried out the way.

"Lilly Mae, please. Y'all have to leave."

As Officer Pete came down the steps, he missed one and tumbled down to the ground. Luckily for him he landed on the ground first with Lilly Mae on top.

"You stupid fool! Can't you see that I'm pregnant! I could have lost my damn baby!" she yelled as she began hitting the officer with a fist full of fury.

In defense, Officer Pete covered his face as best he could. Sheriff Brevard ran over, and pulled her off of him.

"Lilly Mae, you can't be hitting a police officer; it's against the law! Please just leave!"

"We don't have nowhere to go!"

Calmly, Mrs. Pearl looked at Sheriff Brevard and asked, "Can you call Vivian Johnson?"

One hour and fifteen minutes later, Pearl and Lilly Mae were sitting on the curb with all their household belongings. The windows were all boarded up, and padlocks were on the front and back doors. Mr. and Mrs. Johnson slowly pulled up in their pickup truck.

PART TWO

5

*I*T HAD BEEN three weeks since the eviction. The transformation of living underneath someone else's roof was hard for Lilly Mae and her mom in the beginning. As time went on they got used to the big old house. Actually, it wasn't that bad. Lilly Mae and Vivian had a lot of things in common, especially with them being pregnant. They talked about babies' names, college days, how they used to party together, and things they used to do when they were little. They stayed up late at night watching TV and slept half their mornings away. Sometimes they would go out and shop for new outfits for themselves and for their babies. Well, Vivian treated Lilly Mae most of the time because she knew she didn't have any money.

Pearl adjusted by cooking and cleaning all the time. She loved to cook, especially whenever someone said that they were hungry. The Johnson's kept plenty of food in their house. Fruits, vegetables, eggs, butter, milk and such were filled to the brim in the refrigerator. They had a tall deep freezer out on the back porch filled with nothing but meat. They also had a big walk-in pantry that resembled a grocery store.

As Lilly Mae sat at the kitchen table having breakfast with Vivian, she wondered about the Johnson's income, but soon let the thought go. *Look at me sitting here thinking about how much they're making. It's none of my bees' wax really. I should just be thankful that my girl took me and Mama in,* she thought.

"Vivian, we really appreciate y'all letting us stay here for a little while."

Vivian took a sip from her coffee.

"Little while...girl please. It's been some weeks. I wish y'all get out so me and my husband can fuck."

"Girl, watch your mouth! Don't you see mama over there?!"

Eyes big as hell, Vivian quickly covered her mouth.

"I'm sorry, Ma Pearl. I meant to say so we can make love." Pearl didn't even hear her because she was into her cooking.

"It seems like as soon as y'all moved in, his thing just stays limp."

"I'm sorry, but we have been looking for a place to stay. And no one has called mama about a job yet."

"I'm just playing, but not about the sex part."

Her kidding put Lilly Mae's mind at ease, and they laughed.

As they were laughing, Bugalue walked into the kitchen with this bad-ass cream color three-piece suit on. His handsome face was shined from baby oil, and his facial hair was trimmed to a tee. His teeth were pearly white, and his small afro was nice and tight.

"Good morning, ladies. Mrs. Pearl, something sure smells good. Whatever it is, I'll have four of each."

Grabbing a plate from the cabinet, and silverware from the drawer, he placed it on the table and sat down.

"Baby, you sure are decked out and hungry this morning," Vivian said.

Giving his wife a million-dollar smile he said, "I sure am."

"It must be nice to have three women under one roof cooking and keeping the house clean."

Lilly Mae sat with her own thoughts. But after hearing Vivian's statement her silent thoughts slipped out of her mouth by accident.

"Amongst other things."

"And what does that supposed to mean?" Vivian asked.

Lilly Mae looked at Pearl serving Bugalue eggs over easy, country bacon and pancakes.

"Don't be looking at them. I asked you a question. What does that supposed to mean?"

"I mean he's spoiled. Look at all that food on his plate."

With a mouth, full of food, he said, "Don't I work every day? Don't I bring home the bacon and then some? Shit, I deserve to be treated like a king. If it wasn't against the law, I'd have *two* wives."

"Now what would you do with two wives?" his wife asked.

"One would be for having babies, cooking and keeping the house clean. The other would be for whatever I tell her to do in the bedroom, at any given time. You see I just think that women should earn their keep in a man's house and…"

As Bugalue ran off at the mouth with a bunch of nonsense, Lilly Mae started to daydream. All she saw was his mouth moving with no sound coming from it. Her mind went back into time when she was washing dishes at Vivian's kitchen sink one morning. Bugalue had snuck up behind her and squeezed her breast. In a deep husky voice, he whispered in her ear, "You know you got to earn your keep while you're in my house, don't you?"

Putting her head down, she stopped washing the dishes. "Man, I'm pregnant."

"Baby girl, that's what makes that thing sweeter than before. It'll be just like old times. You know, at first I didn't even recognize you with your face being so fat and all."

Giving her a hard slap on the rear, he turned and walked to the kitchen table. He sat down and extended his legs.

"Come on over here and do what you do best," he said as he unzipped his pants. Hesitating, she thought, *why is this happening to me? I don't want to be bothered with this man, but if I don't do what he wants, he's going to put me and Mama out on the street.*

With great bitterness, she gave in.

Throwing the dish towel in the sink, she walked towards him.

"Stop! Don't come to me like that!" he yelled. "I want you to do it like I like it."

Smiling, he displayed his private part to her, and began to rub it. Hatred was written all over her face as she stared at him.

"Come on now, before my wife and your mother get back from the store."

With a disgusted look, she unpinned her long hair, and got down on her hands and knees. Slowly, she crawled toward him like a cat on the prowl while staring into his eyes.

"Yes, daddy," she said, mimicking a little girl's voice.

Throwing his head back, he let out a hearty laugh. *Wow, I can't believe this shit. Here I have my pregnant wife, a woman who may be having my offspring, and a hell of a cook, all under one roof. And just to think, for a split second, I was intimidated by this bitch. This is the epitome of a man being head of household,* he thought.

Lilly Mae's seductive cat crawl was a real turn-on to him. Vigorously, he rubbed his manhood as it began to grow.

"What's my name, little-girl?"

"Big daddy," she replied with a sexy voice.

His manhood was at full attention before her now. It was waiting to be conquered. With his hand on top of her head, he pushed himself deep inside her mouth until he heard her gagging.

"That's right, take that shit. We're going to get along real good up in here. Just like family."

Slowly, he began to reappear and disappear.

"Hold my dick, girl," he said as he leaned his head back.

Faster and faster he appeared and disappeared until his body started to jerk.

"Lilly Mae! Oh, shit, Lilly Mae!" he called as he reached his climax.

Vaguely, she heard her name being called repeatedly. It got so loud that it caused her to come back to reality. And when she did, she saw Bugalue looking at her smiling.

"Don't you, Lilly Mae...? Lilly Mae..."

Slightly confused, she was unsure of what he was asking.

"What? Are you asking me something?"

"Yes. I said, don't you think a woman should earn her keep in a man's house?"

"Oh, I don't know," she said as she took a sip of her coffee.

"Sure you do," he said with a slick smile.

Vivian got up to get some orange juice from the refrigerator.

"Leave her alone with your crazy, silly ideas."

Bugalue laughed so hard his food flew out of his mouth.

"I had y'all going."

Looking at his watch he saw that time was ticking by.

"Man, I'm going to be late for work. I'll see y'all this evening."

After finishing up his food he got up and gave his wife a big kiss. Catching Lilly Mae off guard, he ran over to her and planted one right on the mouth. Shocked and disgusted, she wiped her lips.

"Hey, stop that!"

"Bugalue, you play too much!" Vivian screamed

Playfully, he danced his way towards the kitchen door.

"Well, she is carrying my baby, too."

"Get out of here, crazy!" Vivian yelled playfully as she threw the dish towel at her husband.

"Man, can't I have some fun in my own house?" he said as he ducked the towel.

"No!" they yelled.

Waving them off, he left the house. Vivian sat back down at the table with her orange juice.

"That man plays too much. If I didn't know no better, I'd think he was telling the truth."

Lilly Mae had just taken another sip of her coffee when suddenly she began to choke. Coughing repeatedly, she tried to get it under control. Scared, Vivian jumped up and started hitting her on the back.

"Are you okay?!"

Pearl got a glass of water from the sink, and handed it to her daughter.

"Here baby, drink this!" Lilly Mae took several sips and gave the glass back to her mother.

"You feel better? Girl, you scared the crap out of me."

"I'm fine sis. It just went down the wrong pipe, that's all."

With a smirk, Pearl looked at her and went back to washing dishes.

"Hey, why don't we all go and check out that friend of your husband's, who knows the lady that runs the boarding house?"

"Well, if y'all don't mind driving, that's fine with me. Just let me help Ma Pearl with the dishes, and then we can go."

6

*I*T WAS ABOUT a thirty-minute drive from Vivian's house to David Memorial Church of God and Christ. As they pulled up to the church, they saw kids playing on the lawn. They were running around a big sign that read FRIDAY NIGHT REVIVAL. Mrs. Pearl parked her car in the space that read Visitor Parking Only. They all got out and walked up to a teenage girl who was sitting on the front steps. She was busy folding brown paper napkins for the dinner that was going to be served at the church that night. Squinting one eye because of the glare from the sun, she looked at the approaching women.

"May I help you?"

Sitting down next to her, Lilly Mae began helping her fold the napkins.

"Is Mr. Carter available?"

The girl stared at Lilly Mae's and Vivian's stomachs.

"Is he in some kind of trouble, ma'am?"

The ladies glanced at each other and then looked at how serious the girl was. Reassuring her, Lilly Mae patted the young girl's leg.

"No, baby, he's not in no trouble. We just want to talk to him. Can you go and get him for us?"

Nodding her head, she jumped up and ran into the church. A few seconds later she returned with an elderly woman, walking with a cane, praising God.

"Yes, Lord. Thank you, Jesus…new members. Can I help you, ladies?"

"We are looking for Mr. Carter, sister…"

"Mother Dixon. I is the mother of this church."

"Mother Dixon, it's very nice to meet you. We're looking for Mr. Carter.

"Well, *Pastor* Carter is here. That's his title, you know. He's helping with the cooking for the Revival tonight. Are you all coming? It would be—"

"No, but we would like to talk to Pastor Carter, please," Vivian interrupted the conversation.

"Okay…but it will be a few minutes. I'll be happy to show you to his office, and you all can wait in there."

Lilly Mae got up, and they all followed Mother Dixon into a very nice-looking church. The dark wooden floors were shined and beautiful just like the benches. Hymn books were in every slot on the back of the benches. They also had long, narrow, carpet going up to the podium from the entrance.

She took the ladies to the back of the church, which had several office doors. One was marked "Pastor Joe Carter." She took a single key from her bosom and unlocked the door. They entered into a very immaculate office. There were matching soft, cushion, gray chairs in front of a big, cherry wood desk. Next to a window was a tall, slim fake tree. There were several diplomas on the wall next to it.

"Have a seat. Make yourself comfortable. He'll be here momentarily."

Going over to the Pastor's desk, Mother Dixon pulled on the drawers to make sure they were all locked. As she walked towards the door, she cut her eyes over at the ladies and left. The women looked bewildered by her actions.

Walking down the hallway to the stairs that led to the basement, she had to be careful as she descended because of her bad legs. When she finally reached the last step, she stopped. Taking a deep breath, she called out.

"Pastor! You got some women folk upstairs to see you!"

She waited for an answer but didn't get one. Taking her cane, she hit the kitchen door several times.

Bang! Bang! Bang!

She waited...still no answer. Painfully, she took the last step down. She opened the door to be presented with hot steam from the stoves. Pots and pans were banging and women were talking and laughing up a storm.

Mother Dixon looked over and saw the Pastor cooking at one of the stoves. His back was to her, so when she made her way over, she tapped him on his shoulder.

"You got some folks upstairs who would like to see you."

Pastor Carter didn't turn around. He was adding some seasoning to his big pot of pinto beans and ham hocks, which he was famous for cooking. Everybody loved his beans and sweet corn bread. He took a sip of the broth, and nodded his head in agreement with the taste. While wiping his hands on his apron, he turned to her and asked, "Are these people seeking the Lord, or do they need some kind of assistance?"

"It's hard to say. But if you ask me—" she said with a frown.

Throwing his head back, he looked up at the ceiling for a minute, because he knew that he wasn't going to get a direct answer.

"I am asking you."

"It doesn't look like they in need to me. But if..." He rolled down his sleeves and removed his apron.

"Do me a favor and add a little more butter to this. I'll be right back."

Grabbing the apron from him, she put it on. As he headed toward the door, she went to the refrigerator and grabbed a stick of butter.

"Two of them are pregnant!" she yelled as she closed the refrigerator door.

Removing the thin paper from the butter, she walked back over to the big pot of beans, and threw the whole stick it. She watched it melt and continued on.

"They probably don't know who the daddy is."

"Is that right?" he said as he continued toward the door.

"Their mama probably dropping them off because she don't want to be bothered with them no more."

"Is that right?"

"Kids need to learn to keep their legs closed, and their brains open for education."

"Is that right?" Smiling, he held the door open until she finished.

"And if you ask me—"

"Odessa," he laughed. "I'm not asking you anything."

Not liking to be interrupted when she talked, with one hand on her hip, she turned and looked at him with an evil eye.

"Well, if you *were* asking me, one of the ladies up there looks like Mr. Bugalue's wife."

He smiled, and closed the door behind him.

Turning back to the beans, she took a sip of the broth. Her face became distorted.

"My, my, this stuff has no taste to it. If you ask me, I think it needs more salt."

She grabbed the salt box and poured a lot into the pinto beans. After stirring a few times, she took a sip.

"Hot damn," she said as she slapped her thigh. "Now we're cooking."

In the meantime, the ladies sat in their chairs looking at each other. Tired of just sitting around, Lilly Mae got up and walked over to the wall where Pastor Carter's accomplishments and articles of achievements were displayed in frames.

"It says here that the Pastor received his PhD in Sociology at the Tuskegee Institute."

She looked at another frame.

"It says here that he got his Master of Divinity from Vanderbilt University. He's also a member of the Mississippi Council for Negro Leadership."

She looked at another frame that read "The Republican Club." Another one read "Black and Tan Party."

"Now, I never even heard of that."

When Vivian and Pearl didn't respond, Lilly Mae walked over to the window and stared at the children playing.

"With him being involved in all those organizations, he must don't have much time for his wife."

"That's the reason why his wife left him," Vivian said.

"What! He's not married?" Lilly Mae shouted.

Her mind was running 90 miles an hour, going North. *Here is a man with all of these accomplishments and no wife. Maybe, just maybe...*

Vivian got up and walked over to the frames, and started pretending to read the articles.

"Yep, was married for about five years, and been alone for about three, to the best of my knowledge."

Lilly Mae walked back to her chair and sat down.

"What happened?"

"He was so wrapped up into his work he didn't notice that a man came along and wrapped himself around his wife. She took off with that other man like a bat out of hell."

Lilly Mae moved to the edge of her seat.

"What! Are you serious?"

Vivian continued to talk as she walked to his desk. She picked up and examined a few items then placed them back down.

"Yes girl…left him high, but not dry. She left everything behind. She didn't ask him for a penny. She didn't even ask him for the house. She *had* to have her own money leaving like that."

Pouting and looking disappointed, Lilly Mae sat back in her chair and folded her arms.

"He probably lives in some old shack."

"Shack! Girl please. I heard that Negro got himself a nice-size home and land to boot. It's on a plantation that he inherited form his folks. The Carters were a huge clan during slavery. He thought him and his wife were going to have a house full of children, like his ancestors did."

"He doesn't have any kids?"

"Nope," she said, smiling as she walked back to her seat and sat down.

After hearing all the gossip about Mr. Carter's life, Lilly Mae relaxed in her chair. She didn't say a word. Her mother looked at her, but said nothing. Silence was among them again. Then a light knock was heard at the door.

Knock-knock-knock

The ladies turned toward the door as Pastor Carter entered. He was about 6'2", slim-built with really dark skin. He had a short, curly afro, black as the night. And his cheekbones were high. Lilly Mae quickly sized him up as he walked to his desk. *Ok, he is handsome with good hair, but tall and nerdy-like.* She stared at his pants. *I don't see a print. He probably wasn't hitting that thing right, so his wife dipped out with a man who was.*

He sat down and noticed that his paper weight, in the shape of a flat, gold cross, was out of place. He moved it an inch to the left. He intertwined his fingers, placed them on top of his desk, and cleared his throat.

"Good morning, ladies. How can I be of assistance to you today?"

Lilly Mae stared at him. *Yessiree. I do believe he is going to get got.*

"Good morning, Pastor Carter. My name is Vivian Johnson. You met me a while ago through my husband Bugalue."

"Mrs. Johnson. Yes, how are you? You attended one of our Council meetings, right?"

He sat back and relaxed in his chair.

Smiling hard as hell, Vivian said, "Yes, I did, and it was very interesting."

"I talked to your husband about a week ago, and he did tell me something about a family friend in need of some type of help or something."

Lilly Mae, whose hair was hanging down, turned away from them as they continued their conversation. Taking a few bobby-pins out of her pocketbook, she discreetly started to pin her hair up. She thought to herself that putting her hair up made her look older, and more conservative. After she finished she turned and looked at him with a sad face.

"Not 'or something.' My mama and I need a place to live."

Vivian turned to introduce her, but had to take a double look because of her new hair style.

"Pas—Pastor Carter, this is Lilly Mae Page, my best friend. And this is her mother Mrs. Pearl Page. They're staying with me for the time being."

"Ladies, how can I help?"

Pearl was about to reply, but Lilly Mae cut right to the chase.

"We were wondering if you could talk to the lady who runs the boarding house across town."

He looked down at his hands and then back to Lilly Mae.

"I could, but if you don't mind me asking—what happened? I mean, you don't look like the kind of folks that would stay at a boarding house."

"We're not..." Pearl said before her daughter could say anything else. "But we are in need, just the same. We lost our house when my husband passed away a few months ago. He was head of household. I didn't have to work a day in my life. He took good care of his family. The way a man is supposed to."

With great pride Pearl spoke of her husband. However, Lilly Mae gave her mother a flat-out reality check.

"We lost our house because we thought my daddy was paying the mortgage, but come to find out he wasn't."

Inside, Pearl was embarrassed by what her daughter just said. *Lord, I like to slap the holy crap out of this child right now for putting the family business out like that.* Nevertheless, she held her composure and said nothing.

"Did he have any savings or life insurance?"

"We used the insurance money for the funeral. As far as savings go, he didn't believe in that. His belief was to live for today."

"Well, if you don't mind me asking, how...uh, how—"

"How did he die?"

"Yes."

"He died—" she started, but.

"Diabetic," Pearl quickly cut her off. "He was a diabetic and died of complications."

As if she had seen a ghost, Lilly Mae stared at her mother. *What the…? Where in the hell did that come from? Is there any truth to that, or is she trying to cover something up that I don't know about?*

From her peripheral vision, Pearl saw Lilly Mae looking at her but paid her no never mind. Her eyes stayed focused on Pastor Carter.

"I'm so sorry to hear that," he said softly.

"Why are you sorry? It's not like you knew my father."

"Lilly Mae!" Pearl screamed in shock at her daughter's attitude.

"Well, Mama, he didn't."

"No, I didn't know your father, but I know how it feels to lose someone you love," he said as he put his head down.

There was silence in the room. The atmosphere was so thick you could cut it with a knife. Finally, Pastor Carter looked up and smiled.

"Anyway, I can call Mrs. Dupree to see if she has anything available, if you can give me a few minutes."

"That will be fine," Pearl said as she cleared her throat.

The pastor excused himself from the room. As soon as he left Vivian hit her girlfriend on the arm.

"Why are you being so rude?"

"I wasn't being rude. I'm just sick and tired of people always saying they're sorry for our loss, when they really don't even know me or my family. Oh, here's a saying that just kills me. If you *"need"* anything let me know, and I'll *"see"* what I can do. Knowing damn well they don't mean it."

"Don't cuss in the Lord's house," Pearl said flatly.

Lilly Mae looked at her mother like she was a fool.

"Mama, don't go there—don't even start it with me. Do you know how much crap goes on in 'the Lord's house'? A friend told me that all churches have truth in them, but everything in the church isn't the truth."

As her daughter ran off at the mouth, so to speak, Pearl just sat there as if she didn't hear a word. *Well, Lord you know I've been down this road a many of times. Ms. Diarrhea of the Mouth is trying to go toe to toe with me—again. She just got to have the last say.*

Tired of hearing Lilly Mae's mouth, Vivian got up from her seat and tip-toed out into the hallway. She heard the Pastor's voice coming from another office. Quietly, she walked toward it to eavesdrop on his conversation.

"Yes, yes I understand.... Ok.... No, that's fine. If anything becomes available, just give me a call.... Sure thing. Have a nice day."

Hearing the conversation end, she ran back down to his office. Upon entering the room, she saw that Lilly Mae was still at it. She sat down just as he walked back into the office. Leaning against his desk in front of them, he folded his arms across his chest and took a deep breath.

"Ladies, I talked to Mrs. Dupree, and she doesn't have any room right now. However—"

Before he could finish his statement, Lilly Mae jumped out of her chair, ranting and raving, swinging her arms in every direction.

"Something told me not to ask strangers for help!"

Her outburst caught him off guard. As he tried to stay clear, her elbow made a serious connection to his nose by accident.

"Ouch!"

He grabbed his nose as blood dripped down his shirt.

Pearl jumped up and hurried to him as she pulled tissue from her purse. Placing it up his nose, she guided him to his chair.

"Pastor, sit down and lean your head back!"

"My god, what the hell is wrong with you?! He was just trying to help you!" Vivian yelled.

Lilly Mae sucked her teeth like a kid. She turned her head away from them so no one could see the tears swelling up in her eyes.

"Help, my butt. He was just going through the same-old ritual that everyone else does when they really don't want to help you."

"Well, before you knocked the mess out of me, I was going to tell you that if you need anything to let me know, and I'll see wh—"

"What I can do. Is that what you were going to say? See, Mama, I told you. People are so fake!"

As she walked up to his desk she asked straight out, "We need a place to live. Can we stay at your house?"

Pearl was flabbergasted at her suggestion.

"Girl, what's wrong with you? You can't ask him that. We don't even know him."

"I'm just letting him know what we need. Now I want to see what he can do, which is nothing, cause people say what he said all the time. They don't mean it."

She tried to laugh. However, her emotions overwhelmed her, and she began to cry.

Vivian went to console her with a gentle hug.

"Oh, Lilly, it's ok. You all can stay at my house as long as you want."

"No, Vivian. Our babies are due soon, and that's going to be too much under one roof. I just want my own place. A place *I* can call home."

After Pearl finished wiping some of the blood off the pastor's shirt, she walked over to her crying daughter and hugged her.

"Come on, baby. We'll work it out. God has a plan for us all. Come on, child, let's go."

They all started walking toward the door.

"Now hold on a minute. Just hold on," Pastor Carter said as he stood up, being careful not to let the stuffed tissue in his nose fall out.

The ladies turned and looked at him.

"I know what I was saying before she cut me off, and I meant every word of it. I'm willing to help, if you all just slow down now. Just slow down."

Sitting back down, he cradled his nose.

"How can you help them, Pastor?" Vivian asked.

"They can stay at my house," he said as he pushed the bloody tissue further up into his nose.

"Oh, we can't do that. It won't look right," Pearl said.

Lilly Mae had her head down, praying: *Jesus, why don't she shut the heck up. We're practically in the door. Now I got to piggyback off of...you-know-what....*

"Well, Mama, I guess you're right. I mean, what will his *wife* say?"

"I no longer have a wife," he told them as he took a deep breath.

"Oh, I'm so sorry to hear that. What happened?"

"It's a long story, but that's neither here nor there. Look, the bottom-line is that I have plenty of space."

Vivian was kind of skeptical. She really didn't know the man all that well, and neither did her husband.

"Are you sure?"

"Yes, I'm sure. I'm never home. I'm always busy at work, or attending some kind of meeting. I'll let y'all stay until you get yourselves together, but under one condition."

Got damn it, here it comes... "What's that?" Lilly Mae asked.

"Y'all have got to earn your keep."

Her eyes rolled up in her head. *I knew it.... I just knew it. The man wants me to wax his knob.* Then it dawned on here. *Hey, wait a minute. I'm not volunteering to do a damn thing. He's going to have to come straight out, and tell me that I've got to give the booty up.*

"Ok, meaning...?

"Meaning if y'all cook, clean, and wash my clothes, we have a deal. It's been a while since I've had a woman's touch in my house."

"What if you get tired of them? You know she'll be having the baby soon," Vivian said.

Holding the bloody tissue in his nose, he got up and walked over to the ladies. He gave every one of them direct eye contact.

"I'm a true believer that the Lord puts people in our path for a time, a reason, and a season. That baby is going to need a home with some stability in its life. So now, do we have a deal?"

The ladies looked at each other for a few seconds. Slowly, they began to nod their heads at each other in agreement.

"Ladies, what do you say?"

"Yes, we agree," Pearl said.

With excitement, Lilly Mae extended her gratitude by kissing him on the cheek.

"Thank you, Pastor Carter."

A little uncomfortable, he stuttered, "J-J-Joe. Y'all can call me Joe."

7

*P*EARL AND LILLY Mae prepared to move into Joe's house the next day. Vivian helped them pack their clothes and loaded the car up. Her husband loaded their furniture on the truck. It was a relief to him that they were finally leaving. After sexing Lilly Mae on the down-low as often as he wanted, which was just about every day, he couldn't get it together when it was time to make love to his wife. She started to think that something was wrong with him, because he couldn't get it up. She even told him to go and see a doctor. His ego was shot at hearing those words from his own wife. *Thank God,* he thought as they all drove off.

From a distance, they saw Joe's house, which was about a thirty-five-minute drive from the Johnson residence. They couldn't believe what they were approaching. It was a beautiful, huge plantation-style home. It was painted all white with pillars and plenty of windows. As they got closer, they could see the upper level had a porch with French doors. The driveway up to the house was long.

As they got closer, they saw that there was a circular driveway in front of the house. The grass was a deep, rich green. The house was surrounded by plenty of shade from the weeping willow trees. Lilly Mae was excited. She just knew she had hit the jack pot. *This house is mine!* she claimed silently.

As they pulled up to the entrance, Bugalue blew his horn for Mr. Carter to come out, but he didn't. After waiting a few seconds, the ladies got out and started to remove their luggage. Joe heard the horn from his bedroom. He had gotten up hours ago because he couldn't really sleep. He was excited about his new guests coming to live with him.

The home in which he inherited from his great-great-greatgrandfather, Jean-Louis Pierre Bessette, who was from France. He and his wife left the family textile business, and came to America to seek their fortune. Somehow, they ended up settling in Louisiana, where Mr. Bessette started his own textile business. He had the best of fabric imported from the family business overseas. Within a few short years, his business flourished, and he became an extremely rich man, with many slaves. One of whom he became very fond of was Joe's great-great-great-grandmother Octavia. She arrived via Caribbean Islands when she was just four months old. When her mother, father and siblings were sold off, the slave trade master placed her in a wooden box on the ground and continued his business. She started crying, but the people around her acted as if she wasn't even there.

As Mr. Bessette approached the slave trade block, he heard the baby crying. Once upon her, he noticed that she was alone, so he inquired about the little one to the slave trade master. He told him that she was born on the ship, that he had just sold off her family, and didn't know what to do with her because a baby was of no use to him.

The Bessettes were unsuccessful in having children, so he brought the slave baby for a few coins as a gift for his wife. When he picked her up, she immediately stopped crying and smiled at him. Delighted in her little smile, he started laughing and called her Octavia from the name of the ship she came on.

When he presented the baby gift to his wife, she too was delighted in the beautiful bundle. The baby reminded her of her fine porcelain baby dolls that she once had when she was a little girl growing up in Europe. Her dolls had beautiful shiny black hair. Their eyes were big, with long dark eyelashes, and their complexions were rosy pink.

Mr. and Mrs. Bessette fell in love with the little one. Within a year, they informally adopted her, and she became Octavia Pier Bessette.

They raised her as their own, and vowed that no one would ever know that she came to America via slave ship. They loved her, and educated her in the best of schools in America and abroad.

As the years went by, Mrs. Bessette became very ill. She died at the age of 42 from tuberculosis. The loss of his wife devastated Mr. Bessette, causing him to go into a depression. Over the years, as Octavia grew into a very beautiful young lady, she watched her father become an introvert and a functional alcoholic.

She loved her father very much, but didn't know what to do to bring him back to the living. In need of advice, she went out to seek help from an elderly slave woman who was like a second mother to her. Mr. and Mrs. Bessette couldn't pronounce her real name, so they called her Melba. She was 91 years old, and strong as an ox. Octavia learned to knock on the slave cabin doors before entering. Melba had told her when she was little that just because they were slaves didn't mean that they weren't human. That they sat down to eat, washed their bodies, and loved their mates just like white folks did. She had also told her to do unto others as she would have them do unto her. Octavia had always kept that saying close to her heart and knocked on the door.

"Come in," frail Melba answered.

Upon entering the wooden shack, she could see that there still wasn't much in it from the first time she entered as a little girl. The wooden floor was still covered with fine loose dirt. The fireplace still had an old black iron pot hanging over it. There was a worn out wooden table with two chairs and a small bed with a decayed quilt on it. On a wooden crate, next to the bed, was her old beat up Bible. Everything was still in its same place. Melba had lived here by herself ever since her husband was killed for trying to run away from a previous slave owner. Melba didn't mind being alone. She always said that when you got God in your life, nothing else really mattered.

Octavia entered and sat on Melba's bed. She began to pour her heart out about her father's condition. Melba sat at the old wooden table and listened without saying a word. When Octavia was finished, Melba went and stood before her.

"Love your father," she said very slowly.

At hearing these three simple words, Octavia became confused; she thought she was a loving daughter.

Seeing the expression on the girl's face, Melba explained:

"You are old enough to know the truth. Your father is your father, but he isn't your flesh and blood, nor was your mother. You were brought here by way of a slave ship. No one knows of your real mother or father because you were a baby, and alone when your Master first saw you. You came from the West Indies. Your real father was probably British because of your white skin. Your mother was a Native of the West Indies. Do not be ashamed of who you are. God made you that way for a reason. God loves us all. Seek him first within your heart, and the understanding of life shall come. Your father has fathered many slave children on his property. To him, they are just that—property. But you... You on the other hand, are very special to him; always have been, always will be. Because of his wife and the love, they had for you; he held his manhood from you. Now that your mother is gone, go and bring life back to him. Your mother couldn't conceive a child for him, but you can. You are still young. Go to him, and love him as a woman would love her man. Go to him and comfort him."

Octavia was dumbfounded. She thought, *could all this be true? My mother and father aren't of my own flesh and blood. I am the product of a white man and a slave—but I don't look like a slave. I'm white. My hair isn't hard; it's fine and beautiful.*

"I don't understand these things that you tell me. I'm not dark like the slaves from Africa. My nose isn't wide, and my lips aren't protruding from my face."

Melba smiled because she knew that Octavia was naive.

"All slaves ain't from Africa. Some are from South America, and others are from the Caribbean Islands. You are what they call a mulatto."

There was nothing else to say. That day, Octavia learned the truth about her family and, more importantly, about herself. There was neither fear, nor hatred in her heart. The love that she felt for her father deepened even more. She learned that her father loved her so much so that he raised her as his own. It didn't matter to him that she was a slave. Her heart melted for knowledge of the love he had for his barren wife. Yes, she thought. *I will go and bring life back to my father by loving him as a woman would love her man.*

In the wee hours of the night, Octavia went to her father's bedroom. She stood before him naked as he slept. Silently, she wept because as she stared at him, she realized how much she loved the man she knew as father.

Jean-Louis, who was a light sleeper, heard her small sniffles and woke up. He was surprised at her nakedness.

"Octavia…" he said softly.

She didn't move. They stared into each other eyes for what seemed like all eternity. Her emotions overwhelmed her.

"Papa," she said softly as she covered her face with her hands.

Through tears, she tried to tell him what she had learned about her past from Melba, However, he stopped her.

"Shhh. Octavia, my darling…come."

He removed the covers from his body, and invited her into his bed with open arms. That night they made passionate love. They made a marriage vow between them, and lived as husband and wife. They had five sons and three daughters. They too were well-educated, and lived on the land with all the slaves. As the years went by, some of their children had sexual relations with the slaves. However, his grandchildren were never born into slavery. They grew up free and were well-educated. They had children, and their children had children. That's how Joe became the owner of the huge plantation.

He went down and greeted them with a big smile.

"Good morning. I see you all didn't have a problem finding the place."

"Finding the place was no problem. Wondering if we were going to get shot at for pulling up to this big old fancy house was the problem," Bugalue said.

"Why didn't you tell us you had a big old plantation?" Lilly Mae asked as she walked over to him, with her hands on her hips.

Looking up at his house, Joe shrugged his shoulders and said, "It's just a house. My family lived here all their lives."

Pearl walked past them with her luggage.

"Y'all going to stand out here in the heat and talk all day, or are we moving in? Time ain't standing still, and I got to prepare supper."

They all grabbed the luggage from the car except for Joe. Running past Pearl, he held the front door open for her to enter the house. Lilly Mae dropped her bags at the sight of him helping Pearl and not her.

Bugalue laughed. "I guess he likes older women."

Vivian slapped her husband on the back of his head.

"Fool, it ain't like that. He's just showing respect for the elderly."

Lilly Mae picked her bags back up and started walking toward the house.

"Respect, my butt. That man is going to learn not to be having me carry my own bags."

"What! You're not that man's wife!" Bugalue yelled.

"Right now I'm not, but you wait and see how I train a man like that."

When they entered the front door, they noticed Pearl standing there looking amazed. As they put the luggage down and looked around, they too were amazed. In front of them was a huge, gorgeous mahogany staircase with T-shaped banisters. To the left of the foyer they were standing in was a magnificent dining room. A thick cherrywood table was set for twelve. A beautiful crystal chandelier was hanging over the center of the table. Through an open door in the dining room, they could see part of another room. To the right of them was a huge library, with two big reading chairs and a small table in between them. They just stood there, admiring the beauty of the house until Joe interrupted the silence.

"Let me show you to your quarters."

No one said a thing. Still in amazement, they gathered the luggage and followed him. He first showed Mrs. Pearl to her room, which was down the hall on the left.

"Mrs. Page, this is your room."

When he opened the door, Pearl dropped her bags. *Oh, my Lord... I don't believe my eyes.* The room was big and immaculate. There was a king-size bed with pillars on all four corners. An oval porcelain tub sat on the other side of the room facing one of the three windows. There was a white porcelain flower vase sitting on top of a tall mahogany chest of draws. A beautiful, thick wooden chair and table were positioned to the left of the room. Various old paintings were hanging on the walls. Surprised at how the beautiful room was, Pearl couldn't move her feet. Lilly Mae had to give her a little nudge in order for them to enter the room. Pearl took deep breaths.

"Pastor, I—I can't sleep in this room! I'll get lost in here."

Lilly Mae rolled her eyes at her mother.

"First of all, it's Joe, not Pastor. And how are you going to get lost in a room? That's about the dumbest thing I've ever heard of," she said. "Bugalue, can you bring mama's luggage in here for me, please?"

"Sure. No problem."

When he left, Vivian pushed Lilly Mae on the sly.

"What I tell you about your mouth girl?"

"What I say wrong this time?"

While the ladies talked amongst themselves, Joe showed Pearl the closet for her clothes and linen. He pointed out to her that the tub was an antique and still useable.

"You just have to retrieve hot water from the bathroom down the hall to take a bath in it, and you have to drain the water out from underneath with a pan."

As Bugalue brought the luggage into the room, Joe was asking the party to follow him.

"Yes, with pleasure. Let's leave mama here so she can draw a map of her *room* so she won't get lost."

Everyone except for Pearl left the room and walked down a long corridor. They passed three doors, which were closed. Making a right turn they passed four doors, which were also closed. Continuing down the hall, they made yet another right. This side of the corridor had four doors. They finally stopped at the last door, which faced Pearl's room from across the banisters.

"This is your room, Lilly Mae."

Baffled, she looked at him, and then over to Pearl's room.

"Now, why would you take us all around the mulberry bush just to wind up across from my mother's room?"

He opened the door to a very nice room. To her disappointment, Lilly Mae saw that it wasn't as big as Pearl's room, but nice just the same. The bed was a king size, with big pillows on it, but no pillars. She too had a mahogany chest of draws, paintings on the wall, and a sitting area.

"Where's the tub?"

"The bathroom is right next door," Joe said as he placed her luggage on the bed.

Vivian walked over to the window and looked out.

"Oh my... Lilly Mae come look at this."

Lilly Mae walked over to the window, and saw the colorful flower garden.

"That's nice," she said dryly.

"Gardening was my wife's hobby."

"Well, who keeps it up now that she's gone, or does she come back from time to time?" Lilly Mae asked as she walked over to check out the huge walk-in closet.

"No, she's been gone for some years now. I keep it up myself. It actually relaxes me."

Satisfied with the answer, Lilly Mae walked back over to the window and looked down at the garden again. *Lord if that's what relaxes him; I'm going to have that Negro walking in the daylight with a candle looking for me.* Her attitude quickly changed about the garden.

"You know, Joe, the flowers are beautiful. I had a flower garden once. But when my daddy passed away I just lost interest in it. Maybe I can start it back up," she said softly.

"That would be nice to have someone sharing my interest," he said with a smile, which caused her to blush.

"So Joe what's up with the other bedrooms?" Bugalue asked.

"Nothing. They're just empty rooms for now. I mean…but since Lilly Mae's having a baby she can pick whichever one she wants the nursery to be in."

"Speaking of rooms…where is yours? I know you must have the best room in the house," Vivian said.

"Oh, my room is on the opposite side of this corridor. Pearl's room and mine were the only two rooms that I didn't have modernized. It's the same as it was during slavery time. There's a guest bedroom and a bathroom between us. Pearl's room was the house slave's room."

Not believing what he just heard, Bugalue waved his hands in the air.

"Wait a minute. Hold up! You mean to tell me that your three-times-great granddaddy had the house nigger, which I know *had* to be a light skin female, living in the big house. What did his wife say about that?"

"Oh, I don't know. From what I've been told they didn't even share the same bedroom."

"Get out of town!" Vivian said because she was surprised at the living arrangement.

Joe thought about what he just said. And knowing the history of slavery, it was kind of odd to have a servant actually living in the master's house. However, he could give no explanation for it.

"Man, talk about privacy and service at the same time," Bugalue said with a great big smile.

"Well, that's how he ran the house back then. Everyone knew their place. His wife and kids' rooms I think were on this side of the house because he didn't want to be disturbed by them. I really don't think they slept in separate bedrooms all the time. I mean we *do* have a huge family. My great-great-great-grandparents loved each other very much from what I've been told. Maybe down the line as they got up in age something happened between them."

Bugalue put his hands on his wife's stomach.

"Baby, maybe we should start living like Joe's people did. I can have my own room, and you and the baby can have y'all own room. That way, I don't have to be bothered with neither one of *y'all* when *y'all* start acting crazy."

Vivian made an attempt to smack some more crap out of her husband's head, but missed. Bobbing and weaving like a pro fighter, he threw a few playful jabs at her. Joe escorted his guest back toward the stairs.

"I'll be happy to show you all the rest of the house and the grounds if you like."

Eager to check things out, Vivian agreed.

"Hold up," Lilly Mae said. "Let's get mama first so she won't get lost and panic trying to find us."

They all walked back to Pearl's room. Lilly Mae knocked on the door, but there was no answer. She knocked again, still no answer. She called for her mother as she opened the door.

"Mama...you in there? We're about to tour the rest of the house and..."

Out of nowhere Pearl appeared at the bottom of the staircase, and yelled up to them.

"Whenever you all are ready I got some ham sandwiches and ice cold lemonade for you! And before you come down make sure y'all wash your hands first! You're not eating at my table with no dirty hands!"

Surprised as all outdoors they looked at each other and burst out laughing.

"Well, I guess we're going to have to take that tour a little later. Mrs. Pearl done found her way to the kitchen and conquered it," Joe said

"And I didn't need no map either!" she yelled as she walked back to the kitchen.

Lilly Mae abruptly stopped laughing. Her facial expression clearly showed that she was surprised at her mother's feistiness.

8

AFTER LILLY MAE made the smart remark, about her mother needing a map for her room, Pearl wasn't in the mood to see her daughter's room, nor any other room for that matter. She just wanted to be alone. When they all left, she got down on her knees and thank God for blessing them with a place to live. Once finished, she got up and walked around the room. In amazement, she touched the beautiful mahogany furniture, the thick, white tub that was resting on fancy legs and the porcelain vase. She even smelt the old quilt that was on the bed. Walking over to the French doors, she opened them and saw two white wicker chairs, and a small table on the porch. Leaving the door open for the light cool breeze to come in, she went to her bed and began to unpack her suitcase. Once finished, she put her luggage in the closet and sat on the king-size bed. She stared at the walls for a few minutes. Tired of doing that, she decided to lie down just to see how the bed felt. It was soft and comfortable. Not like her old bed, which was nice but a little too firm for her. She didn't complain to her husband about it because he liked the way it felt.

After a few minutes of lying there she became restless and sat up. Looking at the old furniture, she wondered if it needed to be cleaned. As she walked over to the linen closet to retrieve a dust cloth, she did a two-finger dust sweep on the dresser, and saw that the furniture definitely needed a wipe-down.

So off she went into doing her busy work. And in doing that she came upon an enormous painting of a beautiful white woman, sitting like a goddess on a tree stump. The woman had a very distinctive look. Her lips were full, and her eyes were big and round. Her nose was small and pointy. Her cheekbones were really high, and her hair was a fiery red color with a sea of waves going down her back. She had on a long, fancy, pearl-white, low-cut dress, which showed off her cleavage. Below the painting was the name "Isabelle 'Sea of Fire'" Pearl stared at the woman for a while. She knew from the combined features that the woman was a half-breed and that she could pass for white. The picture caused her to think about her own Native American ancestors; the Iroquois Tribe. They consisted of the Cayuga, Mohawk, Oneida, Onondaga, Seneca and Tuscarora tribes. They were physically strong, spirited, high self-esteem people, who worked in the fur trade business among other things. Pearl's parents and grandparents made sure that she knew and remembered her history.

She stared at the beautiful woman and wondered, *did you denounce your race to survive in the white man's world?*

Pearl wiped the painting clean. When she finished, she stepped back to admire it. That's when she noticed a small horizontal indentation under the name plate. She walked back up to the painting to wipe the tiny area down. However, as soon as she touched it, the painting moved a little to the left. Startled, she dropped her cloth and ran to the bed for protection. As she held on to one of the pillars, she waited to see if something was going to happen. When nothing did, she slowly walked back to the painting and picked up her cloth.

She stared at the small space that was now between the wall of the painting, and the wall next to it. Curiosity had a hold on her.

"Hello...?"

When no one answered, she boldly pushed the bronze indentation all the way in, which caused the wall to open to the size of a door.

"Hello? Anybody there?"

There was no answer. Pearl stepped into the breezeway of the door and saw a descending staircase in the shape of a backwards L. To the right of her was an old, gold candleholder sitting on a small ledge. There were three long white candles, and a box of thick stick matches next to it. Grabbing a match, she struck it alongside the box and lit one of the candles. She placed it in the candleholder and went down the steps. The hidden passage was dark and cold. Spider webs were everywhere. With each step she took, an eerie sound was made. By the time she reached the small platform, she counted 11 steps. Turning to her left, she went down seven more steps. There before her was an old beat-up wooden door with a bronze door knob. She turned it, but it didn't open.

"What the...?"

Turning the knob again she gave the door a little push. Still it didn't open. Pearl placed the candle down on a ledge to her right. Like upstairs it too had a box of stick matches and candles. Looking up the steps, she saw a very faint light coming from her bedroom. She contemplated: *Do I go up or do I just yell for someone to find me?* With her bad hip, it was a little difficult walking down all those steps, and it would be even harder for her to go back up. *If I do yell for help, Lilly Mae is going to have a field day with "I told you so" and "Why didn't you draw yourself a map?" That would make me look stupid in front of everyone.* Envisioning this, Pearl became angry with herself. *Something told me not to go down these damn steps. But ohhh no you had to be nosey. You just had to see fat ass.*

Really pissed-off, Pearl grabbed the doorknob. With all her might she pushed. *Crack!* To her surprise, the door gave way, causing her to fall on the floor. She cried out in pain as she landed with a hard thump.

"Oh crap!"

She hoped that no one heard her. After a few minutes of silence, she mustered up the strength to get up off the floor. Straightening out her dress, and making sure that her hair was still in place, she took a deep breath.

"Now, let's see what room this is."

In observing the room, she saw that she landed in the kitchen. Looking back at the old door she thought, *that must have been the servant door used by the slaves.* Putting her hands on her hips, she admired the big kitchen.

"Well, I'm in the right room so I might as well get to cooking."

Looking across the room she saw an open pantry displaying stacks upon stacks of can goods, peanuts, potatoes, cucumbers, tomatoes, onions and then some. But what really caught her eye were the clear jars of fruit preserves sitting on the shelves. Smiling, she walked over to them.

"Now I know good and well this man didn't do this."

Taking one of the jars off the shelf, she opened it. And behold the aroma of fresh peaches lit her nose up like a firecracker. She dipped her finger into the jar for a quick taste.

"Wow, now these are sweet."

Still dipping her finger in the preserves, she walked over to the sink that had a window with sunflower design curtains. Looking out, she saw rows upon rows of different vegetables. And just beyond that she saw a few run down wooden cabins.

That's where the slaves must have lived while working the land. Abruptly, she turned around and stared at the stair passage that lead-up to her bedroom. *What kind of Slave Master would have a picture of a half-breed in his house?* She pondered this thought until the growling of her stomach brought her back to reality.

"Good Lord. I hope this man got some food in the refrigerator."

When she opened the refrigerator door, her face lit up like a Christmas tree, when she saw all the food in there. Joe had meat, eggs, milk, butter, fresh vegetables, and bread neatly placed on the shelves. Pearl was happy as a jaybird with a worm in its mouth going home to feed its family. She grabbed the apron that was hanging on the wall and went to work. While she was whipping something up for lunch, she started thinking about what she was going to fix for supper already. *This is my kitchen*, she claimed, just like Lilly Mae claimed that Joe was going to be her husband.

9

*W*HEN LUNCH WAS over, they toured the rest of the house and outside property. After that, Joe and Bugalue took the Pages furniture, and placed it in one of the shacks. When all was said and done; Joe, Pearl, and Lilly Mae escorted Vivian and her husband back to their vehicle. They said their good-byes, and the Johnsons were off to their own little world once again. Lilly Mae kept waving bye to them until they were no longer in sight. By the time she went back into the house Pearl had the kitchen just about clean, and Joe was in the library reading his newspaper.

"Joe, is there anything we need to know about the house, or are there any rules that need to be established by you?" she asked as she approached him.

"Um, no, not really. Just the things that I asked for earlier," he answered without looking at her.

"Ok, I guess that's it then," she said smiling, and began to walk away.

"Oh, there is just one little thing that I will not tolerate."

Lilly Mae stopped in her tracks. "What's that Joe?"

"I can't stand to be disturbed while I'm reading. That's all."

Shuffling his newspaper, he went back to reading. Immediately, Lilly Mae took offense to what he said, because she had just done the very thing that he didn't like. She put her pride to the side and apologized.

"Ok, I understand and I do apologize for disturbing you. It won't happen again."

Leaving Joe to his solitude, she walked right into the kitchen and sat down at the table.

"Oh, I can't believe that man."

Pearl stopped cleaning and looked at her daughter.

"What's your problem?"

"Can you believe that man said that we're *not* too disturb him while he is reading?" she said as her left leg shook a mile a minute.

"What's wrong with that?" Pearl asked as she went back to her cleaning.

"What's wrong with that! Mama, are you serious? That's like someone telling you to speak only when spoken to, or be seen and not heard. That's not right. I mean, who does he think he is?"

Pearl tried to stay calm while her spoiled daughter kept going on and on. But finally, she couldn't take it anymore. Using her inner voice, she gave her daughter a piece of her mind.

"Look, girl. That man is head of household here. He opened up this beautiful home to two strangers. Not to mention to a stranger who is pregnant, and don't know who the damn baby-daddy is. Now whatever that man says, *that's* what we're going to do, whether you like it or not. The only thing he said that we have to do to maintain in his house was to earn our keep, and *that's* what I intend to do. If you got any common sense, you'd do the same because I don't see a soul hiring a pregnant woman for work. Now get that broom over there and sweep this kitchen up. And learn to keep your big mouth shut sometimes. No one wants to hear your mouth, child. I like this house. It has a lot of history. And I plan on staying here—with or without you."

Lilly Mae was stunned. Her mother had never talked to her like that before. Rolling her eyes, she got the broom and started sweeping.

PART THREE

10

*T*HE LADIES ESTABLISHED certain rules between themselves when it came time to maintain the house. For instance, when small stuff was needed for the house, like milk, eggs, and butter, Lilly Mae would go shopping for it while Pearl ran to do Joe's business. She did stuff like picking up his clothes from the cleaners, going to the post office to retrieve his mail, having things copied for his town meetings and such. For whatever reason, Pearl didn't trust Lilly Mae to take care of his business for him. That's why she gave her the task of shopping for food just to keep her busy. It was a good arrangement between them both.

It was now Saturday morning; a busy day for the ladies. Pearl was at the post office dropping off a package and checking the mailbox, while Lilly Mae was at the General Store picking up some odds and ends for the house.

Whatever people needed, the General Store had it. The owner, who was Jewish, knew that if he had everything that his customers wanted and needed under one roof, they wouldn't go anywhere else to shop. Furthermore, in observing the colored community, he noticed that as soon as a lot of the men got paid, they were broke by next week. This was due to a spending spree on partying, alcohol, gambling and hookers. It left mothers with no money to feed or clothe their children. Hence, the General Store credit came into being.

The owner was very lenient with the credit because he knew that he was going to get his money back with 25 cents on the dollar. They needed him for hard times and he needed them to keep his business going.

Whenever the store owner was absent from work, he would have an elderly white man named George tend the store. He watched colored folk like a hawk when they entered. At times, he would act like he was dusting the canned goods just to keep his eye on their location. He was from the era of the "NO COLORED" signs.

With a small basket, Lilly Mae shopped for food. In doing so, she faintly heard a familiar female voice in the next aisle.

"Go over there and get us a cart," the lady said.

She saw a little girl who she thought she recognized running toward the silver cart. When the little one got there, she made an attempt to reach the handle, but couldn't. On her tippy toes, she pulled on the handle several times, but it didn't budge. Frustrated, she stopped and took a deep breath. The familiar voice encouraged her.

"Go 'head, baby, try again. Don't give up. Pull really hard."

Spitting on both hands, she rubbed them together and attempted again. She pulled and pulled with all her little might. She kept pulling until finally it came loose, causing her to fall backward onto the fruit stand. She and the fruit fell to the floor. Lilly Mae ran over and tried to catch some of the fruit from falling with her basket, but it was just too many.

"Oh, my God! Roxie, are you alright?!" Vivian yelled as she ran to her niece.

Hearing the commotion, George ran to the little girl and with force grabbed her by the arm.

"Hey! What in Sam hell is going on over here? Get up and clean this mess up now!"

Roxanne started to cry.

"Aunt Vivian, get this man off me! Let me go! Get off me!"

Vivian, who had her newborn baby with her, started hitting George on the back of his head with the baby's diaper bag.

"What are you doing to my niece?! Get your hands off of her!"

"Stop hitting me! She was trying to steal my fruit! Now look what she's done! The fruit is all over the floor!"

"No, she wasn't. She was trying to get a cart and fell backwards when it came loose. No one was trying to steal anything," Lilly Mae said as she picked up some of the fruit.

"Please let me go!"

"Didn't I tell you to get your hands off my niece?!"

Customers heard the loud commotion and began to gather around them to see what was going on. When they saw the little girl crying, they became verbally aggressive toward George. He let the child go and tried to calm them down.

"It's alright, everything is alright. Go back to your shopping."

They didn't move. Still crying, the little one got up and ran to her aunt.

"Look, you can't talk to me like that. I'm the storekeeper you know," George stated as he picked up the remaining fruit and placed it back on its stand.

"Well, you might be the storekeeper, but you're not the owner. Just in case you haven't noticed, you *are* in a colored neighborhood. Now if I go outside and tell everybody how you done grabbed one of their own by the arm, yelled at her, and accused her of stealing fruit, you won't have a store to keep."

"And not only that. All of us standing here will bear witness to everything that just took place," Lilly Mae said.

"That's right!" an elderly lady yelled from the crowd causing everyone else to jump on the band wagon.

"It seems to me like you owe my niece an apology *and* some free candy," Vivian looked down and winked at Roxie, who was clenching her right leg. When the little one smiled up at her, the crowd sighed with relief. Satisfied that she was alright, they all went back to continue their shopping. With a frown, George looked at the ladies then to Roxanne. With much hesitation, he walked up front to a barrel full of Mary Jane candy and grabbed a handful. He put the little peanut-tasting sweets in a small brown bag and walked back over to them.

"Here," he said as he extended the bag to the little girl.

Roxanne immediately turned her head and buried her face into Vivian's dress. Patting her on the back she gave the little one a reassuring smile.

"It's ok, baby. You can take it."

Roxanne looked at the old man and then to the bag of candy. Quickly, she grabbed the bag while still holding on to her aunt. Mumbling underneath his breath, George started to walk away, but Lilly Mae stopped him.

"Hey, excuse me."

"What!" he yelled as he turned to face them.

"We didn't hear you apologize to Roxanne. Vivian, did you hear him apologize to Roxanne?"

Vivian popped a Mary Jane in her mouth after giving Roxie one. "Nope. I sure didn't."

They both stared at the storekeeper as if they were in a silent debate.

"Little girl—"

"Roxanne!" they both yelled in unison.

He took a deep breath. "Roxanne I'm sorry."

The little girl smiled as sugar juice ran down the side of her mouth from the candy.

"Well, that's better. Now things can go back to normal around here," Lilly Mae said with a great big ole smile.

"Damn niggers," George mumbled as he walked back to the counter and sat on his stool.

Vivian and Lilly Mae burst out laughing while giving each other a hug.

"Girl, *that's* what I'm talking about. We women have *got* to stick together," Vivian said.

Their loud laughter caused the baby to cry. Lilly Mae pulled the light pink blanket from her face.

"Ah, she's so cute."

She bent down and kissed Lil' Suzie on her fat, tiny cheeks. Vivian took her candy out of her mouth and rubbed Suzie's lips with it. Instantly, the baby stopped crying and began to lick her lips. Lilly Mae laughed.

"My goodness, look at her. How are you and the little one doing?"

Vivian kissed her baby on the lips.

"We're doing just fine. When are you going to drop that load girl?"

"I'll drop it whenever the good Lord says it's time."

Vivian took the shopping cart that Roxanne had pulled out and laid Suzie down in the small upper part. The ladies began their shopping like nothing had ever happened. Roxanne walked behind them, holding onto Vivian's dress while enjoying her candy.

"So, what's going on with you and Mr. Joe Carter? Did you give him any yet?" Vivian asked as she reached for a box of cornflakes.

"Vivian!"

"What? I know you're not surprised. You haven't changed. Just because your butt is pregnant don't mean a thing."

"Suzie, mama got something good for you," she said playfully as she opened another piece of candy.

She licked the candy first then laid it against her tiny lips. With the sweet taste of sugar, the baby got excited.

"Girl, you can't be giving her sugar like that. Where's her bottle?"

"I left it in the car. This will hold her for right now. So what are you trying to say?

"I don't know. I mean, I walk around the house trying to look sexy with this big stomach and these huge tits, but the man doesn't even look at me."

For about five-minutes, Vivian listened without interruption. When her girlfriend finished, she had her say.

"First of all, you're reading his signs all wrong. He's not like the rest of those men you're used to dealing with. He's a gentleman, and one with class, I might add. You got to step your game up."

"What do you mean?"

"Girl, I can't believe you. That baby you're carrying done slowed your "A" game down. Listen, first of all, you got to have his dinner ready for him when he gets home from working all day. You know, wait on him hand and foot, as my grandma would say. Have his bath water ready nice and hot. Also, have his newspaper and pipe or whatever he smokes, if he does smoke, next to his favorite chair. When he says that his feet or his shoulders are hurting, rub them for him. If you do stuff like that, he's going to know what time it is."

Now in the dairy section, Vivian picked up fresh eggs and milk and placed them in her cart. Lilly Mae put a block of butter in her basket along with some cheese.

"Girl, you crazy"

"Crazy but true. Why you think these black professionals, entrepreneurs and athletes go for women outside their race?"

Lilly Mae waited for the answer.

"It's because they don't have a problem doing whatever it takes to make their man happy."

Lilly Mae laughed at Vivian's perception of a woman's role.

"Oh my goodness." Looking down at Roxanne she told her, "Baby-girl, please don't listen to what your auntie is saying, ok."

"You try it and see what happens. Then after all of that, you slowly start putting that tight, juicy thing on him and he will be eating out of your hands."

"Is that what you did to get your husband?"

"Hell no girl, that ain't for me. My dumb butt got pregnant, so we got married."

"So you all love each other, right?"

"Love...? What does love got to do with it? He got a baby by me, so he got me for life."

Looking at her friend, but dare not say a word, she thought, *you must be out of your damn mind to think that a baby will keep a man for life.*

"Sure you right"

"You d-a-m-n right. Anyway, let's get back to your situation. If you do some crazy, freaky, sexy stuff like suck his toes, or lick him between his—"

"Alright, thank you very much, Mrs. Johnson. I got the picture."

"Alright handle it then. Cause if you do that, you will be Mrs. Joe Carter in no time."

They finished up their shopping, and went to the register to pay for their groceries. The store keeper didn't even give them eye contact. He rang their food up, placed it in a brown paper bag, took their money and gave them their change back without saying a word. They took their bags, and walked toward the door to leave. However, before they walked out Vivian turned around, and said to him with a happy-go-lucky grin, "Have a good day, Mr. Storekeeper." And of course, he didn't respond.

Pearl was just pulling up to the store as they walked out. Her timing was perfect because a few light raindrops had begun falling. A huge thunderstorm was on its way. She blew her horn and Lilly Mae acknowledged by waving.

"Well, there's mama."

Waving to Mrs. Pearl, Vivian yelled, "How you doing, Ma Pearl?" "I'm doing just fine, how you and the baby doing?" Pearl yelled as she waved back.

"We're just fine. Remember Lil Roxie, my oldest sister's little girl? Say hi, baby."

"Hi Mrs. Earl, hi!"

"No baby, its Mrs. Pearl, not Earl."

Lilly Mae laughed and then noticed that it was getting dark really fast. The wind picked up a little too.

"Well, give me a hug. We best to be getting home before it pours down."

"Ok girl, love you. And don't forget to do what I told you." "I'll think about it. Bye, crazy."

11

*I*T BEGAN TO pour down rain as Pearl slowly walked up the front porch steps with Joe's dry cleaning. Lilly Mae was already at the door holding it open for her mother.

"Ma, come on. I got to use the bathroom."

"Hold on now. Don't get your panties all up in a bunch. I can only walk but so fast."

"Mama, come on I can't hold it much longer," she said as she did a little wiggle.

No sooner than Pearl got in the house, Lilly Mae dropped the bag of groceries on the hall table, and ran up the steps like lightning.

"Ma, leave the door open so the storm can bring some fresh cool air in the house."

Doing just that, Pearl went to the hall closet and hung the dry cleaning up. Grabbing the groceries off the table, she went into the kitchen and started to put them away. Within a few minutes, Lilly Mae walked in.

"Man, I was about to burst. So, Mama, what are we having for dinner?"

After putting up the groceries, Pearl went to the refrigerator and pulled out three of the four Cornish hens. She walked over to the kitchen sink, and ran some warm water to rinse them off.

"We're having stuffed hen, brown rice and corn on the cob."

Lilly Mae got a big bowl from the counter, and went to the pantry to retrieve six ears of corn. She brought them back to the table and began shucking them. Pearl was beside herself as she watched her daughter.

"Well, what are you doing?"

"I'm helping you cook, Mama," Lilly Mae said smiling.

Pearl turned the water off.

"I can see that, but why? You never have before."

Lilly Mae's smile faded away.

"It's about time I start learning, don't you think, Mama."

Pearl didn't say a word. She simple turned the water back on, and continued to clean the hens. *I know what you're up to child, and I don't blame you. A good man is sure hard to find.*

Lilly Mae finished shucking the corn and was walking toward the sink, when suddenly loud thunder and lightning roared across the sky. *Boom! Boom!* Startled and scared out of their wits, Lilly Mae dropped the bowl of corn and the hen flew out of Pearl's hands. They screamed and ducked for cover under the table.

Boom! Boom! Boom!

"Hurry and turn the lights out!" Pearl whispered.

Without hesitation, Lilly Mae ran and turned the light switch off and ran back under the table. They didn't move a muscle.

It was taught to folks from way back when to turn all the electricity off in the house and sit still, when it's thundering and lightning. It was also told to children, when it's sunny and raining with thunder at the same time, God and the Devil were fighting. These old sayings were the beliefs of people, and everyone knows that your belief determines your behavior.

They sat there without saying a word until the storm sounded like it was fading away, which was about 10 to 15 minutes later. Even though it stopped thundering and lightning, it continued to rain. Pearl listened for a few minutes more.

"It's passing now. Go 'head and turn the lights back on."

After doing as she was told, Lilly Mae gathered the ears of corn off the floor and put them back in the bowl. Pearl got up and started looking for the hen that flew out of her hands. She looked everywhere for that hen, but couldn't find it.

"Well Lord, we had three hens, now we got two."

She went back to the refrigerator and grabbed the last hen. As she closed the door, the missing in action hen fell to the floor.

"What the…!"

Lilly Mae looked over at her mother and saw her picking up the hen off the floor.

"Didn't you just look over there?"

"Dag on thing flew on top of the refrigerator," Pearl said as she put one of the hens back into the refrigerator.

They continued to do what they were doing before they got the daylights scared out of them. Lilly Mae put the bowl of corn on the counter and took a deep breath. Pearl smiled and started snickering to herself. Lilly Mae looked at her mother like she was a little touched in the head.

"Ma, what's so funny?"

Pearl's snicker became a small laugh. Then it got loud. Soon her mother's laughter became contagious, and she started laughing too.

"We must be some crazy fools doing what we did, baby."

Lilly Mae was bent over laughing.

"Mama, we've been doing it for so long it's just in us. Remember when I was little me and my friends would take a stick and dig a hole in the ground? We would put our ear to it talking about we can hear the devil beating his wife."

They died laughing at the memory.

"And remember I wouldn't go outside because of the saying, 'step on a crack you break your Mama's back'? Man, I was so scared that you would be laying on the floor with your back cracked when I got home."

Pearl screamed with laughter. And Lilly Mae laughed so hard she had tears in her eyes. Pearl had to sit down because her stomach was hurting from laughing. No one noticed Joe standing in the kitchen doorway soaking wet. He cleared his throat.

"Ladies, I see you're enjoying this fine weather we're having."

Abruptly, they stopped laughing and looked at him. Surprised at his condition, Lilly Mae ran over to him and helped him out of his suit jacket.

"What in the world happened to you?" she asked as she placed his jacket on the back of the kitchen chair to dry out.

"The stupid car died on me while I was trying to drive through a small flood. I had to walk all the way from Hudson Street."

"Well, at least you made it home without getting struck by lightning. I'm surprised no one stopped to give you a ride," Lilly Mae said still laughing a little.

"Oh, so you think it's funny."

She tried to stop laughing, but couldn't get it together.

"No, but with the expression you have on your face I couldn't help but laugh. Look at you! You've got mud all on your pants."

He looked down at himself.

"That's what happens when you're running through puddles.

Let me go upstairs and take these wet clothes off."

As he was about to leave, Pearl stopped him.

"Hold it right there. Take them shoes off and put them muddy things out on the front porch. I don't need you messing up the floor no more than what you've already done."

She walked back to the sink. Going back over to Joe, Lilly Mae got down on her knees to take his shoes off.

"What are you doing?"

She looked up at him and smiled.

"I'm taking your shoes off."

Her actions caught him off guard and caused him to be off balance. He had to hurry and grab the wall to keep from falling.

"Hey, wait a minute."

Without saying another word, she got his muddy shoes off and went to put them out on the porch. As she walked back down the hallway, she saw him going up the steps, so she followed him.

"Now what?" he asked.

"I got a surprise for you."

"Surprise?"

"Yes. Come on," she said with excitement.

She attempted to hold his hand, but he pulled back.

"Hold on, now. I got to get out of these wet clothes."

"I know. That's why I'm telling you to come on."

She grabbed his hand and escorted him down the hallway. When they reached the bathroom, she slowly opened the door to a man's dream. His tub was full of hot, steamy water. She had clean clothes laid out on a wooden chair. On the table, next to the chair was a cigar with a cutter, and a box of thick matches. A glass of red wine and a small flower arrangement in a beautiful vase that she had decorated herself were also on the table.

"Wow, this is nice," he said as he walked into his bathroom.

Lilly Mae followed him in and closed the door. She was excited with her little surprise for him.

"You like it? It's not too much, is it?"

Staring at the water, Joe went into a trance. He remembered doing the same thing for his lovely long-ago wife. It was a romantic attempt to win her love; a love that he never had from the beginning.

They were introduced to each other at their church through both of their parents. For Joe, it was love at first sight. For her, he was just another guy. Nevertheless, her parents encouraged her to get serious about him, so she played the game to please them. Within a few months of dating, Joe's nose was wide open for her. She was totally different from the Christian women at church. The way she walked, talked, and dressed blew his mind. The girl had fire in her soul, and she was what folks called a loosey-goosey. Joe had expressed to several friends that he was going to pop the question to her. However, they all told him that she wasn't the type of woman that a God-fearing man should marry. And of course, he didn't care what they said. After all, she was his first love, so he followed his heart. And in just a little over five years, his wife followed another man. Now here he stands, in his own bathroom getting the same treatment he once tried to give to his wife.

"Yes—I mean no, it's not too much. I've never had anyone do this for me before."

Lilly Mae walked over to the water and felt the temperature. She ran the bath water piping-hot when she went up to use the bathroom. It was perfect.

"You deserve it, Joe."

It was as if he didn't hear her. He was still staring at the bath water when Lilly Mae approached him. Standing before him, she loosened his neck tie. Then she unbuttoned his shirt.

"You know, Joe, this is the way a woman is supposed to treat a good man."

"Is that right?"

"Yes. Mama told me that a way to a man's heart is through his belly," she said.

Joe's body became stiff as a board as she walked around to his back and slowly removed his tie and pulled off his wet shirt.

"Is that right?"

Silently, she gasped at his beautiful masculine back. She had no idea of how well defined he was underneath his clothes.

"That's what she said. But you know what I say?"

"What?"

"I say that a way to a man's heart is to first feed him spiritually," she said in a slow, soft whisper and then kissed him gently on the back of his neck.

But he didn't respond.

"To pamper him physically."

She ever so gently licked a small area of his back.

"And make love to him mentally."

She reached around to his soft, hairy chest and caressed it for a few seconds. Then to her own surprise, as she hugged him from behind, she laid her head against his wet back. Joe reached up in an attempt to touch her hands but couldn't. Standing like a statue, he took a deep breath and looked up at the ceiling to prevent tears from falling down his face.

"You feel good, Joe."

"Lilly Mae, I—I don't know what to—"

"Shhh. Don't say a word. Just let me hold you. I appreciate you, Joe. It takes a God-fearing man to do the things that you've done for me and Mama."

"I just did what any ordinary man would do."

She turned him around to face her.

"No, Joe, you did more than that. You took us into your house and we made it a home. You didn't care about what people would say or how things looked to the community. We made it a home because we care about each other."

He looked down at her.

"Do you really care for me, or is it because I saved you and your mama from the streets?"

"Joe, I've been going out of my mind thinking about you. When you're around me, I want to touch you so bad. I want to smell your body and taste you."

As she talked, her lips came within inches of his lips. But, before they could touch, he pulled back. Disgusted with his negativity toward her, she abruptly turned and walked away from him. With her back to him, she continued.

"You don't pay me any attention. I know it's not easy to desire a woman who's pregnant by another man."

On cue, she mustered up all her talent and started crying. Feeling sorry for her, he walked over to comfort her. He made an attempt to touch her shoulders, but couldn't.

"Lilly Mae, its not that. Its just that..." He hadn't touched another woman since his wife left him.

With a face full of crocodile tears, she turned to face him.

"What, Joe? I'll do anything you want me to do."

"Its just that I don't want to get hurt no more. I've noticed you. The first day I laid eyes on you, I thought you were so beautifully pregnant. I've even dreamed of the baby being mine."

At hearing this, Lilly Mae really poured the tears on. She had no idea that this man was feeling her like that.

"That little baby is going to need a daddy. And I so much want to have a family of my own."

Hot damn here we go. The big home run that I've been waiting for. She had an opening and went for it.

"Will you be my child's father? Could you love another man's child?"

Turning her head away from him, she braced herself for his answer. Joe gently turned her back around to face him.

"You know God loves us all. Who am I to judge? I can love yours, ours and anyone else's if it's God's will. Will you be mine, all mines? Will you marry me?"

What! Her heart skipped several beats. She had no idea that her plan was going to work so fast. He grabbed her face with both hands and kissed her tears away.

"What do you say? Will you have my baby? Will you have my children for me and make me a proud father?"

Lilly Mae was on cloud nine. *Wow, I had no idea this man was thinking like this. I can't wait to tell Vivian. I don't have to do a thing but get laid and have this Negro's babies. Hot damn, I'm in the big league now.*

"You're so beautiful. We are going to have us some pretty babies," he said as he touched her stomach with a gentle hand.

Joe walked over to the flower vase and removed one of the little yellow plastic rings that hung from it.

"What are you doing? I made that for you!"

Dipping the plastic ring into the bath water, he swished it around a few times, and wiped it dry on his bath cloth. With his chest stuck out like a peacock feathers, he began to walk slowly toward her.

"Man, are you crazy?"

He continued toward her with southern pride displayed on his face. Standing before her, he got down on one knee, and cleared his throat before speaking.

"Lilly Mae Page, will you marry me?"

When he presented the yellow plastic ring tears of joy ran down her face.

"Yes! Yes, I'll marry you, Joe Carter."

After placing the plastic ring on her ring finger, he got up off the floor, and gave his wife-to-be a big, sloppy tongue-down-the-throat kind of kiss. Lilly Mae was taken aback from his soft, strong lips. She became light-headed and had to hold on to the little chair for balance.

"Oh, my goodness."

Smiling, he threw his head back and gave a howl like you've never heard before. "Yes Lord, thank you Jesus! Yes! My prayers have been answered! Thank you, Jesus!"

Staring into his future wife's eyes like a madman, he held her stomach.

"Baby, we got to get married before this here baby is born. It has to have my last name before it comes into this world."

Pearl heard the yelling going on upstairs and walked out into the hallway. Standing at the bottom of the steps she yelled, "What's going on up there? Y'all bet 'not be messing up my floors."

Joe shot out the bathroom and ran to the top of the stairs.

"Mrs. Pearl, Lilly Mae and I are engaged!"

Lilly Mae wobbled down the hallway to her husband-to-be.

"Joe."

He ran back to her and escorted her to the banisters.

"See Mama, he gave me a ring."

"Ok, well y'all come own down here and engage yourselves into this food I done cooked. Y'all up there playing around while the food getting cold," she mumbled under her breathe as she walked back to the kitchen. "Don't know what to do with yourselves." Half way to the kitchen she turned and yelled, "And hurry up."

Lilly Mae and Joe stood dumbfounded.

"I just told your mother that we were engaged, and it went right over her head."

"I do believe my Mama is getting old."

"And on that note, I think we need a bath," Joe said with a crazy, playful grin on his face.

"No, *we* don't need a thing. *You* need a—"

He picked her up with his strong arms and headed for the bathroom. Lilly Mae was kicking and laughing up a storm. She tried to get out of his arms but couldn't.

"Put me down, Joe! I don't need a bath."

He entered the bathroom and stood a few feet from the tub.

"Oh, yes you do."

"Please, no! I'm pregnant!"

He moved slightly closer to the water.

"That's right, and with our baby."

Lilly Mae continued to plead with him as he moved closer and closer to the tub.

"Are you sure you want me to put you down right now?"

"Yes!"

His smile grew even bigger. He had her totally over the bath water.

"Oh no, Joe!" she yelled and held him tight.

Laughing he stepped into the water.

"No don't put me down. I'm going to kill you. Joe no... Please...!"

Gently, he sat down in the soothing water with her on his lap.

"Why did you do this to me; look at me... I'm a mess."

"Yes, but you're my mess now. You belong to me," he said with a soft whisper as he stared into her eyes.

She melted in his arms. *Finally, I belong to someone.*

Gently taking her face, he brought it close to his.

"I love you," he whispered.

"I love you, too."

That night for the first time they made passionate love.

PART FOUR

12

WEEKS BEFORE THE baby was due, Lilly Mae and Pearl had the wedding set up and paid for. Pearl and some of the women from Joe's church catered the food buffet style. The menu consisted of salad with three types of dressing, a choice of roast beef with red wine, or baked chicken with white wine, green beans, red potatoes, and a variety of rolls. Their wedding cake was prepared by Cecelia's Bakery from across town. It was a beautiful, tall three layered yellow cake, with white frosting. Lilac, made from cream cheese frosting, were placed all around it. The top layer had a plastic figurine couple standing hand-and-hand under a white plastic heart.

Lilly Mae's wedding dress was designed and made by her mother. Mrs. Pearl brought the fabric from a very expensive textile store, over in the white section of town, and worked around the clock to make sure that the dress was ready on time.

No one had seen such a beautiful wedding dress before. It was white with silk lace and faux pearls around the bottom of the gown. Pearl made it really wide so that no one could notice her daughter's pregnancy. The top had a deep V-neck, front and back, with short sleeves that just barely hung off her shoulders. Her veil covered only her face; Lilly Mae wanted her long, wavy hair to hang freely.

Lilly Mae asked several girlfriends to be the bridesmaid in her wedding, and they all agreed until she told them that Joe wasn't paying for their dresses. Only one person came through, and that was Vivian. The others made excuses after excuses instead of just saying they couldn't afford it. So, there weren't any bridesmaids or bridegrooms. And Joe, who wore a basic black tuxedo, didn't mind one way or the other.

The wedding was held at Joe's church on a perfect Saturday autumn afternoon. The sky was clear. There was a light brisk wind blowing. Nature had transformed the trees into beautiful colors. The church was packed with family, friends and uninvited members of the church. Those members only came just to be nosy and to have something to talk about, and he knew this. Therefore, he made up a guest list for the reception way in advance to prevent people from freeloading off his food.

When the music started to play, everyone stood. Joe came down the aisle first. The photographer, who was standing up front, took two maybe three pictures of him. But when Lilly Mae entered the room, his light bulb went off like crazy. No man escorted her down the aisle because her father was deceased, and she didn't want any other male relative to take his place. She carried her father in her heart as she slowly proceeded with a beautiful bouquet of lilac flowers close to her stomach. Even with her gown being wide, she still tried to camouflage her condition. However, there was no need in trying to hide anything, because everybody knew that she was pregnant by another man.

When she finally reached the altar, Joe looked at her and was amazed at how lovely she looked. As the ceremony began his mind began to wonder. *Yes, I could learn to love this woman. No matter what, she belongs to me—and me only. She will be the mother of my children.*

Lilly Mae daydreamed through the whole ceremony. She didn't hear the minister's words about unconditional love, honor and respect. She missed the part about a wife submitting to her husband, and a husband loving his wife. She was thinking, *I'm on easy street. No more worrying about a place to live or food to eat. I don't have to pay no bills or go out and look for a job. All I have to do is get pregnant and have his babies.* She smiled at Joe as the minister said, "Do you, Lilly Mae, take this man…"

They exchanged their wedding vows, and the rings were presented.

Within days of their engagement she asked him what kind of ring he wanted and he replied, "Nothing fancy. I really don't wear jewelry." Lilly Mae didn't hesitate into buying her fiance a plain gold band. When he asked her, she took him to a jewelry store over in the white section of town. She picked out a three-carat diamond ring with matching band. Joe looked at the price of the ring and didn't say a thing. But in his mind, he thought, *this girl must be out of her mind to think that I'm going to put that kind of money on her finger.* He told the jeweler that he would put 10% down to hold it, and that he would return next week to pay it off. However, when Joe did return, he told the jeweler to give him his money back. And instead of buying the three-carat diamond, he purchased a three-carat cubic zirconium that was an exact replica of the diamond Lilly Mae had picked out. He knew from talking to his wife-to-be about the ring that she wouldn't know the difference. As long as it was big and shiny she would be happy, and she was.

The rings were placed on each other's finger, and they kissed. "I pronounce you man and wife," the minister concluded.

The guests stood up and cheered. Mr. and Mrs. Joe Carter turned toward the cheering guests as one, and walked down the aisle. Once outside, friends and family members threw rice at them.

One gentleman ran up and placed a straw broom wrapped in white ribbon before them. They looked at each other, smiled, and jumped over it. The crowd shouted with joy.

A distinguished-looking man was standing next to a horse and open carriage. He had on a black suit with a very tall hat to match. He held the door open for them. This was their ride to the wedding reception, which was being held at the Town Hall. Just as Lilly Mae was about to enter the carriage, she turned around and looked for her mother. She saw her standing on the top steps of the church, crying and waving to her. Lilly Mae threw her a kiss and entered the carriage. Joe stepped in behind her, and the chauffeur closed the door. Running around to the front he hopped up into the driver's seat. He made a little sound with his mouth, and the horses began to walk down the street. Kids ran behind them still throwing rice.

As they rode through town, people walking and in their cars waved and blew their horns with excitement. Lilly Mae loved the attention. She wanted everybody to see her on her wedding day, and Joe didn't object, after all this was a very special day.

After their 15-minute hall of fame ride, they were approaching the Town Hall. From the distance, they could see the crowd of people, already there waiting for their arrival. Excited, Lilly Mae looked herself over.

"How do I look?"

"Like a queen," he said with a smile.

As they pulled up, the crowd began to cheer. The chauffeur jumped down from the driver's seat and opened the door for them. He assisted Lilly Mae from the carriage first. Then Mr. Carter got out. Inconspicuously, he slapped a twenty-dollar bill in his hand. The man didn't even look at how much it was. He just tipped his hat and smiled.

"Congratulations. And thank you, sir."

Holding hands, they walked up the steps and entered the building. The fabulous sound of James Brown greeted them in the lobby. Through the glass double doors of the meeting hall turned reception, they could see grown folks getting down on the dance floor. Kids were laughing and running around kicking colorful balloons that were all over the floor. Their parents had them looking sharp. The boys had on their little three-piece suits with nice haircuts. And the girls had on fancy dresses that came just below their knees with leotards and patent leather shoes on. Their hair was pressed out with Shirley temple curls. They were having a good ole time.

Joe wasn't too happy with what he saw. *All these people*, he thought as he put his head down. He didn't want a fancy reception. He just wanted a nice quiet family dinner with all the trimmings at home. But Lilly Mae wanted to go all out. She wanted to have a big reception. Her and her mother got their heads together and ironed out the details. Once they were finished, Lilly Mae presented the reception arrangements to Joe. He looked it over and was nodding his head in agreement until he turned to the last page and saw the price.

"Oh, hell no. I'm not paying that kind of money for a catering service to feed a bunch of hungry people, nor am I wasting good money on some fancy accessories!" he yelled.

That's why Pearl and Lilly Mae asked some of the ladies from the church to help prepare the food. Lilly Mae gave them a fake story about wanting home-cooked food at her reception. But in reality, Joe gave her a low budget.

Lilly Mae wanted white, fabric tablecloths, but Joe told her, "Use paper tablecloths." She wanted each table to have fresh flowers as a center piece, but he told her, "For what? They are just going to die, anyway. Use plastic ones." She couldn't believe how tight he was with money. Especially after he done bought her an expensive ring, so she thought. She asked for cloth napkins, but he told her, "Use paper napkins. They'll match the paper table cloths." The last thing Lilly Mae was sure that she would get, were the ivory color chairs with a nice cushion to sit on. But he told her, "No. Use the gray metal folding chairs that we use for our town meetings. There's no need to rent chairs when there're chairs already in the building."

Now as far as the head table was concerned, he didn't hold back any expenses because he knew that his mother and father were going to be sitting there. Lilly Mae arranged to have two long tables put together to look like one. She had them placed on a small platform a few feet away from the guests. He allowed her to rent five ivory cushioned chairs. He also let her order four white fabric tablecloths for the table, and three beautiful lilac tablecloths to be placed diagonal on top of the white cloth. Placing them diagonally made it look like three V shapes were hanging in front of the table. They had two nice sized bouquets of real lilac flowers catered from the flower shop across town on the table. Three small ivory candles were placed in between them. His mother brought out the family China, sterling silverware and Champaign glasses to toast with. The head table was immaculate. And in spite of the difference between the head table and the rest of the decor, everything looked beautiful.

One of the guests saw them standing at the door and ran to the DJ. He told him that the bride and groom had arrived. Immediately, the DJ turned the music off and made the official announcement.

"Family and friends, I would like to introduce you to the wedding party. I present to you the groom's mother and father."

Standing at the double glass doors the waiters opened them at the same time. Joe's parents walked in with their arms intertwined with each other smiling. Everyone started clapping. Another waiter was standing by to escort them to the head table. After the waiter made sure that they were settled in their seats, he ran back into position to greet the remaining party members.

"I present to you the mother of the bride."

Lilly Mae's mother walked in smiling. She too was escorted to the head table and seated.

"And now what we've all been waiting for! I present to you Mr. & Mrs. Joe Carter!"

Holding hands, they walked in like they were the king and queen of the world. They waved as the guests clapped and the photographer took pictures. After a minute or two of picture taking, they were escorted to the head table and seated in between their parents.

After the introduction, salads were served. When the waitresses saw that the guests were finishing up their salads, depending on the color of their name plates on the table, they began to serve either the white or red wine to go with their meal.

While this was going on, the head table was being served something totally different from the buffet. They had filet mignon smothered in a creamy-white mushroom sauce; wild rice and asparagus catered from a fancy restaurant across town. A waiter came and presented a red wine wrapped in a white cloth. Joe looked at him as he removed the fabric.

"Per your request, sir," the smiling waiter said.

Joe smiled at the very expensive name on the wine bottle and told him to proceed.

"My pleasure," the waiter said.

As their glasses were being filled, other waiters directed the guests one table at a time to proceed to the buffet. Servers were standing at each container of food to serve them per Joe's request. He didn't want the guests to help themselves because he knew some of them would overstuff their plates.

When Vivian's table was called to proceed to the buffet, she looked around for her husband. He had told her that he was going to the bathroom over ten minutes ago. As the festivities went on, someone tapped on their glass with their spoon. Suddenly, everyone joined in. This was the dainty way for the guests to say kiss the bride. Being a little embarrassed and with laughter, Joe reached over and kissed his wife. Satisfied, the guests clapped their hands excitedly. The father of the groom stood to make a toast.

"Ladies and gentlemen, I'd like to propose a toast to my son and his new wife. May your life be full of everlasting love, peace, joy and prosperity."

Raising their glass, the guest toast.

When it was time to cut the wedding cake, Lilly Mae and Joe stood beside it so that the photographer and guests could take pictures. After cutting the first slice they sat back down and enjoyed the sweet treat. All the other slices were cut and served by the waiters.

13

WHEN BUGALUE SAW the head-table being served, he told Vivian that he was going to the bathroom right quick before the waitress got to their table. He got up and went toward the men's room, but made a detour through the kitchen, and out the back door. Two of his boys were waiting for him outside by the steps.

"How long y'all been out here?" he asked.

"Just got here my man," one of the men said as he looked at his watch.

As he looked back up at Bugalue they heard a truck backfiring in the distance.

"Right on time," Bugalue said with a smile.

A few minutes later an old pickup truck was coming toward them. It stopped just inches from where Bugalue was standing. Two redneck brothers got out and stood in front of the vehicle. Bugalue approached them.

"Where's Big D?" Bugalue asked.

The older of the two men was chewing tobacco. As he put his hands into his dirty coveralls, he spat at Bugalue's polished alligator shoes. Only by inches did the nasty saliva miss.

"He ain't crossing them tracks into Niggerville, boy," he said as he wiped his mouth clear of the dark liquid that dribbled down his chin.

The younger man, in brown corduroys and a dirty white t-shirt checked his nose for gold. Once he found it, he plucked it into the air and said, "Daddy says to tell you that this will be the first and last time we makes a trip over here."

The older brother spat tobacco at Bugalue's shoes again. And it would have made its target if Bugalue weren't quick on his feet.

"You see..." the younger man continued, "the agreement was we'd stay on our side of the track, and you colored folks stay on yours. Now just give us our money, and take this here stuff 'cause I'm ready to go. It smells like a monkey's ass around here."

Spitting at Buglue's shoes for the third time, the older brother missed and walked away. One of Bugalue's boys went for his gun, but Bugalue stopped him. With a grin on his face, he addressed the two men.

"Now look here, Mr. White Man. We ain't trying to start nothing. All that name-calling, and spitting at my shoes ain't necessary. I've been doing business with your daddy for quite some time now and—"

"We ain't got nothing to do with that. Today you're dealing with us! And unlike my daddy, we can't stand you smelly niggers!" the younger man yelled.

"I prefer to be called Negro or black, you white-cracker," one of Bugalue's boys said.

The older brother pulled out his pocket knife, and approached him.

"Who you calling a cracker, boy?"

When Bugalue's boys saw the knife, like a flash of lighting they pulled out their guns. The older brother stopped dead in his tracks. Satisfied with his boy's actions, Bugalue smiled and rolled his neck in a slow circular motion, causing it to crack several times.

"Drop the knife, white boy," he said.

Before doing so, the man looked out the corner of his eye to see if his brother had his back. With great disappointment, he saw that his brother's hands were in the air. He dropped the knife.

"Damn it, Ervin. What did I tell you to do if you ever saw me pull out my pocket knife?"

"Rich, I told you this wasn't going to work. My nerves can't take the excitement," said the younger brother as he expelled gas from nervousness.

They began arguing back and forth until Bugalue couldn't take it anymore.

"Y'all shut the fuck up!"

Abruptly, they stopped.

"Now it's my wife's best friend's wedding today, and I'm not trying to fuck it up by having y'all white-ass spread all over here in Niggerville as you call it. So if you so kindly just give me what we agreed upon, I'll give you what you want. Agree motherfuckers?"

Richard attempted to pick up his pocket knife, but Bugalue advised him not to do so.

"Man, don't you see that my boys got their iron on ready Freddy? Now leave it and get my shit."

Richard went to the back of the truck, and started bringing cases of bottled corn liquor to Bugalue. He looked over at his little brother who was just standing there watching him work.

"You stupid retard come on and help me unload this stuff!"

Ervin snapped out of it and began to help his brother with the unlawful spirits.

Finally, Richard brought the last case in front of Bugalue.

"Ok, there are 12 bottles in each case. Give me my money, so I can get from here. Y'all making me itch."

Ervin laughed at his brother's bluntness. But Buckwheat, who was about 5'4" and husky built didn't think that it was funny. Still with gun in hand, he removed his tooth-pick from his mouth.

"Oh honky don't act like you white folks wash your ass now. Everyone knows that y'all don't believe in washing."

While he was talking, Bugalue pulled out a small pad and pencil and started counting the goods.

Buckwheat continued.

"That's why your poor-looking white-ass is scratching now. And why does society call y'all white when you're pink as a motherfucker..."

Little Man, Bugalue's brother-in-law, who was 6'0", slim built with slanted eyes died laughing at his boy's statement.

"Pink? Man, I thought you just said white. Which one is it?"

Buckwheat shrugged his shoulders.

"Shit...pink, white, yellow. Them motherfuckers all look the same to me. Man, let me tell you something. You know them motherfuckers don't like their own color. Every time you turn around they're out in the sun cooking their skin, trying to get it black and beautiful."

"Preach on brother! Don't get him started, come on wit' it Buckwheat!" Little Man shouted with excitement.

"You see white boy, I'm getting ready to go real deep on your ass now. I want you to hold on, cause the shit I'm about to tell you is going to blow your white-ass away from here. You see I'm one of those radical black brothers who believe in uplifting and educating the black community. Yeah, I know you're thinking that I ain't black cause of the fairness of my skin, hair and eyes. But I'm what'cha call an albino. Now the reason why y'all bathe yourself in the sun so much is because y'all want to be our color. Subconsciously, you know that you're descendants of the black race. In other words, we made you. *We* are the original people of mother earth. When God made man, he made us from dirt. And what color is dirt...? Dark baby! Don't get me started."

He walked away a few feet, then turned around and walked up to Richard's face.

"In the Bible, it says that Jesus's hair was like wool, and his feet were the color of what Little Man?"

Thinking, Little Man scratched his head with the barrel of his gun. Then he shouted, "Bronze baby!"

Before Buck got a chance to finish his Black Education 101, Bugalue called him over. Immediately, he stopped and ran to him. Bugalue whispered something in his ear. Buck nodded in agreement, then ran to Little Man and dropped the info on him. Laughing, Little Man nodded his head also.

"What's up with the delivery? Bugalue asked.

"Say what? You got seven cases. Twelve bottles in each case. That's 84 bottles," Richard said with a frown.

"Seven cases...? Naw my man, it's supposed to be *ten* cases. You're missing 36 bottles, baby."

"Hey, wait a got damn minute here! You ain't say nothing bout no—"

With the butt of his gun, Little Man cold cocked Richard on the side of his head. *Bam*!

"Shut up, white boy!"

Needless to say, Richard fell hard to the ground. His brother made an attempt to help him, but Little Man pointed his pistol at him.

"You don't want to do that," he said as he smiled and shook his head.

Bugalue adjusted his neck tie and spoke to the younger brother now.

"Like I was saying, *ten* cases. Your daddy shorted me with some water down liquor the last time."

"My daddy's not going to like this. He ain't going to like this at all!"

Bugalue told Ervin to get the rest of the cases from the truck.

"And it bet not be watered down," Buck said.

Ervin went and got the rest of the cases and placed them on top on the others. Bugalue took a wad of rolled-up money out of his pocket, and threw it at him. Ervin caught it and looked at it funny. Bugalue knew what he was thinking.

"It's all there. Tell your daddy that it was nice doing business with him, but I won't be needing his services no more. Now go see bout your brother."

He ran over to his brother and slapped his face a few times to wake him up.

"Come on get up."

After several hard slaps, he woke up.

"What...what happened?" he asked with a slurred speech.

"Come on get the hell up. It don't matter what happened. Let's get out of here."

Helping him to his feet, Richard staggered to the truck. After getting his brother into the truck, Ervin ran around to the driver's side and jumped behind the steering wheel. Being pissed off some kind of bad, he started the engine up. As they drove off, Ervin leaned out the truck and yelled, "You ain't seen the last of us you coon! You ain't seen the last of us!"

"Thank you for doing business at Niggerville, and please come again!" Buckwheat yelled back in an animated voice.

Satisfied that all was well, Little Man and Buckwheat put their gun away.

"Man, we better gets this liquor out of site before someone sees it," Little Man said.

Bugalue tossed him his keys.

"Go get the truck from around front and bring it back here. We can stash it there for the time being."

While Little Man ran to retrieve the truck, Bugalue opened one of the bottles to have a little taste. He smelt it first, then took a big gulp and choked like hell.

"Hot *damn* that's some good shit right here boy," he said with a distorted face.

Reaching into his left breast pocket, he pulled out a fancy silver tin container. He filled it up and placed it back into his pocket. He looked down and brushed the tip of his shoes off behind his pants legs. He looked himself over to make sure that he was still Mr. Clean.

"How I look?"

Buckwheat smiled at his boy whom he had known since grade school. "Like a hot buttered biscuit waiting to be dipped in some homemade gravy."

Little Man returned with the truck. Putting the bottled spirit in his back pocket, they all loaded up the truck and covered it with a heavy, gray blanket.

Little Man drove the truck back around the front and parked it. Taking another quick hit from the bottle, Bugalue started doing a two-step dance move to the music coming from the reception. Passing the bottle to Buckwheat, he took a sip.

"Good lord, that's what I'm talkin' bout."

He passed the juice back to Bugalue, and he took a smaller sip.

"I tell you what...if my wife wasn't in there; I *know* I would have gotten me some young tender ass tonight."

As Little Man ran back to them like a galloping horse, he saw them passing the bottle back and forth and yelled, "Hey don't drink all of it! Give me some of that!"

Bugalue gave him the bottle and without hesitation, he took it to the head.

"Hell yeah that's it right there boy!" he said in between coughs.

Laughing, Bugalue took the now empty bottle and tossed it into the woods. He began to search his pockets as if he lost something.

"What's wrong big man?" Buckwheat asked.

"I meant to bring a little something with me to the reception besides my personal stash."

Smiling, Buck opened his suit jacket to show that he had a bottle on him already.

"I'm way ahead of you baby..., way ahead of you."

"Well I'll be a monkey's uncle. When did you do that?"

"You know that boy is a natural-born thief," Little Man said smiling.

Now that their business was over, and they got their hook up for the party, Bugalue concluded.

"Gentlemen, let's go get our party on!"

All three men walked up the back steps to the festive sounds.

14

AS THEY ENTERED the reception, they could see that just about everyone was on the dance floor. As they blended in, a man yelled *A-Phi!* The music went dead and several Alphas formed a line, and started steppin' around the bride and groom. Since Joe was an Alpha man, he couldn't resist joining his brothers. They all stepped high and proud. By the time they finished people were going off with excitement. Lilly Mae's jaws were hurting so bad from smiling at her husband. Excited, she turned to the guest and yelled, *"Skee-Wee!"* And her sisters responded back to her. They all formed a line in front of their Greek brothers and started to step. You couldn't tell those AKAs nothing. They were right and tight. Everybody cheered them on. When they got finished doing their thing, they all hugged each other. The DJ started the music back up with the soulful sounds of Motown. The coordinator for the reception came up to the front of the room waving her hands. "Everyone please gather around. It's time for the bride to toss her bouquet."

The ladies assembled across the room, and Lilly Mae was on the other side. She turned her back to them and threw the beautiful bouquet. The ladies screamed and scramble to catch the flowers. However, a little girl with long pony-tails came out from underneath them yelling and jumping up and down.

"I got it! I got it! Look, I got the pretty flowers!"

Laughing, the ladies all hugged her and walked away.

"Now it's the men's turn," said the coordinator.

Not one man moved from their spot.

"Come on gather around, no need to be shy."

The men slowly gathered on the opposite side of Joe for the catching of the garter belt, which was taken off of Lilly Mae's leg during Bugalue's business deal out back. The Groom turned his back to the men and tossed it. But before anyone grabbed it, a loud gunshot was heard from outside. *Bang!* Everyone screamed and ducked for cover. Within seconds, cocktail bombs were thrown through the windows, causing the curtains to go up in flames. Several men ran to the kitchen, and filled pots and pans up with water to put it out. One man grabbed from the table a bowl full of Kool-Aid, and doused one of the windows with it. Others took off their suit jackets and beat the flames down. A man scared half to death peeped out the window, and saw several white hooded men with torches riding around the building on horses.

"It's the Ku Klux Klan!" he yelled with terror in his voice.

They were shooting their shotgun's up in the air and screaming and yelling. Another cocktail was thrown into the building, and it landed on a little girl's dress. She screamed out in pain. A man, who had just come out of the kitchen with a big bucket of water, saw the little girl engulfed in flames. He took the whole bucket of water and threw it on her.

No one knew what was going on, or why they were even out there. But from past experience, they did know one thing, and that was some serious, funky stuff was kicking off really bad. Nothing like this had happened for a many of years, because everyone stayed in their place.

Years ago, there was so much killing that both sides were tired of the bloodshed. So the KKK and colored folk came to an unofficial agreement. And that was to stay on their own side of the railroad track to keep the peace between them. That agreement was made about 10 years ago. It didn't matter to them what was going on in other parts of the world. Down in the Bayou everyone knew their place.

"Bugalue, come out here Nigger!" one of the hooded men yelled.

By the intensity of his voice, you could tell that he was mad as hell. The people inside the building were huddling down not knowing what to expect. They all started to ask each other who in the world was Bugalue.

"You hear me Nigger! Come on out here!"

Lilly Mae looked at her husband who was crouched down beside her against the wall. When a gunshot was fired again, Joe grabbed his wife's hand, and they ran to the head table where their parents were hiding underneath. He flipped it over and pulled the table cloth over them.

"Everybody ok…" he asked and they replied yes.

"Bugalue…what in the world do they want with him?" Lilly Mae whispered to her husband.

"I don't know, but I'm about to find out."

"Joe don't leave me! Don't go out there!" she yelled, grabbing his arm.

"Woman are you crazy?! I'm not going out there. I'm going to ask Bugalue what the hell is going on."

Lilly Mae got a sharp pain in her stomach and grabbed her belly.

"*Are* you ok…? Is it time?"

"No, go on and see what's happening."

"Be careful son," his father said.

He kissed his wife and left.

Joe first peeped from under the tablecloth to see where Vivian and Bugalue were. He spotted them just a few feet away. They were sitting up against a turned over table with their backs to it. He crawled across the floor to where they were.

"Bugalue…what the *hell* do they want with you?!" he whispered.

Bugalue looked surprised at Joe's question.

"Me…? Man, you got it all wrong. They don't want me. They yelled hoop-dee-do not Bugalue."

"That's right. That's what I heard too Joe," Vivian said.

"They're out there just having fun at colored folk expense," Bugalue said with a slurred speech.

Joe got angry because he knew that was a lie. White folks haven't been in their neck of the woods for years.

"I don't have time for this. I need to know why the KKK, of all people, are at my wedding reception causing a whole lot of ruckus. I can't help you if you don't tell me what's going on."

"Man nothing's… *Bang! Bang!* Two shots went off before he could finish his sentence.

"One last time come on out here Nigger! We got some business to talk about!"

Vivian's mind began to race. She looked at her husband in a questioning manner.

"Business…? What business is he talking about? You did business with the KKK fool?! Lord we are some dead folks for sure."

Joe looked down at the floor, then back to Bugalue.

"Are you going to tell your wife, or am I?"

Stunned at Joe's statement Vivian asked her husband, "Tell me what?"

He ignored her.

"Man, she don't got to know everything. I mean as long as I put meat on the table and a roof over her head...shit I'm the man of the house."

At hearing his nonsense Joe got mad as hell. With his fist, he hit the table just inches from Bugalue's head.

"You're not a man if you lie to your wife. Two shall become as one, remember? That's the way God planned it in the beginning."

Vivian began to bite her manicured nails. She was getting very edgy with what was being said, or rather what was not being said between her husband and Joe. She thought that she knew everything about her husband's whereabouts and business. Before Bugalue did anything, he would let her know what he was doing, and how long it was going to take. With pleading eyes, she looked to her husband.

"Bugalue, tell me what baby? What is Joe talking about?"

He ignored her again.

"Ok... I see...just because you married now, and got a PhD that makes you an expert in relationships...get the fuck out of here."

Joe knew Buugalue was a little tipsy because of his slurred speech. So before responding to him, he took several deep breaths to stay in control.

"No it doesn't. All I'm saying is that you need to tell your wife why those white folks are out there with sheets on their heads, carrying shotguns and acting crazy while calling your name."

Tired of being ignored, Vivian screamed.

"What the fuck is going on...?! Somebody had better give me some answers, or I'm going right out that front door and find out for my damn self!"

Joe looked at Vivian, then to Bugalue. Bugalue looked at Joe, then to his wife. They said nothing.

"Ok fine. If that's the way you want it. I'll find out for myself."

Vivian got up, but Bugalue quickly grabbed her arm and pulled her back down to the floor. He pleaded to her between belches.

"Baby. (Burp). Don't. (Burp) Um, excuse me. Don't go out there."

Vivian's face became distorted from the smell of his breath.

"Oh my Lord…! What is that smell? Is…" She got closer to smell his breath. "Is that liq…are you drunk?!"

Joe had enough of the lies and told Vivian the truth.

"*That's* what he's been doing Vivian. Your husband has been buying moonshine from them."

Bugalue tried to take a swing at Joe but missed.

"Look at him…he's drunk as a skunk."

Bugalue attempted to get up but fell back down.

"Shut up or else I'm going to whip your ass!"

Vivian was livid. With her fist, she rammed them into her husband's chest for lying to her. Upon impact, she yelled and grabbed her hand from the pain of hitting something hard. Joe quickly opened up Bugalue's jacket, and saw the tip of his fancy silver container.

"What the…!"

He grabbed it and unscrewed the top to smell its contents.

"Wow!" he said from the strong smell.

He handed the container to Vivian. She smelled the odor and gagged.

"What is this?"

Joe, who had heard through the grapevine what Bugalue was doing, told her the truth.

"That's what your husband's been buying from them folks outside."

"That's not mine!" Bugalue yelled.

Vivian was shocked. All this time she believed her husband told her everything. Whatever he said she didn't question it; there was no reason to. He was always home by a reasonable time at night, unless he had to go out of town for business. And even then, he would call her when he got to his destination to let her know that he had made it. Now, for the first time, she had to confront lies from her husband.

"You mean to tell me that you haven't been closing deals on houses…"

"Is that what he told you he was doing closing deals? He might have been closing deals., but it wasn't on houses. The market slowed down months ago. He's been buying corn liquor from the white boys and selling it to our community."

Bugalue got pissed now that the truth was out.

"All right that's it. I'm going to fuck you up."

He took a wild swing at Joe, but Joe ducked, and he hit his wife instead. Vivian grabbed her face and screamed. She began to cry uncontrollably. Hearing her girlfriend scream, Lilly Mae got up and quickly ran over to where they were. She saw Vivian holding the side of her face and crying as she rocked back and forth. Enraged, Lilly Mae screamed and started beating the mess out of Bugalue.

"Don't you be hitting her…what's wrong with you?!"

Bugalue tried to block her blows to the best of his drunken ability.

"Man, get this pregnant bitch off me!"

"Bitch. Who you calling a Bitch?!"

Joe grabbed his wife.

"Baby stop, and calm down!"

"You don't be hitting her you hear me! You don't be hitting her!"

Suddenly, pain shot through her stomach. She bent down and grabbed her unborn child.

"O my God… Joe!"

"Baby what's wrong! Come on sit down. You know better than to get upset with your condition," he said as he guided her to the floor and began to rub her stomach.

Vivian stood up shaking the silver container at her husband.

"Is this the reason why you've been staying out all night?"

"Baby look...hear me out," he said as he mustered up the strength to stand up.

If looks could kill, Bugalue would have been dead a long time ago with the fierce smirk Vivian had on her face. She got up and started toward the door.

"Baby, wait let me explain!" he yelled as he attempted to grab her arm, but she jerked away.

"No! Get your hands *off* me! Don't *touch* me! I trusted you!"

"And you still can baby."

"Then why do them white folks out there want you?! Why!" she yelled as she continued toward the door.

Bugalue didn't have a clue as to how to get out of this one. It never dawned on him that his wife would catch him in his web of lies and deceit. H had been lying to her for so long he actually started believing them himself. He created several lies to cover for each other.

"I don't know why they're out there. Maybe it's because they don't want us to have a good time.

"Aw come on...that's bull, and you know it!" Joe yelled.

A shotgun blast came through the window. Everyone screamed except for Vivian.

"Bull or no bull I'm going out there to see what the hell is going on. And so help me God...if it's this shit they're talking about...!" she said as she waved the silver container in the air.

Leaving the comfort of her husband's arms, Lilly Mae jumped up and ran after her best friend.

"Please...don't go out there!"

She grabbed Vivian's arm several times to stop her, but Vivian yanked free each time.

"Lilly Mae let me go! I'm sick of this! I don't even know who my own husband is anymore!"

"Calm down please," Lilly Mae pleaded with a sorrowful look.

Vivian continued walking as if she didn't hear her. Lilly Mae turned and looked at Joe for help, but he didn't want to get involved.

"Let her be. She needs to learn the truth about her husband."

Bugalue thought that Lilly Mae was going to produce some magic words to calm his wife down. But when he saw that it wasn't happening he bolted after her. However, he was a day late and a dollar short. Everything seemed surreal to him from this point on. In slow motion, his wife looked back at him while yelling some choice words as she opened the glass door. When she got to the main door, she opened it and stepped out onto the front. And within seconds, a bullet hit her in the leg. Screaming in pain she went down.

"God!"

"Vivian!" Bugalue yelled as he ran out and fell on top of her to protect her.

"Don't shoot! Please don't shoot!"

Hysterical at the sight of what just happened; Lilly Mae screamed and ran out to them.

"Vivian! Vivian!"

Joe jumped up and ran after his wife.

"Lilly Mae don't go out there! It's none of our business!"

Lilly Mae pushed Bugalue away from Vivian. She tore a piece of her wedding dress off, and tied it around her leg in an attempt to stop some of the bleeding.

"Jesus, it hurts! God help me! I'm bleeding!"

Placing Vivian's head on her lap, Lilly Mae tried to keep her focused.

"Shhhh…it's going to be alright. Look at me…*look at* me… somebody call a doctor! My friends been shot!"

Joe ran to his wife and yanked her away.

"Woman what did I tell you! It's not our business now!"

"But Joe she's been shot! Help her!"

Joe looked at Bugalue as he stared at his wife. Blood was all over his suit. In shock, he looked at them.

"Please help my wife. I… I don't know what to do. She's bleeding bad."

"Joe let me go…let me go…she needs me!" Lilly Mae screamed as she tried to free herself from her husband's grip. However, he refused to let her go.

"Stay out of this baby! We have nothing to do with this!"

One of the white hooded men standing in front of the building pointed his gun at Joe.

"Nigger if I were you… I'd keep that wife of yours still."

He shot two warning shots in the air. *Bang! Bang!*

"Don't nobody move!"

He motioned for a few men on horses to come to him.

"Y'all get round to the back, and stand guard just in case someone tries to leave by the back door."

The men took off.

Keeping his gun pointed at Joe and Lilly Mae, he backed up to where the Grand Wizard was sitting on his horse.

"What now?"

"Which one?" asked the Wizard as he leaned forward.

"That big, black gorilla looking nigger right there," he said pointing to Bugalue.

The Wizard sat back up on his horse and looked at his posse. He saw that they were itching for a scratch. They wanted to do something really bad to these folks. He pointed to two of the members and motioned for them to get Bugalue. As they did so, one had his shotgun ready.

"Come on here Nigger," said the one without the shotgun as he stepped over Vivian's body.

Bugalue didn't even resist. It was like his mind was in another place. When Vivian saw the hooded man grab her husband by the arm, she gathered what little strength she had to stop him.

"Leave him be...you hear me...leave him be!" she screamed as she grabbed the man by his pants leg.

He tried to shake her loose but couldn't. In anger, he took his free foot and kicked the holy crap out of her.

"Nigger get your dirty, filthy paws off of me!"

When she didn't let go, with hatred in his eyes, he kicked her repeatedly until she did. Vivian screamed until she could scream no more.

"Oh God no! Please stop it! Stop it! Stop it!" Lilly Mae yelled hysterically.

Suddenly, Joe no longer had control of his wife. Like a jellyfish, she slipped out of his arms and made a bee-line toward the man. With her hand raised, she was going to slap some God-fearing sense into him, but before she even got close to the man, the butt of the other man's shotgun made contact right square in her stomach. Grabbing her stomach from the excruciating pain, she screamed a horrific sound and fell.

"Joe! He hit me! The baby! Joe!"

"Lilly Mae!" he yelled, as he made an attempt to go to her. But the gunman pumped his shotgun and put it in his face.

"Make a move and I'll blow your damn head clean off!"

Joe immediately put both hand's up in the air and backed down slowly to the floor.

"Ok man I'm cool...I'm cool!"

The commotion caused Bugalue to come out of his trance. After blinking several times, he looked at the hooded man holding his arm.

"What the fuck...!"

He yanked his arm away and gave the man a powerful two piece to the face. *Whop! Whop!* Dazed, the man fell to the floor.

"Get that sumbitch!" yelled the Grand Wizard.

Three men ran up on the porch and tried to take Bugalue down. However, he was too much for them. Growing up in New York, he was in plenty of fights like this. The odds against him were nothing new to him. He beat them boys all the way down the steps.

"Gotdammit...somebody put that big nigger down!" yelled the Grand Wizard.

That's when a gun came out of nowhere and hit Bulalue in the back of the head, causing him to fall to the ground. The man with the shotgun ran over to him and rammed the butt of his weapon into his stomach.

"Got damn you boy...you are one tough sumbitch!"

Several horsemen gathered around him as he vomited something terrible. Holding his stomach, he rolled over and looked up at the dancing flames before him. It was as if they were a thousand feet tall dancing the dance of death.

Buckwheat and Little Man saw all of this from inside the building. They had their guns drawn, but the odds were against them. Buckwheat wanted to go out there and blast every one of them. But streetwise told him to assess the situation first. Peeping out the front window he saw about 15 white hooded faces. He ran to the back-kitchen window and saw about 5 there. They were sitting on their horses with shotguns and torches in hand. They had the place surrounded. Looking out at them the realization of the situation kicked in. It was just him and Little Man with two guns apiece, limited ammo and no back up. There were women and children. And the other men had no guns. He decided that he had no choice but to lay low and wait for an opportunity to help his boy.

He ran back to the front and peeped out the window again. They now had Bugalue on his knees in front of the Grand Wizard. He closed the curtain and banged his head against the wall.

"Damn! Damn! Damn!"

Being from the South, Little Man didn't say a word, because he already knew that the situation was going to get worse.

In a slow, sickening, southern drawl, the Wizard spoke.

"Alright listen up! What we have here is a *situation*! This here Nigger has wronged my family, and he thought he could get away with it! Well…he was wrong! You see…this here is America and we white folks are the true Americans. We have allowed you coons to live a somewhat decent life here in the Bayou. And I say somewhat, because you people ain't nothing but animals to us, and you don't deserve to breath the same air as we do. Now, my boys came down here to conduct some business with your kind, and for whatever reason, this big, black Nigger thought that he could get one over on us…wrong!"

As the Grand Wizard spoke, one of the Klansmen got down off his horse, and grabbed a thick rope that was hanging from his saddle. He walked over to Bugalue and told him to put his hands behind his back, but he didn't move.

"Put your hands behind your back boy," repeated the Klansmen.

Bugalue still didn't move. He was in a praying position, with his head down and his hands on his lap. The bad-ass suit he had on was now bloody with vomit all over it. The Klansmen jumped up in the air and brought the rope down across Bugalues face full force. Vivian screamed as her husband fell to the ground. He laid there as if he was dead. Two Klansmen rolled him over on his stomach. The guy with the rope straddled him like a hog and tied his hands behind his back. In a daze, he laid there not saying a word or moving a muscle. From the corner of his bloody eye, he saw a Klansmen throwing a thick rope with a noose, over a big oak tree branch. Vivian and Lilly Mae saw their intention and began to scream. When Bugalue heard them, he began to struggle to get to his feet. But the guy who tied his hands up gave him a swift kick to the stomach. The kick was so hard Bugalue threw up blood and stumbled backward to the ground.

The Wizard had not been talking while all of this was going on. He didn't believe in speaking when he didn't have folk's full attention. So now that the matter was under control he continued.

"Thank you, son. Now as I was saying…we try to deal with you people as little as possible because (1) We don't like niggers. (2) You're here to stay. But if we could kill every one of you to keep America pure, we would. And last but not least, we just hate your kind. It's that simple. You don't belong here. You need to go back to the jungles that you came from. You're so got damn dumb, but you think you're smart. You think you're so smart, but you're stuck on stupid."

The Wizard jumped down off his horse and walked over to Bugalue. He pulled his head back by his hair and yelled in his face.

"You stole liquor from my family, you sumbitch and thought you could get away with it?!"

The Wizard hit Bugalue in the face with his fist.

"Lord have mercy on my husband soul! Lord, have mercy!" Vivian screamed.

Lilly Mae could only hold her stomach and deal with the traumatic pain she was feeling. Silently, she prayed to God to protect her unborn child. Joe lunged forward in an attempt to help Bugalue, but one of the men saw his attempt and shot him in the leg.

"Keep still boy!"

"You motherfucker!" Joe screamed out in pain as he grabbed his leg and fell down the steps.

"Joe! No, no, please don't hurt my husband!"

The Wizard walked over to Joe and stood over him like a gigantic monster; being 6'2" and weighing about 337lbs.

"Joe Carter, we don't got no problems with you. You know your place. It's a lot of you Niggers that know your place down here, but this here boy ain't one of 'em. He needs to be taught a lesson," he said as he pointed his finger at Bugalue. With a long and precise pronunciation, he said as his body twitched with excitement, "You don't *fuck* with the KKK. Rope him up boys!"

The posse became wild and crazy. It had been a while since they had fun like this. Two Klansmen dragged Bugalue over to the big oak tree. They took the noose and placed it over his head and made sure that it was nice and tight around his neck.

With a bloody, busted up face Bugalue looked over at his wife. With arms reaching for her husband, she cried out to him.

"Bugalue!"

He looked at her with tears in his eyes as if asking for forgiveness.

Joe tried his best to ignore the pain from the bullet wound and pulled out a hand full of money from his pocket. He presented it to the Grand Wizard.

"Mr." he said with a shaky voice. "You don't have to do this. We… we can work this out. How much does he owe you $50.00, $60.00…?" Insulted by Joe's action toward the Wizard, a Klansmen ran up to him and hit him across the face with his gun; causing blood to spill from his mouth.

"You stupid coon! It's not about the money…it's the principal of the whole thing!"

A Klansmen took the other end of the rope that was tied around Bugalue's neck and tied it around one of the horse's neck.

"Ready!" he yelled.

The Grand Wizard walked back to his horse. He turned and looked at the situation he had created. With a disturbing grin, he admired the control, power, and fear he created among the people. He saw that it was good, because the people inside the building were peeping out the window with a frightened look on their face. With the thought of what was about to transpire, his smile became broader. He looked over at the Klansmen who was waiting for the signal. The Wizard nodded to him.

"Yee haw!" yelled the man while smacking the horse as hard as he could on his back side.

Frightened, the horse took off running until he couldn't run any more, thus causing Bugalue to rise off the ground. His legs dangled, and his eyes rolled to the back of his head. He looked as if he was trying to scream, but the rope was too tight around his neck. They all stared at him for several minutes until his body went limp.

Satisfied, the Wizard jumped on his horse.

"Look at him! Look at him *real* good! This here is a Nigger who crossed the line! You all learn to stay in your place you hear! Let's ride!" he yelled to the members.

As they rolled out they threw more cocktail bombs into the building. The building became engulfed with flames, causing everyone to run outside. In doing so they saw Bugalue hanging from the tree. The realization of what just happened hit them hard. Nothing had changed with the white folks. No matter how much time went by, they were still hated because of the color of their skin. The past is still the present, and the now is still way back when.

It seemed just like yesterday when a young girl ran to her mother, when she found the head of her oldest brother laying by the edge of a corn field. He had been missing for four days. Some say he was caught by some white boys with his head between a white girl's legs, so they cut it off. No one really knew what had happened to him, and it seemed like no one really cared.

The men slowly walked over to Bugalue's hanging body. They didn't run to get him down because they all had seen this too many times before. They grabbed his legs and cut the rope from the horse and sent it on its way. Gently, they laid his body down on the ground. A young gentleman took off his jacket and covered his face with it. Even though they didn't know this man, one of the elderly men said a prayer for his sins.

"Shouldn't we put out the fire?" asked one of the men, no one in particular.

They all looked up at the Town Hall, which was now engulfed with flames. They then looked at all the people and saw Pearl, Lilly Mae, Joe, his folks and Vivian resting against a tree a small distance from the building.

Sadly, one of the elder men said, "Son, there's no use in doing that. It's out of control. We're just going to have to rebuild as we've done in the past."

They all stared at the flames in silence until they heard Lilly Mae scream out in great pain.

"Lilly Mae...baby!" Pearl yelled as she looked down and saw that her baby's dress was wet. Her water bag had broken.

"Somebody run to the shed and get me some water, rags, paper... anything! This baby is on its way!"

The women ran to the shed with all the little children who were crying and scared to death. They planted them right outside the shed's door and told them not to move. There were no containers to put water in, so the ladies gathered old dirty rags from the floor. They wet them from the old water pump that was in the back of the shed. As they ran toward Pearl, they heard her screaming.

"Lord Jesus, help me! Please God help me with your child!"

Pearl looked down at Lilly Mae whose breathing wasn't under control. She told her in a comforting manner to take deep breaths to help control her breathing and to calm down.

"Baby when I tell you to push, you push as hard as you can. But when I tell you to stop, you do so...ok."

Lilly Mae nodded her head as she grabbed and squeezed one of the lady's hands. With the other women standing by, Pearl told her to push and to push hard. As she pushed through clenched teeth, she screamed.

"God help me!"

PART FIVE

15

*T*IME PASSED BY since that dark day at the Town Hall. No one was ever charged for the murder of Bugalue Johnson. There were some questions asked by the police in the community, but there were no answers. Those folks knew not to talk about a lynching to the policemen. For all they knew they could have been one of the hooded men that night.

Bugalue's mother, sister and brother, who lived up North, came down with the people who were going to transport Bugalue's body back home. Very few questions were asked by his family. They knew that they were in a different world down in the Bayou.

Bugalue's mother asked her daughter-in-law if she and the baby were going to attend the funeral, and if she wanted to come and live with them in NYC. Vivian told her mother-in-law that she had said her good-byes before their local funeral home embalmed him for the trip. She also told her that she was a southern girl and up north wasn't the place for her. With that being said, the Johnson's gave Vivian a hug and kissed the baby good-bye. It would be several

years before she, and her daughter took a trip up north to see them. Truth be told, Vivian never really cared too much for her in-laws.

When Bugalue first introduced Vivian to his family, she couldn't understand a word his sister and brother were saying because they talked too fast. And every other word that they used was a cuss word. Also, the street slang that was used by them sounded so ignorant to her ears. Bugalue's sister Mary told Vivian straight out that she dressed funny and sounded country as hell. Then she had the nerve to burst out laughing right in her face. Vincent, his brother, came out the mouth with explicit comments about what he had heard about New Orleans women and sex. Bugalue asked them both to shut up from talking crazy, but that request went right over their heads. The only one that had any common sense was their mother, Lisa Johnson. She was very quiet and polite.

She was born and raised in the South Bronx by her parents, who came to New York City via Mobile Alabama looking for work. They were strong Christian folks dedicated to God's word. Every Wednesday, Friday and Sunday they attended church.

Her parents put her in the Youth Choir when she was only 5 years old. Some say that girl had a big voice to be so small. When she had a solo to sing the director of the choir had to use a milk crate for her to stand on, in order for her to reach the microphone. When Lisa got older, she joined the Young Adult Choir. That's when she first saw a young man by the name of Alex Johnson, who had just got back from Connecticut. He was a tall, slim, dark skin brother with pearly white teeth. All the young ladies thought he was handsome as hell.

His parents, who owned Johnson Dry Cleaners over on Lexington Avenue, kept that boy in church when he was little. But during his adolescent years, he became bored with church. He also became unruly at school. Rumor had it that he started hanging out with a group of older boys on the street, and that they introduced him to the drug game. He often played hooky from school just to be with them. From being around the negative atmosphere his demeanor changed for the worse. He started lashing out at his parents and became hell on two feet. He had gotten so bad that his parents didn't even know who he was anymore. All they could do was pray for him.

And the Lord must have heard them, because one afternoon Alex went to Queens with a few of his boys to cop some dope from a third-party connection. To make a long story short, the deal went bad, two men got shot dead, and Alex was charged with accessory. The judge sent him to a juvenile facility up in Connecticut until the age of 21.

The age or penal system must have rehabilitated him, along with the prayers his parents sent up to God, because Alex had a new attitude on life when he was released.

He took over the daily dry cleaner's responsibility so that his parents could rest. He also started attending church again. He even joined the Young Adult Choir. That's where he first saw and introduced himself to Lisa. With both parent's approval, they started dating. And within no time, they were married with three children, Bugalue being the oldest.

Life was beautiful for the Johnson family. Lisa, for some reason, started disassociating herself with old friends and started mingling with new uppity ones. She even started to throw dinner parties for whatever occasion she made up. Doing this made her think that she was a part of the "in" society. She had developed the Johnson's name into importance by using her husband's family money and who she associated her family with.

As the years went on and the family business grew, it seemed to people that she totally forgot where she came from until one day she had a rude awakening. It was discovered by her that her beloved Alex had died from a drug overdose. Yep…she found her loving, church going; God-fearing husband laid out on the bathroom floor in one of the four dry cleaners they owned, with a dope needle stuck in his arm.

Alex didn't get rehabilitated from that time he spent up in Connecticut; he just got streetwise like no other. It was taught to him by some nineteen-year-old Sicilian in Connecticut doing time with him, that the real money was in real estate not the streets. The Italian told him that if you buy real estate, and owned your own business, you could hide and do much bigger things on a larger scale when it comes to making money.

And Alex did just that. He got back into the drug scene without missing a beat. He conducted his drug business on the down low through the dry-cleaning business and started using his own product. No one who was close to him knew what he was doing. All they knew was that the money was coming in; he was buying real estate and opening up more dry cleaners. He got so good at it, that he started laundering dirty money for the same dude that he met up in Connecticut. Come to find out later, the dude that he met up in Connecticut was a family member of a serious big time crime organization.

16

*T*HE CARTER'S DIDN'T give Bugalue's death a second thought. He was an outsider in their eyes. Lilly Mae supported her girl Vivian through her rough times, but other than that... nothing was missed. Life continued on for them.

Lilly Mae gave birth to a beautiful 7lb 9-ounce baby girl named Betty Jean. Folks say she was light, bright and damn near white with the prettiest eyes. Her hair was light brown and soft to the touch. As time went by, Lilly Mae thought her baby girl's hair would change its texture, but it didn't. It just got longer and longer.

Vivian would bring her little Suzie, who was now three, to the Carter's house every Saturday morning, so they could play with each other. This little visit would also give Vivian a chance to see her best friend, who was now pregnant for the third time.

Six months after Betty Jean was born, Lilly Mae became pregnant with Joe's first child. She went her full term and had a baby boy.

They named him Malcom Duane Joe Jr. However, a few months after the baby was born, something terrible happened. Lilly Mae had just finished breast feeding little Joe and laid him down in his crib for an afternoon nap. A few hours went by and Lilly Mae's breast became engorged with milk. It was feeding time for the baby. She walked up to the baby's bedroom and put her ear to the door to hear if he was crying. But she heard nothing. She opened the door and walked up to the crib expecting to see him wide awake, smiling and kicking. But she didn't see that at all. He was sound asleep. At first, this baffled her, because like clockwork, the baby would start crying as her breast became engorged. She brushed it off thinking that the baby must be real tired. She didn't wake him up for his feeding and left the room. She went back to her bedroom and used a breast pump to relieve the pressure from her swollen breast.

A few more hours went by, and her breast became engorged again. This time she went into the nursery calling little Joe's name in a child-like manner. There was no response from the baby. Lilly Mae walked up to the crib expecting to see her baby boy wide-eyed and smiling. But what she saw horrified her. Little Joe's face was pale as a ghost and his lips were dark blue. Lilly Mae screamed and grabbed the baby. She shook him like a rag doll in the air. Not one sound came from his little lips. Pearl heard Lilly Mae's scream and ran into the room to see what was going on. She saw her shaking her grandson and that his body was limp. She ran over to her and snatched him from her arms. Pearl grabbed his blanket, wrapped it around him and ran to the car. Lilly Mae ran to her bedroom; grabbed Betty Jean from her playpen and ran behind her. They jumped into the car and rushed to the hospital.

When they arrived, two paramedics were standing outside the emergency door talking. Pearl stopped the car right in front of the door and yelled to them that her grandson wasn't breathing. The men ran over to the passenger's door and yanked it open. They grabbed the baby from Lilly Mae's arms and rushed him into the emergency room. Doctors and nurses responded to his bedside. They did everything they could to bring life back to Little Joe, but it was too late. Joe Jr. was dead. It was determined that he had been dead for several hours. The doctor explained to them, that when a perfectly healthy baby dies for no apparent reason, it's diagnosed as SIDS (Sudden Infant Death Syndrome), and nothing could be done about it.

The news shocked Pearl and Lilly Mae. When Joe arrived at the hospital and heard the terrible news from them, he was in disbelief. In anger, he yelled and tore his shirt off. He didn't understand how such a thing could happen to a little one. Even though Pearl and Lilly Mae were still in shock, they understood God's way. Their belief was that even though people were born into the world to families, ultimately, you belonged to God. They tried their best to console Joe by telling him this knowledge and that Gods Will shall be done. However, Joe didn't want to hear none of it. He just wanted his son back.

After this terrible loss, Joe became a bitter man and was mad at God for taking his first born away from him. The loss also put a strain on his marriage. Talking was at a minimum with his wife, and he stopped sleeping in the same bed with her. However, in spite of what happened, he still went to his wife at night and did his business without any type of foreplay, love or affection. It didn't matter to him if she was tired from a day's work of house cleaning, cooking and taking care of Betty Jean. Sex was just a routine to him. And Lilly Mae just laid there with her head turned toward the wall, concentrating on a little spot, while he grunted and sweated all over her. The only thing he was concentrating on was getting back what God had taken away. Once she conceived, he didn't bother her at all. For the last few years, it was pure hell for her.

17

*N*OW PREGNANT, LILLY Mae sat on the front porch with her mother, as they prep the night's dinner. From a distance, they saw two small figures coming up the long driveway. One of the figures was smaller than the other, with something hanging from its hand. As they got closer, their dog King, a German shepherd, Joe had brought after his son died, stood up and started barking and wagging his tail. He acknowledged the two figures before Pearl, and Lilly Mae did. It was Vivian and Suzie coming up the driveway. He ran off the porch and headed toward them. Suzie saw King running and took off running to greet him. Her little feet were just a getting it. When they met up with each other, King playfully knocked her and her little doll baby down. He licked her all over her face. Suzie laughed with delight as she tried to get up. But being so excited at seeing his little friend, King kept knocking her back down. When Vivian reached them, she had to yell at the over-zealous dog.

"King, stop that! Go on, stop! Let her up!"

Barking, he ran circles around them a few times, then took off running back to the house. Still laughing, Suzie got up and ran after him.

"Lord what am I going to do with these two," she said as she looked up to the sky.

She began a little trot to keep up with her daughter.

"Suzie, slow down now! You're going to hurt yourself!"

Her daughter didn't stop running because she was having too much fun with King. When the little one finally reached the front steps, she said to the ladies with her tiny voice, "Good morning Mrs. Carter."

"Good morning Suzie."

"Good morning Mrs. Pearl."

Pearl smiled at Suzie and held her arms out for a hug. Suzie loved herself some Mrs. Pearl. When she saw the invitation, she ran up to her and gave her a big, little person hug. Pearl rocked her back and forth and gave her a kiss on her fat, little checks.

"How's my sweet little Suzie Q doing today?"

Suzie could barely get her words out because Pearl's big breasts were covering up her face.

"F…Fine."

"And who do we have with us today?" Pearl asked as she looked at her doll.

"This is Candy. My mama brought her for me." She looked at Mrs. Carter and asked, "Can BJ come out and play with me and my new doll?"

"Mrs. Pearl, Lilly May…how y'all doing?" Vivian asked as she plopped herself down on the steps from being a little out of breath.

Suzie walked over to her mother and sat down next to her. Lilly Mae stopped breaking the ends off the green beans and looked at Vivian.

"Girl I know you're tired from waiting on that bus in this heat. When is the truck going to be fixed?"

Vivian took out a handkerchief from her pocketbook and wiped the sweat off her neck.

"About another week, they say. Girl I tell you...as soon as I get one thing fixed something else goes wrong."

Pearl poured a glass of fresh, ice cold lemonade she had on the table next to her.

"Suzie, give this to your mama."

She got up and took the glass of lemonade and handed it to her mother.

"Look at my baby. That long walk up here didn't bother her not one bit. I wish I had her little energy...thank you baby."

"You welcome Mama."

Vivian took several sips of the refreshing drink and handed the rest back to her.

"Go ahead baby and drink the rest."

Suzie did so, but wanted more. Turning the glass upside down, she shook it.

"Ma, can I have some more please?"

"Is it ok Mrs. Pearl?"

Pearl reached out for the empty glass, and Suzie happily gave it to her.

"Here baby just a little more."

Suzie took the sweet lemonade and sat back down next to her mother. She started to drink it nice and slow. After she finished, she looked up at her mother and smiled. Vivian smiled back.

"Consider that a little treat. Because you know Mrs. Pearl believes that little people should drink more water and less sugar. It's healthier."

Suzie got up and handed the glass back to Mrs. Pearl and directed her attention to Lilly Mae.

"Can BJ come out and play now?"

"Yes, baby she can come out and play with you. Cotton-top, come outside! Suzie's here!"

Lilly Mae waited for an answer, but there was none.

"She'll be right out baby."

Suzie began to play with her doll.

"Mrs. Pearl did you see what April had on during Friday night service? Now you know that didn't make no kind of sense."

Pearl was never the one to gossip. She said gossiping was a sin and the devil's playground for the mind. When she did respond to such talk, she always tried to bring something good out of it.

"Well you know she wore what she had. Everyone isn't as blessed as the next person. The important thing is that she showed up for service. That's all that matters."

"And you know the Lord looks at our heart not our clothes," Lilly Mae added. "Cotton-top, come on out here!"

"That's true. But the girl's dress was so short. You could see the dirty underwear she had on. And not only that...a little of her booty was showing. My goodness that girl was stinking too. And I was two rows behind her."

Lilly Mae burst out laughing as she remembered seeing April, who was drunk, swaying back and forth while standing during a prayer given by one of the members.

April was just an average girl who started drinking beer, with the football team during her 11th grade year, after the high school football games. She thought that it made her popular with the guys, but it didn't. The team looked at her as being a dumb-ass. She had sex with just about every guy on the team, to get to this one particular guy whom she really liked. His name was Terrance

De'Ogblow. He was a tall, handsome guy with black curly hair, light-brown eyes, and a fair complexion. She had heard from his pass girlfriends that he was well endowed, so she wanted to find out for herself. And indeed, she did. So much so, that he became like a sex habit to her. When, where and however, he wanted to have sex with her she did it. She thought being at his beck and call would win his heart.

When she got pregnant, she told him, and he laughed at her, saying that it wasn't his. He claimed that she was trying to latch on to him because he came from a good stock, and because he got accepted to Penn State on a full football scholarship.

His negative response devastated her. Because while they were having sex, he told her several times that he loved her, and that she was the only one for him. And of course, she truly believed him.

When she told her parents that she was pregnant, they told her to get an abortion. But she wasn't having that. She kept her baby against her parent's wishes.

While Terrance was away in school, April had a baby boy. She heard the baby cry, but didn't get a chance to see or hold him. Because, for some reason, the nurse immediately took him away; talking about some type of complication.

That girl laid in that hospital bed for hours waiting to see her baby boy. Finally, the doctor and the same nurse came in to check on her. When April asked when she could see her baby, the doctor looked at her bewildered. He looked at the nurse, but she avoided his eyes by staring at the floor. The nurse's action spoke volume to him. He knew right then and there that no one had told the young mother the bad news. So, he informed her that the baby was still born. Not believing them, April went off. She jumped out of bed and started throwing things at them. She screamed hysterically that they killed her baby; that she felt her baby moving all through her pregnancy. Even while she was in labor, she felt the baby kicking up a storm, and she heard the baby cry when it was born. They tried to calm her down but couldn't, so additional staff members were called in to assist. April believed that Terrance's parents paid the doctor to kill her baby to protect their son's future.

She was only sixteen when all this happened. There was no support from her family or friends. When she did try to talk about what happened to her, people always told her to forget about it and to move on with her life. But she couldn't. The only thing that consumed her mind was her little baby boy being gone forever. This caused her to go into a depression, and eventually she dropped out of school. She also started drinking heavily without her parent's knowledge. By the age of 21, she was a functional alcoholic.

During Terrance's senior year of college, she had heard through the grapevine that he got picked up by the NFL. Hearing the news caused her to go into an even deeper depression, and she tried to commit suicide. However, God intervened so she didn't succeed. Her parents admitted her to a mental hospital. And while she was there she recognized that the Lord was knocking at her door, and she finally let him in.

Now she wasn't perfect, and she didn't pretend to be because she still drinks.

But you best to believe, every time the church opened its doors for service, she was right there. Pearl knew the girl was trying her best with what life had dealt her.

Y'all stop laughing. Just stop it. That ain't right talking about folks like that."

"Mama what's not right is her wearing a dress above the knees to church. Cotton-top, come on out here, Suzie has a new doll and wants to play!"

"You know what that was all about girl," Vivian said.

Just as Vivian gave her two cents worth, Betty Jean burst out the screen door with something long and white protruding from her little fingers.

"I'm going to eat you...Grrrr!" she yelled as she ran to get Suzie.

Suzie saw her coming and screamed with delight. Giving her doll to her mother, she took off down the steps running from her little playmate. With arms stretched out, Betty Jean ran after her. King got excited with the girl's activity and started barking. It was total pandemonium whenever those two little ladies got together. Poor Pearl didn't know what was going on.

"Lord...what in the world?"

Lilly Mae was surprised too. She jumped up from her chair, causing the green beans to spill all over the porch.

"BJ come here! You get here right now this instant!"

Betty Jean didn't hear her mother's voice. How could she...? She was no longer Betty Jean, but a big scary monster with long claws. Her mind was on catching her prey, which was Suzie. Vivian laughed at the little one's facial expressions as she chased her daughter. It was a beautiful sight to see her only child full of joy and laughter.

Even with her truck in the shop, she knew that she wasn't going to miss her weekend visit with the Carter's. Ever since Betty Jean was born, Vivian visited Lilly Mae on Saturdays. She enjoyed being with them. They really helped her adjust to the loss of her husband and being a single mother.

Vivian looked at Lilly Mae trying her best to catch up with the little ones.

"Girl, look at what your daughter has on her fingers!" she yelled.

Lilly Mae stopped running to catch her breath. As she gave her daughter a looking over, she realized what exactly was on her fingers and got pissed.

"What the hell… Cotton-top, get your damn ass over here now! I'm going to whip your behind when I get a hold of you!"

Hearing the foul language, Vivian immediately stood up with her mouth wide open. She was flabbergasted at the language her friend used toward her own daughter, not to mention around her little Suzie. She didn't like that at all, and called for her daughter to come to her.

"Baby, come here!"

When Suzie heard her mother, she ran to her.

"Yes Ma'am!"

As Betty Jean continued to run to catch her prey, she didn't notice her mother getting close behind her. Within arm's length, she grabbed the back of her dress.

"Got'cha!"

Betty Jean screamed from the sudden pull and fell on her butt.

"Why you do that…? You made me fall." She began to cry.

Not liking what she heard and saw, Pearl got up from her chair and descended down the steps.

"Don't you hurt that baby!"

Ignoring her mother, Lilly Mae yanked Betty Jean up like a rag doll and spanked her butt in unison with every word she said.

"What in the world do you have on your fingers?!"

Even though she knew what they were, her eyes got big at the site of her tampon holders on her daughter's fingers.

"Oh my goodness…Mama, do you see what this child has on her fingers!" Yanking every one of them off, she threw them at her daughter's head.

"You stop hitting that child like that! She's just a baby! She didn't know no better! And stop calling her Cotton-top! She can't help that her hair was white when she was born!" Pearl yelled as she walked over to them.

"She knew better! She's just like her damn daddy..., always getting into things that don't belong to her!"

Dumbfounded, Pearl stepped back. She cocked her head to the side, and balled her hands up into a fist and placed them on her hips.

"And just what does *that* supposed to mean? You know who the daddy is all of a sudden."

Realizing what just slipped out of her mouth, Lilly Mae slowed her demeanor down.

"Nothing Ma," she said under her breath. "BJ, pick this stuff up right now."

Betty Jean, who was still crying, began to pick up the tampon holders. Suzie was just about to run over to help her little friend, but her mother pulled her back.

"Well...I can see you all are busy, so we'll just come back next week."

Lilly Mae didn't say a word. She was too wrapped up in her own anger. Vivian took a deep breath and looked down at her daughter, who still wanted to play.

"Come on baby let's go get some ice cream. Would you like that?"

Suzie nodded without looking up at her mother. Then a great big smile came upon her face.

"Can my friend come with us?" she asked as she looked up at her mother.

"No baby. Betty Jean can't go this time.

Suzie looked at her best friend with a sad face and waved good-bye as they started down the driveway.

"Bye BJ."

Betty Jean stopped picking up the tampon holders and looked at her best friend with a sad face.

"Bye Suzie," she said and continued to pick up the holders.

As Vivian walked down the driveway, she kept looking back at Lilly Mae. She was trying to figure out what was going on with her. *Why was she so upset with two little girls playing…and what's up with the tampon holder thing? It's not like she'll be having a period anytime soon.*

Pearl was disturbed by her daughter's action because BJ was only a child. Instead of explaining to her granddaughter that it was wrong for her going into her mother's personal things, she just stood over her like an oak tree and watched her pick up the holders.

"Betty Jean, leave the rest there and come to me."

Instead of giving the holders to her mother, Betty Jean threw them right back to the ground, and ran to her grandmother. She grabbed her leg for dear life.

"Everything is going to be alright baby. You didn't do nothing wrong," Pearl told her as she patted her little head for reassurance.

Betty Jean felt safe when her grandmother was around. The two of them were closer than she and her own mother. It was as if Lilly Mae resented having her. Pearl noticed the negative disposition about two weeks after Betty Jean was born.

Pearl gave her daughter a no-nonsense kind of look. "Now I suggest you tell me what's on your mind and stop taking it out on this here baby."

Lilly Mae rolled her eyes at her mother as she began to pick up the holders.

"What are you talking about…I'm not taking nothing out on no baby."

"Yes, you are!"

When BJ heard her grandmother's voice rise, she began to cry. Seeing that this upset the little one, Pearl got down on her knees and looked BJ straight in the eyes.

"Oh, baby I'm ok."

Smiling at her little pumpkin, she pulled out a grape Wheel Barrel candy from her apron and presented it to her.

"Look what *I* have. Do you think you can open that for me?"

Betty Jean wiped her tears away and nodded. She took the candy and attempted to open it several times, but couldn't. It was so hot out, that the heat melted the clear wrapper.

Pearl smiled at Betty Jean's determination.

"Baby, go up and sit in my chair. Make sure the entire wrapper is off before you put the candy in your mouth."

Betty Jean gave her a great big smile, because she knew that candy before supper was a real treat. Putting her little hands on her grandmother's shoulders, she said with her cute little voice, "Babaw (She called her this because she couldn't pronounce grandma) I sorry…I sorry. I not do that no more k."

Pearl gave her little sugar lump a big hug and pinched her fat cheeks.

"It's alright baby. You didn't mean no harm. You're just a little person with a *whole* lot of energy."

Betty Jean smiled and pointed to herself.

"I'm a little person and you're a big person?"

"That's right," Pearl said as she got to her feet. "Now, go sit in my chair while I talk to your mother."

Betty Jean ran to the chair as fast as her little legs could go. King ran behind her barking up a storm. It was as if he was warning her to slow down before she fell. She made it to the porch without falling and made several attempts to climb up into the chair. When she kept falling from her attempts, she began to cry.

"I can't… I can't get…get up!"

"Yes you can. Take your time!" Pearl yelled.

After several tries, she got up in the chair. "I did it!"

"Yes you did baby." Pearl clapped her hands for her little one.

BJ looked at her mother as if she knew that she wasn't going to be excited for her accomplishment. In a teasing manner, she shook her candy at her. Lilly Mae stared at her daughter like she didn't even know her.

"Ma, I don't know why you baby her so much. You'd think you had her."

"With the way you treat her, I wish I had. You look at that baby like she was a demon child."

"Well she is her father's child," Lilly Mae said with a laugh.

"And who is the.... You know what...never mind."

On that note, Pearl walked back to the porch.

"Jesus all I can do is pray. Lord, all I can do is pray for this family."

Picking BJ up, Pearl placed her on her lap and held her with so much love.

After getting the wrapper off, Betty Jean went to town on that candy. Sweet juice ran all down the side of her mouth. Smiling at her little sugar lump, Pearl began to sing BJ's favorite hymn "Jesus Loves Me." BJ smiled at the sound of her song and began to clap her hands. Looking at the both of them, Lilly Mae thought they were a sight for sore eyes.

Placing the holders in her pocket, she walked back to the porch and sat down. She didn't bother to pick up the fresh beans that were scattered all around them. She just stared off into the distance listening to the hymn. Soon, her mind wandered. She left the present and traveled back into time. To a time where she saw herself sitting next to her mother during a Sunday church service, which they attended every time she was home from college.

It was packed with believers and non-believers of God. Meaning… some people went to church to get a heavy dose of the good word, and some went because they were programmed from generation to generation to do so. Anyway, the Holy Spirit was really moving in God's house. The music had everybody dancing and shouting. At first, the music was nice and mellow. But as the song was ending a lady got the Holy Ghost, and that was all she wrote. The drummer and piano player started cutting up to their own tune. Folks started jumping and screaming Halleluiah. Other folks got the Holy Spirit and started dancing to the beat of the drums.

During this entire emotional exhibit for the Lord, Lilly Mae and Pearl just sat there fanning themselves. They stared at the Pastor, whose name was Matt Abler IV. He was a tall, slim, red hair, deep blue eyed handsome man. His descendants from Ireland have lived and ministered in the Bayou for what seemed like forever. The Ambler's weren't rich with worldly things, but they considered themselves rich in what mattered the most, and that was the word of God.

As the spirit music died down, Pastor Abler walked over to the podium and said with a great big smile and loud voice, "Praise God! Can I get an Amen?!"

"Amen!"

Not satisfied with the response, he repeated himself.

"I *said*…can I get an Amen!"

"Amen!"

While the congregation took their seats, the Pastor made an announcement that the offering was about to begin. With wicker baskets in hand, two young female ushers walked up to the front of the church and stood before him. As he began to speak about giving from the heart and supporting the church, one of the ushers looked up at him and smiled as she reached into her low-cut dress and pulled out a dollar bill for the offering. From where the Pastor was standing, he had a nice bird's eye view. Even though he was mesmerized by the voluptuous site, he didn't miss a beat with the service.

"Let us pray. Lord, thank you *Jesus* for the wonderful view…I mean for the wonderful offering that we are about to receive. In Jesus name, Amen."

The ushers went and stood at the end of each row and waited for the collection plate to be returned to them, so they could move on to the next row.

While this was going on, the pianist played a slow song, and the people began to sing softly.

Pastor Abler continued to speak.

"Y'all know that if you give from your heart the Lord will bless you. And if you can give just a *little* more, please do so because the Lord is going to bless you ten folds Amen. Also, if you haven't paid your tithes yet please do so at this time."

The offering plate came upon a single mother and her teenage son. The son placed 15 cents into the basket, and the mother gave an offering of $5.00. The boy looked at his mother like she was crazy.

"Mama, what are you doing? That's all the money we got till next week."

"The Pastor says we going to be blessed for given extra," she said smiling as she patted her son's leg.

"What we going to do for food?"

His mother was so wrapped up into the Pastors words; she could care less about food. She believed every word her Pastor said.

"Baby if he says the Lord will provide, then he will provide."

Pastor Abler looked out into the congregation and noticed that only a few people were giving offerings. And that wasn't good because he had church bills to pay amongst other things. Instantly he began to speak in tongue. And for some reason, the church folks got excited and started giving more money. He said as he spoke in between tongue, "The spirit is moving family! Keep your offerings coming! Keep it coming! The Holy Spirit is *here... right... now!*"

The people got so excited with all the hoopla going on, they gave up their last bit of money to make the Pastor happy. After church was over, he would go stand outside the front door and do a meet and greet, which consisted of shaking hands, giving church hugs, and a big smile.

"Thank y'all so much for coming. Good to see you. Thank you for supporting God's church."

Pastor Abler loved the meet and greet, because it gave him the opportunity to watch the young ladies' backside as they walked down the steps. And when it came to Lilly Mae, he always gave her a hug a little longer and tighter than the others.

"Sister Lilly Mae don't forget about the Praise & Worship at 6 o'clock Wednesday night."

"Are you going to be their Pastor?"

"I will be there to assist in any way I can," he said with a very broad smile.

As he was talking to Lilly Mae, a young lady with very wide hips passed by them.

"Yes Lord, assist in any way I can," he said staring at her backside.

That Wednesday night the pastor got there early because he knew that it was going to be a huge turnout. It was now 6:25pm, and people were still arriving. Pearl had arrived and did a disappearing act, while Lilly Mae went straight to the front and began to tarry.

With her eyes closed, she asked for forgiveness of her lustful thinking. She was crying and carrying on so loud it got the attention of Sister Smith, who was standing just a few feet away from her. She looked at Lilly Mae and thought, *I don't know...maybe this girl don't believe that the Lord can forgive her sins with the way she's going on.* Next thing you know, within a blink of an eye, Lilly Mae screamed and fell out.

"Lilly Mae, are you alright?!" Sister Smith yelled as she hurried over to her. But Lilly Mae didn't respond.

"O Lord, come on baby get up, it's going to be ok. Whatever it is, it's going to be alright!"

She tried to lift her up, but she was too heavy. She looked around the crowded room to see if Pearl was anywhere near to help, but didn't see her. However, she did see the Pastor talking to a female member just a few feet away.

"Pastor Abler, please come over here and help me with Lilly Mae!"

The Pastor looked at Sister Smith confused. Turning back to the young lady, he told her to keep her faith and that God has control of everything. After anointing her with oil, he ran over to Sister Smith.

"Lord Jesus what's wrong with her?

"I heard her talking about the lust of her flesh and asking for forgiveness. Then the next thing I know, she just fell out."

"Where is her mother?"

"I don't know. I looked around for her and didn't see her."

While shaking his head in disappointment, he anointed Lilly Mae's forehead. Afterward, he told Sister Smith to help him get her up.

"We need to get her to the bathroom and put some cold water on her face. That should bring her around."

They got her to her feet, and assisted her to the lady's room. Moaning a little and feeling weak, she told them that she needed to sit down. A small, gray, iron chair was in the lady's room, so they sat her there. The Pastor gave her words of encouragement.

"Come on now. God has his hand on you. He sees all, knows all, and forgives all."

Sister Smith, who had gone, and wet a brown paper towel, placed it on the poor girl's head.

"Sister Smith where are you?!" yelled a young girl from the hallway.

"I'm in here! I'm in the bathroom with the Pastor and Sister Lilly Mae!"

Upon entering the bathroom, and seeing Lilly Mae's condition, the girl asked, "What happened to her?"

Sister Smith started to answer her, but decided against it. *That's all I need to hear. A bunch of he said, she said going around about what I said.*

"Don't matter…what do you want?"

"A girl just vomited all over the floor."

"O Lord what in the world is going on here? Ok get some paper towels and go on back up front. I'll be right out."

The girl got the towels and just stood there being noisy. "You need some help?"

"No. Go on now, we don't need you back here." Reluctantly, the girl left.

"Pastor, can you stay until she feels a little better?"

"Go on back out front and help God's people," said the Pastor as he waved her off. "She'll be just fine."

Just before she exited the bathroom, Sister Smith abruptly turned toward them.

"Pastor, please give that girl some Godly advice about her situation. Lord knows she needs some help."

Coming around, Lilly Mae grabbed the back of her head.

"What happened?"

"I don't know…you must have fallen out from exhaustion while asking the Lord for forgiveness."

Lilly Mae stood up, but immediately sat back down because of dizziness. Pastor Abler grabbed her arm to support her balance.

"Are you alright? Do you need anything?"

"It's hot in here. Can you help me to the sink? I need some cold water on my face."

Slowly, he helped her to the sink. She tried to turn the cold water on but she was just so weak to do so. She began to sway back and forth, and was just about to fall backward when the Pastor grabbed her by her waist.

"Lilly Mae come on now, you have got to snap out of it."

When she didn't respond, he held her up with one arm around her waist. With the other, he turned the cold water on, and made an attempt to splash her face. But the water got all over her blouse. Lilly Mae screamed from the extremely cold water. Thinking that he was helping her soul, Pastor Abler continued to throw water on her.

"That's right come on out of her devil! Release her in the *name* of Jesus!"

Lilly Mae screamed not only because of the ice-cold water, but because he was holding her too tight. The combination was killing her.

In the meantime, Sister Smith and the girl were getting the vomit up. The person who did the nasty deed was nowhere to be found. As they were finishing up, a little boy came running to them.

"Sister Smith, I just heard a girl scream from the lady's bathroom."

"And where were you?"

"I was getting a drink of water from the water fountain in the hallway."

As they were talking, a young lady came up to them.

"Sister Smith, Mother Pearl wants to know if you want her to start playing the piano music now, cause it's almost 9 o'clock."

And yet here comes one of the Elders.

"Sister Smith, where is Pastor Abler. I have a young man who wants to be saved."

Sister Smith, who was responsible for all the church functions, lost it.

"Got damn it…is I the only one in this church that knows how things are done around here?! Yes, tell Mother Pearl to start the music." The lady ran to deliver her message. "And I think the Pastor is still in the bathroom with Sister Lilly Mae. My goodness he's been in there for a while now. She must have confessed to him, and he must be blessing her."

"And knowing him he is going into over drive with the word," commented the Elder.

"Amen," they all said.

The Pastor continued to splash water on Lilly Mae as she struggled to get away from him. In the process of struggling, her shirt buttons popped off, causing her white cotton bra to be exposed. The shirt was two times as small for her big boobs in the first place. She knew this but didn't care, because the too small shirts always got the attention she desired from the men of the church. After the brief struggle, he finally let her go.

"Look what you did!" she yelled angrily.

The Pastor didn't hear her words. He was too busy staring at her hard nipples protruding through her wet bra. Instantly, he became aroused at the sight of them. Lilly Mae couldn't help but look down at the slight lump in the front of his paints. She remembered the gossip the ladies in church were saying about him and became very curious. It was rumored that he had a big python in his pants. She decided right then and there that she would satisfy her curiosity. Immediately, she put her game plan into action. While slowly backing up against the wall, she felt her breast in a seductive manner.

"Oh Pastor look at me. I'm a mess," she said in a child-like manner.

Poking her lips out she hopelessly slid down the wall. She raised her knees to her breast causing a little of her white panties to be displayed between her legs.

"I know the Lord isn't going to forgive me know."

The Pastor fantasized at the pretty white sight between her legs. He began to sweat profusely. With what he was thinking, he became a little paranoid and looked around the bathroom to make sure no one else was in there. He grabbed his handkerchief from his breast pocket, and wiped the sweat off his lips and forehead. He contemplated on how he was going to get his manhood in between Lilly Mae's sweet young legs.

The Pastor didn't care for his own kind. He loved colored women like no other. He loved their different skin tone, their shapely body, their walk, their talk, and their hair styles. On the weekends, he would always be at this joint called Sweet Sugar, in another parish, cutting loose. And yet when it was time for him to be at church on Sunday, he was right there sitting like a Saint.

"Sister let me pray for you. The Holy Spirit is telling me something *right now*. He is telling me what I must do *to you*, and it will be good *for you*."

He walked over and held his hand out to her.

"Let me help you up."

Sadly, she looked up at him and took his hand.

"Now I don't feel that this is right with what I'm about to do. But it's not about my feelings. It's about doing God's work. We all have to fellowship and help each other out by whatever means necessary. You must remember…" he said as he turned her around to face the wall. "You must remember that this is *God's* work not mine."

As he lifted her skirt up and pulled her panties down, his breathing became fast and his heart pounded even faster.

"Amen," he said as he bent her over exposing her beautiful, voluptuous rear end.

"Girl, the Lord is telling me to purify you from a sex demon that possesses your soul. And since I'm the Pastor, and pure at heart, it is my God-given *duty* that the Lord uses me as a vessel to do his work"

Lilly Mae's mouth dropped open. She couldn't believe what he just tried to pull. But…because she knew what she wanted, she went along with his little game. Unbeknownst to him, she was playing her own little game as well. She prayed to God. "O Lord, please purify 'my soul. Lord, please save me. Whatever you have the Pastor do unto me Lord, I know it's from you."

He unzipped his pants and placed his manhood inside her paradise. He blessed that poor girl's soul with a vengeance.

"In the name of Jesus! In the name of Jesus!" he shouted with every stroke.

The pleasurably pain caused Lilly Mae to go into a frenzy.

"Lord yes, thank you Jesus, thank you Jesus! Oh, my God yes! Pastor I know this has got to be from the Lord, cause it feels like heaven!"

Pastor Abler blessed her faster and faster.

"Child, when Sister Smith told me that you were having lustful thoughts of the flesh…as your Pastor…it is my *duty* to beat that sex demon out of your flesh, so you can overcome all of your iniquities."

Sister Smith, the young girl and the Elder were standing outside the bathroom with their ear against the door. They were listening to all the noise coming from inside.

"My goodness he must really be blessing her," said the young girl.

Sister Smith pressed her ear harder against the door.

"Sounds like it to me. Let's leave them alone. We don't want to interrupt God's work."

"Amen," said the Elder.

"Praise God! Oh, yes Praise his Holy name! In the name of Jeeeesus!" They heard the Pastor yelling as they walked away.

As he yelled Jesus, the blessing of Lilly Mae came to an end.

Mentally, Lilly Mae heard the pastor yelling. But literally, she also heard her daughter's voice yelling at the same time. *What the hell...* Blinking several times she brought herself back into the now. She looked at her daughter, who was singing from the top of her lungs. "Jeeeesus!"

PART SIX

18

*I*T'S BEEN EIGHT years since Betty Jean's monster days. She was 11 years old now with two half-sisters and two half-brothers. Their names were Jackie, Jamie, Johnny and Jimmy. They were the pride and joy of Joe Carter's life and his reason for existence. They made him feel complete. He worshiped the ground they walk on. Especially the boys; in his eyes, those boys could do no wrong simply because they were his boys.

Everyone around town knew of the Carter's family, mostly because of the contrast Betty Jean brought to them. Compared to her siblings, who were dark skin, people were saying that Betty Jean was white. People always stared at them whenever they all went out as a family.

One time during a community picnic, while standing in line to receive a hot dog, Joe overheard a group of ladies talking bad about his family. They were also making fun of how he was taking care of a white man's child. Now Joe had already heard through the grapevine that people were talking about him and his family behind his back. But to actually hear it with one's own ear was just too much for him to bear. Disgusted, he began to think that his family name, image within the community and pride were tarnished. Overtime, he became deeply ashamed of his step-daughter and extremely resentful toward Lilly Mae for not telling him who the father of her child was. The thought of what folks were saying about his family consumed him every minute, every hour, of the day. However, Betty Jean, who had heard the non-sense, could care less about what folks were saying. She had so much other stuff to worry about, like the everyday choirs her mother gave her to do.

When the family started to grow, her normal childhood stopped. There was no more sitting around playing with dolls, playing hide and go seek with her friends, or stuff like that. She had too many things that her mother wanted her to do, as far as taking care of her younger siblings. It got to the point that she dreaded every time her mother popped up pregnant. She just knew that it would be her who would be washing baby clothes by hand, or changing their nasty diapers. And as if that wasn't enough, she had to bath them. Nope… no more fun for Betty Jean. However, she still had to try her hand.

On this one particular morning, while sitting at the kitchen table having breakfast, Betty Jean asked her father, "Daddy, can I go to Suzie's pajama party this weekend instead of doing choirs?"

"No." he replied.

Upset with his answer, she waited until after school to ask her mother the same question.

"Ma, Suzie's mother is giving her a pajama party this weekend. Can I go?"

"What did your father say?"

"But Ma…all my friends will be there," she whined.

Her mother ignored her. It was as if Betty Jean was talking to a brick wall. Her mother's silent attitude pissed her off some kind of bad.

During dinner that night, Betty Jean huffed and puffed trying to get a reaction out of her parents. But it didn't work. They acted like she wasn't even there. So when she was finished eating, she asked to be excused to get the bath water ready for her youngest sister and two brothers.

"You may be excused," Joe said without looking at her. "But the next time you come to my table, you leave that little attitude of yours somewhere else."

"Yes sir," she said under her breath as she stormed out of the dining room.

As loud as she could, she deliberately stomped up the stairs. When she got to the bathroom door, she kicked it open and slammed it shut behind her. Lilly Mae jumped at the loud sound, but it didn't bother Joe. He continued eating without saying a word.

"I'll go talk to her," Lilly Mae said as she stood up.

Calmly, Joe motioned for her to sit back down and to finish her food. Once dinner was over, Joe would retire to his favorite chair, a fresh pipe, and the daily newspaper in the library. Jackie and Lilly Mae cleaned the kitchen, and Pearl took her grandchildren upstairs to Betty Jean for their bath.

At hearing the kid's laughter coming down the hallway, Betty Jean jumped up from sitting on the floor. With tears in her eyes, she ran to the open window and pretended to be interested in the stars. When Pearl entered the room, she heard Betty Jean sniffling a little. And right away she knew that she had been crying, but there was nothing she could do about it.

"Here they are baby."

The kids stood at the door looking at Betty Jean. They were waiting for her to come and help them take their clothes off. When she didn't, Pearl gave the little ones a nudge.

"Go ahead and take your clothes off."

Betty Jean didn't turn around or even acknowledge her grandmother.

With their clothes off the kids walked over to the warm bath water and got in. They started playing with their toys as usual. Sorrowfully, Pearl stared at Betty Jean. *Lord how long will she hold on...how long will this child hold on.* Pearl lowered her head and slowly closed the door behind her.

At the sudden sound of the door being shut, Betty Jean ran and opened the door to cry out to her grandmother. But all she saw was the bottom of her long dress turning the corner. Head down and with the greatness of ease, she closed the door. Leaning her back against it, she stared at her siblings with much hatred. She despised bathing them. She never understood why she had to bath her mother's children. *They ain't my kids. So I shouldn't have to bath their little butts...?*

One day Betty Jean got her nerve up and asked her mother why does she have to bath them all the time. Her mother told her that because she was the oldest, it's her responsibility to do so.

"What kind of an excuse is that shit. I'm only eleven years old. I can't go and have fun with my friends or nothing. She always got me doing something around the house," she said out loud.

Betty Jean didn't have any concerns about what outside people were saying. But within herself, she became very bitter toward her family over the years. It had gotten to the point where she hated them all, except for her grandmother. She was the only one who showed her unconditional love.

At times, she sat on the front porch with her grandmother, thinking of ways to harm her father and mother, because of how they didn't allow her to have any fun. She would think that the best way to deal with the responsibilities put upon her, was to just simply kill everyone. Mentally, she would often leave the realization of her situation. She would travel to a bazaar world of torture and suffering; to a world where she received pleasure from dispensing hurt and pain to others. She wanted people to feel the pain that she was feeling.

As she stared at the kids playing in the water, a negative entity began to have a field day with her imagination. Thoughts of drowning them, and shoving their toys down their throats came to mind, just to get them out of her life. Her thoughts became so wicked she couldn't even believe what she was thinking. *They're just little kids...she* thought to herself. But the negative entity didn't care about that, it wanted harm to come to everyone. She fought the terrible thoughts by hitting her head with her fist. She did this until she heard laughter and splashing of water. Taking several deep breathes, she got herself together and walked over to the tub. Grabbing the washcloth from its holder and the soap from Jamie, she began to wash her up. Mechanical she performed her duties.

As she did this, she began to daydream. Happy thoughts came to mind; things like attending a basketball game and riding a bike with friends. She even dreamed of having her own home with a white picket fence. Her kids were on the front porch laughing and playing. The joyful sounds became so loud that she had to tell them to quiet down, but they continued.

"Shut up!" she yelled several times.

Hearing her own voice screaming brought her back to reality. With her hand over her mouth, she realized that she was actually screaming at her sister and brothers. Jimmy took a handful of water and threw it on her.

"You shut up!"

Surprised at his actions, she lost it.

"Boy what you do that for!"

She pushed him down in the water, and held his head underneath for several seconds. When she let him up, he was laughing up a storm.

"That was fun! Do it again!"

"Boy, you are just as dumb as a jay bird," she said while rinsing her sister off. "Stand up. Come on boy it's your turn. Jamie, sit down and play until I get this nappy headed boy clean."

She plopped right down in the warm water, and started playing with the toys.

As she washed Jimmy, she noticed Johnny from the corner of her eye. He was sitting still in the water, making weird faces, and not saying a word. Betty Jean recognized what he was trying to do.

"Boy! Get your butt out the water and go use the toilet! Why you got to be so nasty?!"

Jimmy burst out laughing at his brother. He knew that he was trying to put a long, brown log into the water to see it float. As Johnny jumped out of the tub, he fell to the floor. His butt was up in the air as he laid there hurting from the fall. Betty Jean couldn't resist the opportunity of playfully kicking him in his rear end.

"Stop!" he yelled as he got up, and ran to the toilet.

"That's what you get for being so nasty. Now sit there and do your do while I finish with your brother."

Putting his head down, Johnny folded his arms and began to concentrate on his bowel movement.

While her attention was on Johnny, Jamie grabbed the thick bar of soap and began to lick it. For some reason, she always thought that the soap was vanilla taffy. She began to choke from the suds in her mouth. Betty Jean turned and instantly smacked the soap out of her hand.

"What the hell...! You are such a little dumb-ass! Keep that soap out of our mouth!"

Grabbing her hand from the sting of being hit, she began to cry.

"Don't be hitting my little sister!" Johnny yelled from the toilet.

"Shut up boy!" She continued to wash Jimmy. "I don't know why I got to wash y'all anyway. Y'all ain't none of my damn children."

"Awwwww, you cussed! You used the devil's word!"

"No I didn't!"

Taking a deep breath, Johnny yelled with all his might. "Yes you did, and I'm telling daddy!"

"Go head and tell him! That's y'all daddy! He ain't none of my daddy!"

"Yes he is...he all our daddy!"

Betty Jean grabbed Jimmy's little arm and placed it against hers.

"Boy, look at my color and look at his...you see that? I'm way lighter than all y'all."

She grabbed her hair.

"You see this? My hair is sandy color and soft. It's not black and kinky like y'all is."

Forcefully, she pushed Jimmy's arm back down.

"So..." Jimmy said smartly with a soft-spoken voice.

"So people say that makes me better than you; all y'all. And your daddy ain't my daddy cause he too dark"

"No you're not better than us, and he is your daddy!" Johnny yelled as he made an attempt to wipe his butt, but got most of it on his hand.

"Yes I am, and he's not!" she yelled back in a taunting manner.

Johnny screamed back distinctly pronouncing each word. "NO YOU AIN'T BETTER!"

Laughing, Betty Jean mimics him, "YES I IS BETTER!"

Taking up for his big brother, Jimmy licked his tongue out at her.

"Well...at least we know who our daddy is," he said teasingly while shaking his butt.

His words hit Betty Jean's heart like a ton of bricks. Before she knew it, she slapped him across the face like there was no tomorrow.

"You little nappy headed fool, shut your butt up!"

From the force of her slap, he fell in the water.

"I'm going to tell daddy on you!" he yelled and began to cry.

When Jamie saw her brother crying, she started crying too. Johnny became furious because he always thought of himself as being the big, little protector of his younger sister and brother.

"Don't you be hitting my little brother!"

With tissue lodged in between his butt, he jumped off the toilet, and ran over to Betty Jean. He yanked her long hair and started hitting her in the face. She screamed and slapped the crap out of him.

"Boy…you better stop before I knock the holy shit out of you!"

Her slap bounced right off him. He continued to hit her with his powerful little fist.

"You're the devil! You're the devil! Ma said that anybody that cusses is the devil!"

Jimmy grabbed another part of Betty Jean's hair and pulled it. He began hitting her in the face too.

"Don't you be hitting my big brother!"

Even though Johnny and Jimmy were small in stature, they were strong as all outdoors. Betty Jean tried to fight them off as she sat on the edge of the tub, but lost her balance and fell into the water. She screamed out as they continued to hit her.

"Stop it! Get off of me! What is wrong with y'all?!"

As she tried to get the boys off of her, Jamie took her big, yellow, rubber hammer and commenced to beating the mess out of her sister's head.

Joe heard the noise coming from upstairs and tried to ignore it, but it got louder and louder. He tried to maintain his composure by looking up at the ceiling. Taking a deep breath, he attempted to read the paper again, but the commotion was unbearable.

"Lilly Mae go see what those kids are doing up there!"

"Betty Jean is bathing the children Joe!" she yelled to him from the kitchen.

"I didn't ask you to tell me what was going on up there. I said go see. Now put the dishes down and go see…now!"

"I'll go Mama," Jackie said.

Frustrated, Lilly Mae slapped the dish rag down on the counter.

"I got it baby; finish up the kitchen for me."

Pissed off, she wiped her hands on her apron, and started toward the stairs. *Like I don't have nothing else to do. Maybe you should go see what the hell is going on up there your damn self.*

As she started up the steps, Joe yelled again.

"Hurry up! I'm trying to read!"

Lilly Mae stopped in her tracks, and shook her head in disbelief. Taking a deep breath, she threw both hands up in the air as if giving up. She realized that there was nothing she could do to make Joe help out around the house. Tired, she slowly continued up the stairs.

Walking down the hallway, she saw a lot of water on the hardwood floor. As she got farther down the hall, she saw that it was coming from the bathroom. *What in God's creation?* When she opened the bathroom door, she couldn't believe her eyes.

"Betty Jean what are y'all doing in here?"

The bathroom floor was covered with water. Soap was all in the kid's eyes and hair. All the towels were soaked and thrown everywhere. Wet toilet tissue was all over the place. Betty Jean was soaked from top to bottom. Lilly Mae couldn't believe the awful site. She walked in and began to pick up the wet towels.

"You know, all I asked you to do was to bath the kids. Why is all this water and stuff on the floor?"

"Ma, Betty Jean said the devil's bad words!" Jonny yelled as he ran to his mother.

"No I didn't boy!"

"Yes you did! Yes, you did!" Jamie yelled as she jumped up and down in the water with excitement.

"Shut up little girl!"

Lilly Mae looked at Jimmy, who was climbing out of the tub. He was always the one to ask if you wanted to know the truth about something. He was a very soft-spoken boy until you pushed him to the limit, which would normally take a whole lot of pushing.

"Jimmy, did you hear Betty Jean say a cuss word?"

"Ye…" Was the only sound you heard him say before he slipped on the floor. He landed with one foot on the tub, and the rest of his body lying flat out on the floor. They all burst out laughing at him as he laid there motionless. Even Lilly Mae couldn't resist the laughter that rose up inside of her. He didn't yell or anything. He just laid there looking up at the ceiling.

"That's what you get." Pointing at him, Betty Jean was laughing like crazy.

Hearing the unison of laughter put Joe over the edge.

"Lilly Mae, shut that noise up, I'm trying to read!"

This time his wife didn't respond. She was actually having a good laugh with her kids.

"Lilly Mae!" Joe yelled again.

No answer. The hearty laughter coming from his family pissed him off even more.

"Don't have me come up there!"

He paused for a minute to see if she would acknowledge him, but she didn't.

"Lilly…woman…I'm warning you; don't have me come up there!"

He waited again for a response, but all he heard was laughter. Feeling disrespected, he jumped up and threw his newspaper on the floor. Unbuckling his belt, he started toward the stairs.

"I just told you three days ago, that I don't want to hear no noise in my house when I sit down to read!"

As he walked up the stairs, he pulled his thick, black leather belt from his paints and wrapped it around his hand. When he reached the top of the stairs, he couldn't believe his eyes.

"What in God's name is going on? Why is water on my hall floor?"

Lilly Mae and the kids were laughing so hard, they didn't hear Joe yelling, until he burst through the door. *Bam!* He opened the door so hard, it sounded like a shotgun went off. Startled, Lilly Mae and the kids jumped right out of their skin.

"Lilly Mae, didn't you hear me calling you! Why is my bathroom in such a mess?!"

"Daddy! Betty Jean said that she was better than us, and she said the devil's cuss words too!" Jonny yelled as he immediately ran over to him.

Lilly Mae tried to take up for her daughter.

"Now that's not true. She didn't say no such thing."

Joe looked down at his son, then to Lilly Mae and Betty Jean. Slowly, he walked over to Lilly Mae, and got up in her face.

"How would you know if she didn't say what my son just told me...were you up here?"

Lilly Mae took a few steps back from her husband, because unbeknown to anyone, Joe had become physically abusive to her down the years. But now, here, in front of everyone, the secret was no more. Like a flash of lighting he slapped the dickens out of her. She screamed and fell to the floor. Knowing what was to come next, she took both hands and tried to protect her face. But it did no good, because when it came to him and that black belt of his, he knew how to work it. He hit Lilly Mae every which way but loose. He beat her like there was no tomorrow.

Seeing their mother being beat for the first time caused the kids to cry.

"Stop it! Stop it!" Betty Jean screamed.

Joe didn't hear a thing. He was in his element. *Whop! Whop!* The belt went with every word he said.

"I told you about doubting my kids say when it comes to that girl of yours didn't I!"

Still screaming, Lilly Mae got up and tried to run out the door. But Joe was right on her tail. *Whop! Whop!*

"Bring your butt back here!"

He got to the door and kicked it shut before she got to it. He continued to beat the mess out of her. Silently, she screamed for her mother.

Pearl had dozed off once she dropped the kids off for their bath.

Grandma! She heard a voice scream, but thought she was dreaming. The scream became stronger and louder. Grandma! Grandma! The frantic voice jolted her out of her sleep. Grandma! She heard Betty Jean scream and sat right up.

"Betty Jean!"

"Grandma, make him stop!"

With urgency, Pearl jumped out of her bed. Grabbing her robe, she ran down the long hallway.

"Betty Jean I'm coming!"

Pearl ran to her oldest granddaughter's room and burst in the door.

"What's going on in h....?"

But no one was there. Confused, she started walking toward one of the kid's room when she heard the frantic voice again.

"Grandma!"

Pearl took off running.

"Betty Jean! Child what's going on?!"

As she got closer to the noise, she heard her daughter yelling, "Joe, stop it! I...I didn't mean nothing by it! Please, don't hit me no more!"

Pearl knew that Joe and Lilly Mae were having marital problems. However, it was never displayed in front of the children. They always kept their disagreements behind bedroom doors, late at night after the kids were asleep. She never told Lilly Mae that she knew about their late-night squabbles because…well, that was between her and her husband. But now, that same noise was coming from where the grandchildren were. *Lord not in front of my babies.*

She entered the bathroom.

"Lilly Mae what's…"

To her dismay, she saw her daughter hunched over on her knees, covering her face with her hands.

"What the hell is going on in here?" she shouted.

Joe was standing over his wife like a gladiator who just defeated its enemy.

"Stay out of this Pearl. This is my business!" he said as he pointed his finger at her.

Betty Jean ran over to her grandmother crying her heart out.

"Grandma, Joe is beating on mama again."

Pearl cocked her head to the side. *Again…Lord how long has this child known about her parent's fights? And what about the little ones…do they know too?*

Joe walked over to Betty Jean and got in her face.

"And what does telling your grandmother supposed to do…stop me?" He slapped her across the face. "This is my house understand!"

"Mama!"

Pearl immediately grabbed her, and drew her close for protection.

"Come on now Joe you didn't have to do that," Pearl said with sorrowful eyes.

Before she could say anything else, Joe for the first time verbally attacked her.

"Shut up Pearl and mind your own business! This is my family, and they are to do as I say!" He looked over at Lilly Mae. "Now get this place and these kids cleaned up!"

Lilly Mae was afraid to move.

"I said now got damn it!"

Slowly, she got up off the floor while wiping tears from her eyes.

"BJ, go get yourself cleaned up."

Irritated by the sound of her voice, Joe walked over to her.

"Did I tell you to talk?"

Bracing herself for another physical attack, she closed her eyes and lowered her head.

"No." she said softly.

Acting like he couldn't hear her, he moved in closer and pulled on his ear.

"What's that...? I can't hear you?"

"No." she said a little louder.

No one said a thing after that. The atmosphere was very intense. A few seconds went by with no one saying a word, which seemed like all eternity. The grandmother tried to perk things up.

"Come on children, let us help you get dressed," she said gleefully.

Grabbing their pajamas, the children ran over to Pearl and Betty Jean. Lilly Mae didn't move a muscle. Still afraid, she kept her eyes glued to the floor.

After putting the kid's pajamas on, they started to leave. However, before they could exit the room, Joe stopped them.

"Y'all hold up. Betty Jean, I need to have a few words with you."

Betty Jean legs became weak at the sound of him saying her name. It felt like she was about to pass out. *Lord, won't he just die.* Slowly, she turned around and looked at her pathetic mother, as she had done so many times in the past. She used to look at her in a pleading manner. It was as if she was saying silently, *Mother you know what's going on... help me please.* But her silent plea for help fell on deaf ears. It fell on a hopeless woman who couldn't even help her own self. Lilly Mae slightly looked over at her daughter, but quickly put her head back down before Joe saw her.

"Go on Pearl," Joe said as he walked over to the edge of the tub and sat down. "Put them children to bed."

Pearl quickly took the kids hands and walked out the bathroom as if nothing happened.

"Come on y'all. I've got some fresh-baked cookies downstairs. I'll tuck you in and then I'll bring you all a cookie and some nice warm milk, before the sleepy angel come and get you."

The children jumped up and down with joy because they loved grandma's homemade cookies.

With a sinister smile upon his face, Joe looked at his wife and Betty Jean. He was enjoying the power that he had over them. They couldn't do a thing in his house, unless he gave them approval. The more he looked at them, the sinister smile faded, and he became disgusted with how sickening they looked.

"Lilly Mae go finish cleaning the kitchen."

Without hesitation, she got up and walked toward her daughter. She whispered into her ear, "It's going to be alright. He's your father. He just wants to talk to you."

As she said these words to her daughter, Joe walked over to the toilet. Putting the lid down, he had a seat and stared at them. It was like he saw them, but didn't see them. He sat there thinking, *they in my house, depending on me for everything. They don't own a thing in their name. They didn't come from a good stock like I did. My mother and father almost disowned me for choosing a woman like her as my wife.*

Joe's parents always believed in having the best of everything. They wore the finest clothes. Their son attended the best schools. They were invited to all the social parties. Everything had to be perfect. They even picked out their son's future wife.

As mentioned earlier, Joe met his first wife Claire at church through his parents. She was the daughter of a prominent socialite in their community. She was beautiful and educated. Her eyes were light brown. Her hair was a long, brownish color and silky smooth to the touch. Her body was the shape of an hourglass. She was the epitome of a beautiful woman to a lot of men.

She had the best of everything and then some. Their wedding announcement was even in the local newspaper. They called it "The Event of the Year." Nothing was spared when it came to the wedding decor and food. The flower arrangement cost just as much as the wedding cake did.

Their marriage went well for the first year. So much physical love was being displayed between them; no problem in that area.

However, once the sex was over, they had to converse and go about daily life as a couple. That's when the problems kicked in.

On the surface, it looked all so beautiful. But behind closed doors, their marriage was falling apart. Joe came to realize that he really didn't know his wife. He thought that her high sex drive was wonderful at first. But soon, it got old to him because she wasn't doing anything that a wife was supposed to do. Things like cooking, washing clothes and keeping the house clean. As soon as he got home from a hard day's work, instead of having his dinner ready, she wanted to have sex. One day he flat out asked her, "Baby, when are you going to cook for me? And she responded, "What…oh no, I don't cook." They really were the complete opposite of each other. They weren't "equally yoked" as the bible states the way a man and woman should be. She was a drinker of all sorts of alcoholic beverages; he wasn't. She wanted to hang out at the Pub and enjoy the night life; he didn't. He wanted to have kids; she didn't. She even stopped going to church. He asked her, "Baby, why don't you attend church anymore?" And she responded, "I really don't like going to church. The only reason why I attended in the first place was so that my parents wouldn't cut me out of their Will." Her parents warned her that if she didn't go to church; do as they say and act like a lady; they were going to cut her out of their money. Every time Joe mentioned to her about going back to church, she would start an argument big time.

To avoid being around her, he got heavily involved in his work and after that he would attend meetings. His routine went on for about five years, until one day he came home and found a "Dear John" letter on the hall table from his wife. It read...

Dear Joe:

> *I no longer can stand living with you. The only reason why I married you in the first place was because my parents told me to do so. They said that you had money. Well... if you do, I can't tell because you don't do anything but go to work and attend meetings all day. I've met a man Joe. I've been seeing him for about two years now. He doesn't mind me not cooking; he loves to cook himself. He also doesn't mind me not wanting any kids. He just wants me to be me and for me to be happy. Good-bye and take care. Maybe you will find the women of your dreams one day.*

That's it...? He thought to himself. *Just like that, it's over. She just up and disappears? Not to me you don't.* He called his in-laws to find out what was going on. When her father answered the phone, he was very distance with him and for good reason. Joe found out that Claire had told her parents that he was beating on her, and that she had bruises all over her body. That's the reason she gave them for not attending church anymore. She also told them that he made her have anal sex, and that he wanted other women to join them, while they made love.

Joe was blown away when he heard the lies. She slandered his name just to stay in the good grace of her parents and their money. He bit his tongue several times to keep from responding to her ridiculous lies, until his father in-law insulted him.

"I knew something wasn't right about you. You have your Degree, but you're still ignorant. You're not even pure like my little Claire."

Joe was livid. He yelled in the phone like the brimstone from hell was raining upon earth.

"You think just because your daughter looks white that she's pure! You think that she's better than me because I'm dark skin! Well, I got news for you *sir;* your daughter is a whore! Yes, that's right a whore! And she drinks like a sailor! And you know what else I found out about your daughter..., I found out through the grapevine that *your* daughter got pregnant in her last year of college! Yes, that's right pregnant! And she was so afraid to tell y'all, because she didn't want y'all to cut her out of you all's Will! So instead of her going to the hospital to get an abortion, she took a coat hanger and rammed it up inside of her, causing her to lose the baby! And you know what else...I don't think she can ever bear children anymore. Because with the way we've been *fuckin'* that ass should have been pregnant! So fuck *you* and light bright too sir!"

He slammed the phone down. And that was the end of that.

Returning back to reality, Joe looked at Lilly Mae.

"Come on now, go on down stairs and close the door behind you."

With her head toward the floor, and feeling helpless for her daughter, she walked out the bathroom closing the door behind her. But for some reason, she didn't go down stairs as her husband told her to do. She stood outside the door to hear what he had to say to her daughter.

Emotionless, Betty Jean stared at the closed door and accepted her mother's abandonment again. At one time, she used to plead, cry, and beg for her mother to save her from her father's wrath, that would flare up out of nowhere for no reason.

Joe told Betty Jean to turn to face him, but she didn't move a muscle. She hated to look at him. She hated the sound of his voice. She stood frigid.

"I'm not going to say it again."

She turned her soaked body around with her arms folded over her breast. Her body language told him that she was on the defensive.

However, that didn't matter to him, because he knew that she was subservient just like her mother and grandmother.

In a calm manner, he told her, "Put your hands down to your side."

Reluctantly, she did so. Joe saw her nipples protruding through her soaked, thin, white shirt. His staring at them made her feel very uncomfortable. In shame, she turned her head away from him.

He began to lecture her.

"I know I'm not your biological father. Truth of the matter is… you don't know who your father is and…"

"I know who my daddy is," she said with a nasty attitude.

"You may know of him, but you don't know who he is. And if you cut me off like that again, I will beat that pretty white skin of yours until it turns black and blue. Do you understand me?"

"Yes sir," she said with protruding lips.

As the chastising continued, Lilly Mae stood outside the door with her ear against it listing. She grabbed her chest from the anxiety she felt. She knew that her little girl was going to get a whipping, but to what extent she didn't know, because she never stayed around to find out. Joe was pissed off to the max this time. And the only thing that she thought she could do for Betty Jean was to pray for her. Pray that her little girl got through his beating in one piece. Silently, she slid down to the floor and began to cry.

Joe continued. "I don't know who you think you are, or why you think that you're better than anyone of these kids. You're all the same in God's eyes. I treat you like you are my own for your mother's sake. The only reason you're still here in this house is because you're your mother's child. Now, like I said time after time, my daddy always told me why I was going to get it, and now I'm going to do the same for my own. I'm giving you a whipping because of what you said. I'm also whipping you to keep that attitude of yours in check."

"Man...you should hear how you sound. I'm not one of your own. I'm my mother's child. *That* I do know," she said with a smirk. "It's a wonder you know who your daddy is from what folks say about your mother."

Expressionless, he stared at her. Joe used to get upset when she talked about his family, but not anymore. He learned to stay cool as a cucumber. He knew about the rumors of his mother running around back in the day on his father, but he didn't care about that. All he cared about was that both parents raised him. They stayed together regardless of who did what. He was loved, and was always taken care of.

"For God's sake, I'm going to ignore what you just said to me girl. Because if I took what you said to heart, I'd hurt you in ways you couldn't imagine."

"Hurt...? You can't hurt me no more than what you've already done. My innocence is gone thanks to you... *Daddy*."

"And thanks to you taking care of me *daughter*...is the reason why you, your mother *and* your grandmother still have a roof over your heads. Now get your ass over here," he said hatefully.

Hesitantly, she walked over to him and stood before him in defiant. She stood tall with her head held high, and her shoulders squared. She refused to let her so-called father break her spirit. With his hands on his thighs, he sat up with anticipation.

"Take your pants off."

As if she was on auto pilot, she took them off, and laid across his lap for a spanking. There was no need for him to tell her to assume the position, because he had been spanking her this way for some time now. With eyes closed, Joe raised both hands in the air.

"Now, remove your panties."

Obediently, she raised her butt slightly up in the air and removed her colorful, butterfly, cotton panties. Even though Joe whipped Lilly Mae with his black belt, he never used it on Betty Jean. He preferred to use his hands. Slowly, he lowered his arms and placed one hand on her hamstring, and the other on her buttocks. In a pleasurable state of mind, his body received a huge surge of energy every time he touched her in that manner. With eyes still closed, his hands linger in their position. After a few seconds, he took a deep breath and opened his eyes. Looking down at her perfectly round butt, and as if kneading dough, he began to caress her buttocks over and over ever so gently. He partook in this action for several minutes. And then without warning... *Whop!* He struck her hard as hell and lingered his hand there to receive the sting of pleasure. He tilted his head back and smiled. *Whop! Whop! Whop!* The faster he hit, the harder his hits became. He began to drool from the pleasurable sensation of the sting.

Betty Jean tried to hold back tears from the pain, but it was unbearable. She finally cried out for her mother's help.

"Mama, make him stop! Make him stop!"

Her cry intensified his pleasure. He began to move his body back and forth. Faster and faster his body went with every word she cried. *Whop! Whop! Whop! Whop!*

"Yes…yes make daddy stop Claire, make daddy stop!"

"My name is Betty Jean, not Claire!"

"Shut up! You're fucking up my…"

He pushed his thumb into her mouth to shut her up.

"Suck it bitch. Suck it and shut the fuck up!"

Her cries were muffled as he continued his action.

Lilly Mae heard her daughter's cry and wanted to help…but how? Joe told her to go down stairs. Not being able to stand it any longer, she quietly looked through the key hole to see what he was doing to her daughter. Horrified at the sight, she put her hands over her mouth to prevent herself from screaming. She fell to the floor. She was taken aback at what she saw. Her baby girl was lying across her husband's lap, with her butt exposed. He was spanking her and rocking back and forth as if he was having convulsions. She grabbed her apron and vomited in it. Her body felt like it was on fire. Her hands were sweaty, and she had shortness of breath. Her heart felt like it was about to explode. Dizziness over whelmed her. Crying silently, she repeatedly beat herself in the chest. Now, she knew why her husband never touched her anymore. Now, she knew why he didn't even look at her in that special kind of way. Now, she realized that she had made a terrible mistake of using a man's kindness for self-gain. Her selfishness caused her Betty Jean a terrible life of pain and misery, and she will never be the same. This was the life she endured from her parents. Now the vicious cycle of mental degradation and sexual abuse continues.

PART SEVEN

19

*T*IME STOOD STILL for no one. Sometimes the passing of time can make things better, or it could make things worse. In Betty Jean's case, it made things better. As she got into her teenage years, she had learned to tolerate the family's attitude toward her. She came to the conclusion that she didn't have any support from the family, when it came to her complaining about the beatings from her father. To make it easier on herself, she stopped with the smart mouth and the defiant attitude. No more resistant body language. Subservient was the name of the game, and she played it very well. That's all Joe wanted, and loved it.

The family was getting along for what it was worth. Lilly Mae stayed in her place, for the most part. And Betty Jean was way into puberty thus developing into a very beautiful young lady. Folks thought that she was a model. She was the talk of the town. All the boys wanted to date her. Even some of the college boys wanted to take her out. But when she told them to ask her dad, they backed off. Reason being, they heard rumors about Joe Carter and his big wooden stick. A few times when guys did get up the nerve to pay

Betty Jean a visit, he would run them off the porch with that stick. If you weren't fast enough you got it right upside the head. No sir, guys stopped asking her out and dropping by. Still, they admired her from afar.

The lack of mingling with her peers, made Betty Jean miss out on a whole lot of childhood experiences. Things like puppy love; your first slow dance; hanging out at the playground watching guys play basketball with their shirts off. Whenever she wanted to go anywhere, she had to get permission first. And when she did get the green light, she couldn't go by herself. Her mother or Pearl had to go with her, because Joe demanded it.

A prime example was on a Saturday morning, while she and her mother were in the kitchen. Lilly Mae needed to run to the general store to pick up a few things. But she also needed to type up the minutes from the meeting Joe had last night at the church. Seeing her mother's dilemma, Betty Jean volunteered to help.

"Ma, I can run down to the store on my bike for you."

Lilly Mae smiled at her. She really wanted to send her daughter on an errand like all the rest of the parents do with their children, but she didn't want to hear Joe's mouth.

"Oh baby, that's so sweet of you wanting to help, but you know how your father is. Plus, the store is way too far for you to go on your bike."

"Ma, he doesn't have to know...he's asleep."

Lilly Mae thought about it for a few minutes. But she got scared just thinking about the consequences.

"No baby, I don't think so."

Disappointed again by her mother, Betty Jean walked away with her head down. Feeling bad, Lilly Mae called out to her.

"BJ, tell you what...let's all go to the General Store. You go on upstairs and put on a nice fancy dress. I'll get the kids together."

Betty Jean jumped up and down with delight. Excited, she ran down the hallway and half-way up the stairs, before she abruptly stopped and thought, *what about grandma...* Turning around she ran back down the stairs to her mother.

"What about Grandma...is she coming too?!"

"She's not feeling too well this morning."

"Ok." Betty Jean said and ran back up the stairs.

Even though she really didn't want to go without her grandmother, she was happy about getting out of the house. *Who knows*, she thought. *I might see a few of my school friends hanging out.*

They all arrived at the General Store, and to Betty Jean's dismay, she didn't see not one of her friends. She wanted to show off her pink fancy dress with the ruffles around the collar and hem. She had on white patent leather shoes with white and pink ruffle ankle socks. BJ looked real fancy. She even tied a big white bow on the side of her head.

Everyone looked at her and smiled. But as soon as they passed her, it was another story. Their facial expression went down south. They were wondering why she had on what looked like to them her Sunday best, instead of regular clothes at the General Store. If Betty Jean did notice the funny looks on their faces, she didn't acknowledge it. She was just as happy as a Jay Bird out of its cage. Being out somewhere other than school or church was a blessing in her eyes.

Lilly Mae went and got one of the food carts.

"Here BJ take this and the list. You can do the shopping."

Betty Jean happily took the cart and pushed it down the aisles. Her brothers and sisters were running around like they had no type of home training. Lilly Mae felt embarrassed.

"Y'all stop that running around in here; you're acting like fools in hell water," she said using her quiet voice.

They kept on laughing and running off at the mouth. Johnny grabbed a bag of peanuts and opened them halfway.

"Ma, can we have these nuts?"

Seeing that he had opened the bag up before asking, she snatched them out of his hand and threw them in the cart.

"I guess so, now that your dumb butt done opened them up."

As they continued down the aisle, Betty Jean saw her favorite cake mix and picked it up.

"Look Mama...can we have chocolate cake for Sunday dessert?"

"No. I don't have money for that."

"But Ma, daddy just got paid."

Lilly Mae stopped dead in her tracks. *What!* With a surprised look on her face, she put her hands on her hips and addressed Betty Jean sarcastically.

"And how would you know when your father's payday is?"

Feeling a little uncomfortable, Betty Jean stared at the floor.

"I don't know; I just know."

Out of anger, Lilly Mae tapped her feet.

"What else is it that you know, that you just don't know how you come about knowing?"

Betty Jean looked up at her mother.

"I know he's been sleeping in the other room for a while," she said shyly.

Surprised, Lilly Mae's mouth dropped open. With her head held high in the air, she turned and walked ahead of Betty Jean. Betty Jean put the cake mix back on its shelf and followed her mother. Lilly Mae wanted to hear more of what this child knew about her business.

"And..." she said over her shoulders.

Betty Jean continued while putting food in the cart.

"When you and grandma were spelling them big words in you all conversation, I knew what it spelt when I was real little."

Lilly Mae continued to look straight ahead.

"Is that right...what else?"

On that note, Betty Jean told her mother all the family business she had known all these years.

"Well let's see. I know daddy has high blood pressure. I know that he doesn't take his insulin when he is supposed to. One time when y'all were out eating; he fell out on the floor at the restaurant because his sugar was low. He doesn't like bathing. You wish that you could have gone to school to be a French Interpreter, instead of having all of us. And that..."

"All right child! I see I'm going to have to watch what I say and spell around you. You're just too damn smart."

Her mother's statement caused Betty Jean to smile.

"Daddy says that I'm smart and pretty just like he is."

Lilly Mae was bewildered by her daughter's statement. She stared at her.

"You do know that he's not your biological father, don't you?"

With hatred, she stared into her mother's eyes. *What the hell... how in the world could this woman say this to me? I'm fucking 16 years old; you don't think that I don't know that this man isn't my real father by now? Unfucking believable.* Holding back tears that were swelling up in her eyes; she looked away from her mother. Picking up a can of peas, she pretended to read the label.

"Ma, I know that already. Why are you rubbing it in? Besides... he tells me that all the time, so it doesn't even matter."

"What doesn't matter?"

Disrespecting her mother on purpose, Betty Jean put a twist in her hip, and shrugged her shoulders as she walked away to finish the shopping.

"Nothing Mama...it don't matter."

"What do you mean?"

Before she could answer her mother, she heard Jimmy further up the aisle.

"Look! The ice cream parlor!" he yelled with excitement.

Totally forgetting about the conversation and grocery list, Betty Jean and her siblings ran up to the Ice Cream Parlor.

"Oh my goodness, look at all the different flavors! I love me some Rocky Road!" Betty Jean yelled with delight.

Jamie rubbed her stomach and swayed her butt at the same time.

"I love Butter Pecan, mmm!" she said while licking her lips.

Jimmy looked at Johnny…

"Vanilla is my favorite ain't it Johnny?"

"No, you like Strawberry like me."

Jackie smacked Johnny upside the head.

"Boy, how you going to tell somebody what their favorite ice cream is dummy."

"BJ wait I don't understand…!" her mother yelled.

As she was yelling, a lady who hadn't seen the Carter family in a while approached her.

"Lilly Mae… Lilly Mae Carter how you doing? I see you got your family out here shopping. I haven't seen you in a while. You don't play bridge no more? Is everything ok with you? How's your husband doing? I've been attending his Friday night meetings. Girl, that man is gifted by God. Are you coming to fellowship this Sunday?"

Agitated, Lilly Mae responded with a short answer.

"Yes."

She walked a few feet away from the lady.

"Betty Jean, come back here!"

"Go head Mama, we'll be right here at the Ice Cream Pallor waiting for you," she yelled without looking back at her.

"But you don't have any money!"

Betty Jean took off her shoe and pulled out two quarters.

"Yes, I do! Daddy gave me 50 cents the other day!"

Disturbed, Lilly Mae's mind screamed. *What?! Did she just say my husband gave her some money? Since when did he start doing that? Why didn't he discuss giving money to the kids with me? How long has this shit been going on?* The more she thought about it, the madder she became. Joe was excluding her out of family activities and decisions altogether.

While Lilly Mae and Betty Jean were yelling back and forth, the lady pulled out her wallet to show her how big her son had gotten. Smiling, she walked over to her.

"Look at Ralf's picture. See how big he's gotten."

Lilly Mae stared at the picture, but didn't see a thing. The young lady was talking about her son, but Lilly Mae didn't hear anything. Her mind was running a mile a minute. *Does he plan on replacing me with my own daughter…?*

20

WHILE THEY WERE at the store, Joe woke up from a good night's sleep. Feeling refreshed, he got up and took a shower. Then he headed downstairs for a wonderful breakfast. When he walked into the kitchen, he expected to see his breakfast and coffee on the table. But what he saw was nothing.

"Lilly Mae!" No answer.

He walked out to the backyard to see if she was out there with the kids.

"What the hell?"

He walked back into the kitchen and stared at the stove.

"Pe...."

He began to yell, but decided against it. He knew she wasn't feeling well, plus it was his wife's job to have his breakfast ready when he got up.

Pissed off, he grabbed the thick, black, iron skillet from the cabinet under the sink and slammed it on the stove. He went to the refrigerator and yanked the door open. After grabbing the eggs and scrapple, he slammed it shut. He walked to the cold stove and turned it on. For the first time in his marriage, he had to cook his own breakfast. *This don't make no fuckin' sense. A man has to cook his own got damn food. I told that woman she had to earn her keep.*

Within an hour, Joe had fixed his breakfast, cleaned the kitchen and was now cutting the grass. He always tried to cut the grass real early in the morning, because the weather was much cooler at that time.

However, today his timing was off because he slept a little late. It was about 10:00 a.m. and the sun was blazing hot already. While removing his shirt because of the heat, he heard a car coming up the drive way. As the car got closer he heard the children laughing, but paid them no mind and continued to cut the grass.

"Y'all get the food and stop playing so much," he heard Lilly say as she popped the trunk.

The kids jumped out and ran to get the groceries.

"Last one in the house is a rotten egg!" Johnny yelled as he grabbed a bag and hauled tailed it to the house.

The rest of the kids quickly did the same and were right on his heels.

Getting out of the car, Lilly Mae stared at her husband's physique. Noticing that he didn't even look her way, she slammed the door shut just to see if he would look over at her. But he didn't miss a beat and continued to cut the grass. A little upset, Lilly Mae sucked her teeth and went inside the house. As she placed her purse on the hall table, she heard her mother telling the kids to calm dawn.

"Ma, what are you doing out of bed?"

She walked in the kitchen and saw her mother prepping dinner.

"Well I heard Joe calling for you, so I decided to get up."

Rubbing her temple, she felt a headache slowly creeping up, due to the kids yelling that they were hungry.

Lilly Mae reached into one of the bags and took out apples for the kids.

"Here...y'all take this and go out on the front. You gettin' on my nerves and you're giving mama a headache."

Pearl sat down at the table.

"No baby they're alright."

"There you go again mama, letting these kids have their way."

Johnny, Jimmy and Jackie grabbed their apples and ran back outside.

Acting like a baby, Jamie pulled on her mother's dress.

"Ma, I don't want this. Can I have an orange please?"

Lilly Mae snatched the apple from her and threw it back in the bag. Betty Jean got an orange out of one of the other bags.

"Here girl. Now get outside with the rest of 'em."

Snatching the orange out of her hand, she sarcastically said, "Thank You." And ran outside.

"Ma you see that?!"

"Come on now, I'm not having none of that. We got work to do. Go head out."

Betty Jean began to take the food out of the bags.

"I'll stay and help with dinner."

"No...you too...go outside!"

Betty Jean looked at her mother like she was crazy.

"What's wrong with you? I was just trying to help."

She grabbed an apple and stormed out the kitchen.

Taking a deep breath, Lilly Mae grabbed an orange and walked over to the sink. Leaning against it, she began to peel her orange.

"Ma, have you noticed anything different about Joe?"

Pearl started to put the rest of the food up.

"Like what?"

Lilly Mae shrugged her shoulders.

"Oh I don't know...anything."

Pearl stopped putting the can goods in the pantry and looked at her daughter.

"Well if you don't tell me what to look for that's different, I ain't going to notice nothing that is."

Looking out the window, she saw Joe working up a sweat.

"I don't know… I mean look at him out there. He has no shirt on; he's never done that before."

Her mother went back to stacking the canned goods.

"First time for everything you know."

"His chest has gotten bigger."

"And…! Girl I don't look at your husband like that!"

"Ha, husband please. That's an understatement."

Pearl stopped doing what she was doing and turned toward her daughter.

"What…? Let me tell you something. That's *your* husband, whether you like it or not."

Lilly Mae threw her orange peels in the trash can and sat down at the table.

"I don't like it Ma. He gives those kids more attention than he does me, especially Betty Jean."

Pearl sighed. "Maybe he is just trying to be nice. Maybe he is making sure that he's not showing favoritism between the kids."

"No Ma, not like that. He gave her 50 cents the other day."

"For what?"

"I don't know, she didn't tell me."

Pearl's curiosity deepened. She walked over to the table and sat down.

"Ask her."

Lilly Mae sucked her teeth. "No Ma."

"Why not…?"

"What I look like asking my daughter why her father gave her some money?"

"Because you are her mother, and you want to know. That's why you asking."

Silence filled the room. Seeing that she was getting nowhere with her daughter, Pearl got up and started putting the rest of the food up. Lilly Mae thought about what her mother said, but decided against it.

"No, I don't want to get nothing started. It's been peaceful in this house for a while now."

A question hit Pearl that would solve the matter.

"Did he give the other kids money?"

"No, I asked them that on the way back to the car, and they said no."

Pearl walked back over to her.

"Did she hear you ask them that?"

"No, I waited until she was a few feet away from them."

They were quiet for a few minutes. Both minds were racing across the board of past times. Pearl was thinking of her husband's behavior toward Lilly Mae. The times she felt left out and alone. Lilly Mae was thinking about the special treatment she received from her own dad.

They both took deep breaths at the same time.

"So why her Ma?"

Pearl wanted to end the conversation now. She wanted her thoughts from the past to go away. She didn't want to relive it through her daughter.

"Maybe it's because she's older than them. She is a teenager in high school."

Lilly Mae's face lit up. To her, that reason made perfect sense.

"Yes that's it, but he should have discussed it with me."

At the tail end of her words, Joe walked into the kitchen. Sweating profusely, he grabbed one of the dish towels from the wall and ran cold water on it from the sink. He laid it on his face for a few seconds and then wiped his neck. He looked at the ladies.

"Discuss what with you?"

Caught off guard, they looked at each other. They were surprised that he heard the tail end of their conversation. Not knowing what to say, Lilly Mae searched for words.

"Ummmmm that you should have…"

Pearl responded quickly.

"That you should have those boys out there helping you."

"No, not right now; they got time to learn. Right now, they just need to be boys as my daddy used to say."

He put the wet cloth in his back pocket and walked over to the refrigerator. He opened the door and smiled at the ice-cold Coca-Cola waiting for him. With the refreshing sound of a cold metal can being popped opened, he took it to the head and gulped the whole thing down, within a matter of seconds. Afterward, he let out a deep, long belch.

"Man, ain't nothing like a cold Coca-Cola on a hot day."

He walked over to the trash can near the table, and threw the empty can away. That's when Lilly Mae noticed the scratches on his back.

"Baby, where did you get those scratches from?"

Ignoring her, he walked back to the refrigerator to get another cold pop.

"The scratches Joe-where did they come from?"

He walked over to the mirror on the wall and tried to see what she was talking about. He twisted and turned to see, but couldn't. He gave up and took the second pop to the head.

"I don't know. Maybe something bit me."

Going to the refrigerator, he hesitated for a minute before opening the door. With all the food in there he didn't know what to eat.

"Pearl, what are you going to whip up for lunch? I'm hungry."

Pearl said nothing. Slowly, Lilly Mae got up and walked toward him.

"Joe, if something bit you, it would have left bite marks not scratches," she said with a soft voice.

As he continued to look at the food, Lilly Mae reached out to touch his back. But when he felt the heat of her hand, with the speed of lighting, he jerked away. She gasped at his reaction. She knew their marriage was estranged, but....

"Stop now. What are you doing?"

"I was going to see how bad it was."

He closed the refrigerator door and walked away from her.

"It's nothing; don't worry about it. It'll heal up."

Eager to please her husband, Lilly Mae ran to the small medicine cabinet on the wall and got the peroxide and cotton balls.

"Here...let me clean it for you," she said as she ran back to him.

She opened the jar and saturated a cotton ball. She tried to wipe his back, but he put his hands up and backed away.

"Go on now, stop it."

Not taking no for an answer, she insisted.

"Just a little will clean that cut up."

Joe became angry with her persistence and smacked her face really hard; causing the peroxide to fly right out of her hands.

"How many times do I have to tell you woman!"

Lilly Mae fell to the floor screaming. In shock, Pearl ran to her baby.

"Lilly Mae!"

Joe was mad as hell. He paced the floor as he yelled.

"Now see what you made me do! I told you no! Now get up and clean your own damn face with that stuff!"

Pissed off, Pearl turned on him for the first time.

"She was just trying to take care of you!

Dumbfounded by Pearl's tone of voice and words, Joe stood in the middle of the floor with his hands on his hips. He questioned himself. *Did she just say Lilly Mae was trying to take care of me?*

Did this woman just yell at me? Yeah…I think she did. He laughed a hearty laugh.

"Ha! She stopped doing that a long time ago!"

Lilly Mae was devastated at how rude and nasty her husband was to her. She screamed at him as her mother helped her up.

"I hate you! Get out! Get out my house!"

Her words made Joe laugh even harder.

"Excuse you… You mean *my* house, don't you…? When your daddy died, y'all lost everything. So being the Christian that I am, I took y'all in."

Lilly Mae didn't like the reality check that he was giving her.

"What does that have to do with the way you treat me?"

Staring at her, his jaws twitched from the fury that was running over inside of him. He was fed up with his life with her; fed up with the frustrations he held in; tired of just maintaining in his own house for the kid's sake. He couldn't take it anymore and went off.

"It has a lot to do with it. You should have told me that you were with child by a white man!"

Lilly Mae was shocked. *Is this what he's been thinking all these years? Because of my little girl's skin color, you're pissed off. Because she looks white and not black, you're holding it against me…against her… My God she's just a child.*

"I didn't think that mattered. She's just a *child*. She didn't pick her skin color or hair or anything she has."

Joe said with a smirked on his face, "You would think that wouldn't you. We'll let me tell you something, I have a lot of pride. I'll take care of my own responsibilities and my own people. But because of *you*, I have to deal with rumors about *your* daughter. Do you have any idea of how it feels when you enter a room, and all the people in it stop talking and stare at you? It makes me feel like *I* did something wrong. Do you know I've heard people say that *you*-my wife, had been fucking around so much so, that *you* really don't know who the baby's daddy is. Rumor has it you've been out having sex with a whole lot of white men."

"Calm down Joe," Pearl pleaded.

Joe snapped back.

"Don't tell me to calm down Pearl! I've had this bottled up inside me way to long."

He looked at Lilly Mae like he wanted to throw up.

"Look at you; you make my stomach turn."

"I had four children for you!" hysterical she screamed.

Joe burst out laughing. He laughed so hard and loud that his side began to cramp.

"For me...no you didn't. You had those kids by me to secure a place in this house for you and your mama. Yeah, I know you thought that I was green."

Pearl looked surprised.

"Oh what...you thought I didn't know that Pearl? Don't look so flabbergasted. You know how your daughter is, because y'all are two peas in a pod."

"That's not true!" Lilly Mae yelled.

But Joe stood fast to his belief.

"Yes, it is!"

Lilly Mae began to cry harder to convince Joe that she really loved him. He smiled at her tears and started clapping his hands.

He went and grabbed the wild flowers off the table and presented them to her.

"These are for you Mrs. Carter. You're the winner of the Screen Actors Guild Award for best actress."

Frantic, Lilly Mae jumped up and threw her arms around his neck. She held on for dear life.

"No, it's not true; it's not true. I love you!"

But Joe wasn't having it. He immediately pulled her arms from his neck and pushed her away.

"Girl, you don't know what love is. You think spreading your legs is love. Is that what your mama taught you?"

Feeling defeated, she slumped to the floor.

"No Joe. Please believe me."

He walked over to her and stooped down to look at her face to face.

"Well…tell me this; when you first came here, why were you walking around here half naked, with your breast all out on display? You did it to get my attention…right?"

Lilly Mae didn't respond and continued to cry.

"OK, tell me this; why did you continue to sneak into my bedroom late at night, after I asked you to stop?"

He didn't wait for an answer and got up. He looked down at her.

"You told me that you couldn't sleep because you kept seeing your father's face."

Pearl's heart began to beat fast.

"I don't need to hear this." And she started toward the door.

Pointing his finger at her, she stopped immediately.

"Stay where you're at Pearl. You're going to hear how your daughter tricked me into marrying her."

Lilly Mae was still on the floor crying. She mustered up all her tricks to get Joe to believe her, but it wasn't working. Yes, she was crying her heart out. But it wasn't because of Joe not believing her. It was because she knew the gig was up. All hell was busting loose, and she was trying to hold on.

"I was scared Joe!"

"Scared…! Are you telling me that you were so scared, that you came into *my* room, several nights a week, with barely anything on, smelling all good and hair placed just right, because you were *scared*… or because you wanted to secure a place to stay?"

Realizing that her husband wasn't as dumb as she thought he was, she gave up the acting and got to her feet.

"You're a mean man Joe Carter."

"No, you're a sick person. You seduced me. You took my kindness for my weakness. You knew what you were doing back then with the bath water being all nice and hot. Me *mean...?* No, I'm not mean. I'm just the man you created by your lies, deception and greed. Now get your pathetic self together before the kids come back in here."

21

*L*UCKILY, THE KIDS didn't hear a thing. They were all out on the front porch playing except for Betty Jean. She was pissed off at her mother for not wanting her to help put the food up.

She just makes me sick to my stomach sometimes. I was just trying to help you out.

Hearing a vehicle from the distance brought her out of her thought. Looking down the driveway, she saw an old beat up truck coming up to the house. As it slowed down coming into the driveway circle, a man was yelling from the window fresh fish...fish for sale!

The truck stopped in front of the house, and the man got out. Before he could introduce himself, Jackie ran up to him.

"What kind of fish y'all got?"

"Oh, we got catfish, cod fish, sword fish, rock fish, flounder and salmon," the old man smiled and said as he pulled on his suspenders.

Another man, only younger, got out of the driver's side of the truck. He continued the spiel.

"We got orange fish, red fish and black fish."

Sucking her teeth and folding her arms, Jackie thought that he was trying to pull her leg.

"Ain't no such color fish."

"Yes it is; you got your Orange Ruffian, your Red Snapper and your Black Drum."

As Jackie and the men talked, Betty Jean's heart skipped a beat when she saw the younger man. She was like, *Daaammmmmmnnn that brother is fine*. He was about 6ft tall with short, curly, jet-black hair. His complexion was so dark, colored folks called it blue-black. And he had a smile like no other.

Slowly, as if in a trance, she got up out of her chair and walked toward them. As she got closer, the younger man noticed her, but continued to talk to Jackie. *Daaammmmmmnnn, now that's a thing of beauty,* he thought. Betty Jean was about 5'4". Her complexion was like Ivory Soap. He thought her hair resembled a beautiful, sandy brown beach with long deep weaves as the sea. He could tell that it was soft to the touch, by the way the gentle breeze blew it. Her eyes were like little light brown marbles. And even though she had on a funny-looking dress, he could tell that she had a nice little figure.

"What's your name?" she asked him as she got closer.

"James Henry Smith Jr," he said with a broad smile.

He was the son of James Henry Sr.; owner of Smith Fish on Wheels. Every so often, his dad would gather up his load of fresh fish and sell it to the local folks. He hadn't been in Joe Carter's neck of the woods for a while and decided to venture on up the road to try his luck.

"James Henry Smith Jr...? I ain't never seen you before," she said smiling.

The father noticed how they were staring at each other and spoke up for his son.

"Oh Miss I guess you were just starting high school when my boy went away to college."

Jackie didn't like the way they were looking at each other. She looked James Jr. up and down and asked with an attitude, "So are y'all here to sell fish or what?"

She turned to Johnny and yelled for him to go get their father. He jumped up from the steps, and haul tailed it into the house.

"Daddy, the fish man outside! Daddy!"

Betty Jean was intrigued by the young man attending college.

"Wow...I wouldn't mind going to college."

This was the first-time Betty Jean had ever mentioned anything about continuing her education after high school.

"Well I plan on having my own business, and I want to educate my people; so education is the key. It's a lot of studying and stuff involved."

Betty Jean sucked her teeth.

"Please...my GPA is 3.8," she said with pride.

He laughed at her cockiness.

"Hey that's good. Maybe you should check out my school. It's an HBCU."

Betty Jean and Jackie looked at each other and frowned.

"HBCU...? What the heck is that?" Betty Jean asked.

Playfully, he took a step back.

"What! Get out of here! Y'all don't know what HBCU stands for? It stands for Historical Black College University."

"And what HBCU do you attend?" Jackie asked with attitude, as she looked him up and down.

"Ioward University," he said proudly.

Bewildered, the girls looked at each.

"And where is that at?" Betty Jean asked.

The young man couldn't believe his ears. Laughing, he turned and slapped the truck, then turned and looked back at them.

"What planet are y'all from? It's in Washington, D.C., the Nation's Capital."

Feeling dumb, Betty Jean had to come back with something smart. She didn't want this fine educated brother to think that she was smart and stupid at the same time. She winked her eye at him.

"I knew that. I just wanted to see if you were telling the truth."

"I know that's right," the old man said laughing at her quick comeback.

James Jr. continued.

"You got a lot of HBCU schools out there. You got Hampton University, Tuskegee Institute, Norfolk State, Morgan, and Grambling. You also have Spelman, which is for girls only."

Jackie frowned.

"Girls only...?"

"Come on sister's work with me here...yes. Morehouse, which is an all-male school, is like right across the street. You got Clark, Morris Brown, North Carolina A&T and Alabama A&M. The list goes on and on."

Betty Jean's mind was spinning out of control with all the wonderful info she just received. She had always dreamed about going to college, but didn't know the first thing about the process. That's how bad her father kept her sheltered from the outside world.

"Holy moly, I didn't know that!"

With excitement, the father clapped his hands after each school was mentioned.

"Break it down to 'em son!"

"Alright...I'm on a roll now," the young man said as he cleared his throat. "Not only that, you got your sororities *and* your fraternities too."

Betty Jean and Jackie laughed at the sound of those two words. "What the H E double hockey sticks is that?" Betty Jean asked. The young man's mood changed with the quickness. He became really serious.

"Girl, you need to get on the ball. Are you graduating this year?"

"Yes."

"And you don't know *any* of this stuff?"

"No."

He began to walk around in a circle. He looked at the ground and then to the heavenly sky. His dad started doing the Ali shuffle and backed a few feet away from his son.

"Oh…look out now. Here it comes!" Henry Sr. said.

"Alright y'all listen up, because you're getting ready to get a crash course about the Greek Family by an Omega Man."

"Omega wh….?!" The girls started to say, but were cut off by him making the sound of a great big dog barking.

Slowly, yet strong and hard, James Henry began to stomp his feet.

"That's what you call steppin," his father said.

His hands began to move with great precision with his feet, and his face was serious as a heart attack. His performance began to increase with speed. Words accompanied the rhythmic of his moves. Body unity displayed at its best.

Jimmy and Jamie, who were now standing next to Jackie, tried to mimic his moves. His dad was having a good time watching his son do his thing. He clapped to the beat his son was making.

"Yes! Go head son! Do the thing!"

He finished the performance with several loud barking sounds, and the kids loved it.

"Oh…my…goodness!" Betty Jean said repeatedly.

James Jr. was hyped-up.

Standing at attention, he yelled, "Yeah boy! What! I'm a member of Omega Psi Phi Fraternity Incorporated! It was founded by my forefathers at Howard University in 1911! Our colors are purple and gold!"

"Show 'em the brand son!"

"Oh Dad they don't want to see that."

"Yes we do! Even if we don't know what it is, we want to see it!" Jackie yelled, as she jumped up and down with excitement.

Reluctantly, yet with pride, he pulled his left short sleeve up to his shoulder blade. There was, what looked like, an upside-down horse shoe branded on his shoulder. The children were amazed. Betty Jean walked up to him and touched the puffiness of it.

"Does it hurt?"

"Nope." he said as he put his sleeve back down.

He dared not tell them all the stuff he had to go through to get it there; especially Hell Week. That was a bitch for him.

"So what other Sororities and Fraternities are there?"

But before he could answer Betty Jean, Johnny ran out the front door yelling, "Daddy said to give him a few minutes. He'll be right out!"

"Ok young man," the father said as he walked to the back of his truck. He started setting up his fine fish for display.

"Come on son help me out."

James Jr. continued to talk as he helped his dad pull the thick gray cover away from the iced fish.

"As far as the names of Sororities, you got Delta Sigma Theta, who was founded in 1913 at Howard University. They are our Greek sisters. You got Alpha Kappa Alpha, Sigma Gamma Rho and Zeta Phi Beta...just to name a few. As far as Fraternities, you got Alpha Phi Alpha, Kappa Psi Phi, Phi Beta Sigma, and Iota Phi Theta. It's a whole lot of Greek Organizations."

Holding her head, Betty Jean rolled it around in a playful manner.

"Man...this stuff sounds like a different language to me. It's a lot of stuff I don't know about. I better get on the ball."

"You sure better. It's a whole new world out there just waiting to be explored."

"I'm surprised your parents didn't tell you about this stuff. Somebody at your school should have told you all of this. Don't you have a counselor?" Henry Sr. asked more out of curiosity then concern.

Betty Jean thought hard about what he just said. *Here I am, a 3.8 student and no one said anything to me about college...that's odd. And my parents are college grads...* She started to wonder why her teachers nor her guidance counselor didn't inform her of this new world she was just introduced to. *What's really going on...?*

"I'm surprised too. Maybe they were going to tell me later in the school year," she finally said.

Henry Sr. hung his old scale up over the fresh fish.

"Later in the school year... Young lady, you graduate in a few months. Did you take the SAT or ACT Test yet?"

"What's that?"

"What's that...?!" James Jr. asked.

Ashamed, she turned her head away.

"I don't know what that is," she said softly.

"What about your paperwork for Financial Aid to pay for school?"

"I didn't do anything," she said sadly.

"You play any sports?" Henry Sr. asked trying to lighten things up.

Jackie laughed, but said nothing.

"No. Well, I mean our daddy don't believe girls should play sports. He says a women's place is in the kitchen."

Both men looked at each other and said nothing. They put two and two together and assumed that their father was domineering. Henry Sr. brushed it off and continued to work.

"I tell you...with your GPA you probably could have gotten a scholarship to go away to school. I mean..., but you still have to take your SAT test and get a score like 1250 or higher for acceptance of the best school and all."

Betty Jean's head spins again. All she heard were the words go away. *Go away…go away from here…as much as I can't stand being in the south, and being stuck in the house. That's all I've ever thought about; was to go away; but how with no money and nowhere to live. And now, here before my eyes, two men telling me that education can get me away from my father; away from my nappy headed sisters and brothers.* Stuttering a little from being nervous, she had to make certain what she just heard.

"You do mean to another state; away from here, right?"

The dad looked at his son, and his son looked at him, then to Betty Jean. He answered for his dad.

"Yes."

That answer turned Betty Jean into a silent raging bull. She balled her hands into a fist and walked around in a circle. Huffin' and puffin' she said to herself, *Oh, that's not right; that's not right. Why lord, why. My parents make me sick. Make my heart go 246. Not because I'm dirty, not because I'm clean, not because I kissed a boy behind a magazine.* Without saying good-bye, she took off running toward the house. She ran up the steps two at a time. She almost ran into Joe as he was coming out the door.

"Hey slow down now. You almost knocked me down," he said as he dodged out of her way.

"Sorry!" she yelled back as she ran into the house. "Mama! Ma guess what I just found out!"

Walking down the steps, Joe extended his hands to greet the men.

"Henry my man; its been a long time. What's going on; how've you been?"

"I'm good, just trying to make a dollar out of 15 cents. You remember my son James Jr., don't you? He's home for the spring break."

Joe stepped back to get a full view of the young man.

"I remember you when you could barely stand up."

Smiling, he shook his hand. Mr. Carter, how you doing sir?"

"Just fine, fine, I can't complain. The good Lord woke me and my family up this morning."

"Amen to that," Henry Sr. said.

The young man pointed to the fish.

"Sir, we got some fresh fish for you today. What do you need?"

While Joe looked the fish over, Jackie picked up several fish and smelt it.

"They smell fresh Daddy."

"They sure do baby-girl," he said as he picked up a nice size flounder and took a good sniff.

He weighed it in his hand for a few seconds and then placed it back down.

"You know the wife just came back from the market."

Not wanting to miss out on a sale, Henry Sr. responded like he was a car salesman.

"O.k., but did she buy any *fresh* fish like the ones right here *today*?"

"I don't know. You know I leave that to the woman of the house. Baby-girl, go ask your mother if she brought any fish."

Instantly, Jackie saluted her dad.

"Yes sir!" she said with a stern voice.

Turning on her heels, she ran to the house; taking the steps two at a time.

"Mama, daddy wants to know if you…!" Her voice faded off as she entered the house.

While they all waited for the word of sale or no sale, Joe made small talk with the men. He grabbed a small hand full of ice and wiped his neck with it.

"So, how is school coming along son?"

"Just fine sir; I graduate this year."

"Good. What are you majoring in?"

"Criminal Justice, sir"

Joe grabbed another hand full of ice and tossed them in the air.

"Well isn't that something."

"He doesn't know what he's going to do with it yet, but it'll be something," his father said.

James Jr. took a deep breath, because he was a little irritated at his dad's comment. He had told him several times, that he was going to continue his education and start his own law firm.

"I'm going to study law at Georgetown University sir. Then after I receive my Masters…."

As he went on and on about his plans for the future, Joe stared at him, but really wasn't interested in his plans.

"Oh yeah, well after you get those degrees, maybe my girls can work for you down here in the Bayou. Betty Jean is smart as a whip."

"Yes sir, I was just telling her that with her GPA, it's possible that she could get some kind of scholarship to go away to school."

Joe's mind snapped like a tooth pick when he said that. His thoughts ran in slow motion, *go away, go away…what the…is he talking about my Betty Jean going away?* The realization of the possibility of her going away, hit him like a ton of bricks. He was so astonished at the possibility of Betty Jean leaving him, his body temperature began to rise. His face was hot. He became light-headed and felt like he was about to pass out. In the midst of his mental turmoil, he heard Jackie's voice.

"Daddy, mama said to get some catfish if they have any. And get some salmon and flounder too."

In trying to pin point his daughter's voice, he turned and saw Henry Sr. looking like a deformed man; as if he was standing in front of one of those fun house mirrors. And to make matters worse, he was doing the jig as it seemed to him in slow motion, with a great big ole smile.

"Coming right up; hold your britches little lady. Coming right up," Henry Sr. told Jackie as he grabbed some brown paper and started wrapping the requested fish.

Joe heard him talking, but his words sounded distorted. At less than normal speed, he saw his children at what he thought pointing and laughing at him, which enraged him. In trying to release whatever had a hold of his mind, he shook his head several times. He grabbed a hand full of ice and wiped his inflamed face. Doing it several times seemed to help a great deal. As he came back to reality, he heard the young man calling his name.

"Mr. Carter, are you alright? Are you ok sir?"

In a silent rage, Joe looked at him and threw the ice on the ground.

Using his quiet voice, he responded in anger, because he didn't want anyone to hear that he was upset. "You down here trying to put ideas into my daughter's head son?"

Bewildered, James Henry turned and looked behind him to see if someone else was there, because of the way Joe was talking to him. When he didn't see anyone, he turned back around.

"Excuse me sir?"

Highly pissed-off Joe started walking toward the front of the truck, because he didn't want the young man's dad to hear their conversation. This was a private matter as far as he was concerned. He thought as he was walking, *all that damn work and money I had done put out to her school and people, to keep my daughter right by my side, and now this educated fool done come down on my land and messed all my plans up. He's done put some crap into Betty Jeans head about leaving the Bayou.*

Not liking his attitude, James Jr. walked up behind him and touched him on his shoulder to get his attention. Joe stopped and turned around. Trying to intimidate the young man, he stared him square in the eyes, and James Jr. stared back at him equally so.

"Excuse me…do you have something to say sir?"

"You heard me boy. Are you trying to get my Betty Jean up north where you are, so you can have your way with her?"

"What!"

His outburst got the attention of his dad. Putting the fish down, he pepped his head around the truck.

"Son…, is everything ok?"

Without looking back, he waved his hand.

"Yes Dad, everything's cool."

Trying to play the boy's outburst off, Joe smiled at his dad.

"Yeah Henry, me and your boy just having us a little conversation about life up North. Go on and wrap two or three more of them catfish up for me."

When he heard the word more, he jumped right back to doing what he does best, and that's selling fish.

"Sir, with all due respect, I don't even know your daughter. I was just given her some advice about college."

Joe looked back at the truck to make sure his dad wasn't looking. Satisfied that he wasn't, he continued.

"When and *if* I want your advice, I'll ask for it. Until then…I don't want to catch you around my daughter, nor my property; you hear." And walked away.

"Man what is your problem?"

Joe ignored him and approached the young man's dad like nothing happened. Henry Sr. was just finishing wrapping up the fish.

"Here you go Brother Carter, fresh as the morning dew."

Joe took a huge smell of the fresh fish and smiled.

"Yes indeed, fish fry here we come."

He turned to the kids.

"How bout it kids…you think we should do a fish fry next weekend?"

"Fish fry! Fish fry! Fish fry!" Jumping up and down the kids yelled with excitement.

The young man knew that he was being ignored on purpose, so he went and got into the truck. In anger, he slammed the door shut. He just couldn't believe what just happened to him. Henry Sr. heard the door slam and was about to go see what was going on with his son. But Joe hurried up and pulled out a hand full of money to distract him. He peeled off a $20.00.

"Here you go my man. This here should cover it just fine and keep the change.

Henry Sr. took the money and stuffed it into his pants pocket. Grateful for his business, he shook Joe's hand.

"Alright we be seeing you. Maybe I'll see you at the Shack."

"You know I don't go to places like that. Never have, never will."

"You know what they say about that…?" Henry Sr. asked as he walked to the passenger side of the truck.

"What?" Joe responded as he walked toward the house without turning around.

"Never say never!" he yelled as he got into the truck.

Henry Sr. hit the outside door twice and they pulled off. Playfully, the children run behind them until they turned onto the main road.

22

JAMES JR. STARED at the road ahead. Total confusion engulfed him.

Someone accusing him of a wrongful deed and attempt had never happened to him in his life. He had always tried to help people, for as long as he could remember. That's the way his parents raised him. Plus, it was just part of his demeanor. That's why he chose Criminal Justice as his major; to help people. His heart was no longer focused on Betty Jean; it was focused on his crushed pride. His dad noticed that he wasn't as talkative like he was earlier.

He looked at him and then back to the road.

"Fish! Fresh fish today! Fish for sale!" he yelled out the window to break the silence.

Laughing, he looked at his son; expecting him to be laughing too. But what he saw was a look of confusion on his face.

"Son what's wrong? You look disturbed."

At first, he wasn't going to say anything. Then he thought, *hell... I've never kept anything away from my old man before, so why now.* Taking a deep breath, he looked at his dad, who he considered his best friend.

"The weirdest thing just happened back there."

"What's that son?"

"Mr. Carter and I were having a nice conversation, and as soon as I mentioned about Betty Jean going away to school…he accused me of wanting to get her up north so I can have my way with her."

"What…! Are you serious son?!"

"Hell yeah I'm serious."

His father didn't say a word. Boiling mad, he turned his head and looked out the window. In silence, they continued on down the road.

Several thoughts were running through the young man's head, as he recalled the conversation he and Joe Carter had. He was trying to make sure that he didn't say anything disrespectful, or anything to insinuate that he liked Betty Jean.

When he first laid eyes on her, his heart skipped several beats. But you couldn't tell because he had learned to hide what was going on in his heart, by hanging out with some of his school friends from the Nation's Capital.

D.C. was full of the finest sisters one could ever see at one time. And before he learned the ropes, he used to drool after every pretty girl he saw.

Within the first few days of arriving at Howard University, just about everyone knew that he wasn't from the city by his heavy, southern accent. And from hanging out with the brothers, they really noticed how excited he got when a fine sister, with a nice backside, walked pass him. No matter where he was at, or what he was doing, whenever he saw a bunch of beautiful sisters, he turned his head to get a bird's eye view of their rear end.

On this one occasion, while standing in line to pay for his food in the school cafe, he couldn't keep up with all the beautiful sisters surrounding him. Excited, he kept turning in every direction to look at them. He was turning his head so fast, he got dizzy and fell out. On the other side of the cafe, his roommate and his boys saw him hit the floor, and fell out laughing. Being concerned, they all ran to him to make sure that he was alright. When they got to him, he was smiling so hard, you would have thought that he died and went to big booty heaven. They all helped him up.

"Man, we're going to have to show you how to represent D.C. style, before you get-got by these fine ass, educated sisters up here. All that glitters ain't gold you know," his roommate said.

The brothers brushed him off and started putting it down, on how one should carry one's self when it comes to women. So much knowledge was dumped on him at one time, he had to take his pen and pad out to take notes.

Throughout his school years at Howard, he did get-got several times by the ladies. But as time went on, he mastered the art of being cool when he saw a fine female.

Satisfied that he didn't do anything wrong, he looked at his father. "Dad, something's wrong with that man."

Henry Sr. still didn't say nothing, nor did he look at his son. He could tell that this situation really bothered his boy. Hell...it bothered him too for that matter. And he didn't like it not one bit. When his son hurt, he hurt. He loves his son like no other. He loves him so much so that he worked from sun up to sun down, just to make sure he got a good, decent education unlike himself.

And it's not like he didn't want a good education, he really did. But, at a young age, he saw how hard it was for his folks to maintain their crop. So while in the 8th grade, he asked his parents if he could drop out of school for a little while to help out. Against better judgment, his parents agreed; telling him that it was only for a little while. However, he never went back to school, and they didn't try to make him go back.

What little crop the Smith's did harvest, was sold to the local folks in town; right off the same truck they drove to this very day. Farming the land wasn't too bad of a living. They made just enough to be comfortable and maybe had a little extra for those special days during the year.

When Henry turned 16, his parents allowed him to take the family truck into town by himself to conduct business. That's when he met Sue Ann.

She was 15 years old, an only child and a loner. Both her parents died in a freak car crash when she was just 10 years old. Her parents meant the world to her. They did everything for her. She wanted for nothing and always had her way with them. After the accident, her grandmother on her mother's side, who had eight children of her own, took her in and tried to raise her as best she could.

For five years, while living with her grandmother, Sue Ann was never happy. She always complained about this and that. Then one day, out of nowhere, she just up and left. No good-bye, no packing up clothes or anything. Her grandmother didn't even try to find her.

She thought that with her being 15 and all, she was old enough to take care of herself.

Since leaving her grandmother's house, Sue Ann didn't really speak to no one. People thought that her mind wasn't wrapped too tight. At times, they would see her sitting on the edge of the sidewalk talking to herself and staring at people.

On this one particular day while sitting on the curve, her eyes came upon Henry. He had his produce truck set up right across the street from her. He was a short, stocky, dark skin, nappy headed young man. Liking what she saw, she approached him and asked him his name. He told her with a song and dance.

"My name is Henry, Henry bow finley, banana fan-na bo-did-ley, fee-phi moe men-ley, Henry…"

She died laughing at him. She hadn't laughed like that since her parents were alive. They hit it off right away. From their first conversation, the biggest thing they learned that they had in common, was that they both dropped out of school at a young age. He was talkative, and she was a good listener. Unbeknown to folks, there wasn't anything wrong with her; she just didn't like talking to folks after her parents died.

That evening after selling his produce, Henry took her home for himself. His parents were up in age and were glad to have her for their son. Every weekend, she would go with him to town just to be by his side. Within a year, they got married, and she conceived a son, naming him James Henry Jr. And he vowed from that day forward that his son would be educated and become somebody.

"Turn this truck around," Henry Sr. demanded.

His son paid him no never mind. He kept driving; eyes straight ahead. He already knew what his dad wanted to do.

"Turn this truck around right now!"

"For what Dad?"

Henry Sr. hit the side of the truck with every word he spoke.

"Ain't no man going to accuse my son of something like that. Turn this truck around right now. I'm going to whop his ass."

He laughed at his father's cussing.

"Dad, its whip not whop ok. No but seriously, that's not necessary. We got to be men about this, so just calm down."

"Don't tell me to calm down. I'll calm down when I whop his ass!"

"Pop stop it. Now who is acting like the father and who is acting like a child?"

Realizing he was the one acting like a child, he calmed down. He had always told his son that two wrongs didn't make a right; to just leave bad situations in God's hands. Let go and let God was his motto.

Playfully, he nudged his son with his elbow, as he looked out the window.

"Well...you still can't beat me," he said under his breath.

"Ouch! That hurt!" his son cried out with a smile.

He nudged him again.

"Yeah that's what I thought...still a sissy I see"

His son smiled because he knew that his dad was trying to make light of the situation. He gave his dad a little shove back.

"Oh yeah, who you calling a sissy?"

Henry Sr. smacked the back of his son's head.

"You onion head."

"Onion head...man, I'll drop you like a hot potato old man." Excited, his father started to stutter.

"Who yoooou caaaalling old man...young buck."

James Jr. burst out laughing and mimicked his dad's speech impediment.

"Yyyou, old man!"

Playfully, his dad started acting like he was really upset.

"Pull this truck over right now. I'm going to whop *your* ass. Your mama not here now to protect you."

They both started to shove, punch and call each other names playfully like little boys. Laughing, they were having themselves a good time; father and son; best of friends together forever.

23

"MAMA! MAMA!"

Betty Jean yelled as she ran into the kitchen, but stopped dead in her tracks. She saw her grandmother on her hands and knees, cleaning up a big spill with glass in it. Pearl looked up at her granddaughter with that you know what happened look. Feeling disappointed, Betty Jean went and sat down at the table.

"Mama and daddy had a fight again?" she asked sadly.

Pearl took the rag and dipped it into the bucket of hot water.

"They had a disagreement."

Betty Jean put her head into the palm of her hands and leaned on the table.

"Then why are you on the floor, if they had a disagreement?"

"Your mama dropped the peroxide."

Betty Jean closed her eyes and visualized what happened.

"You mean daddy knocked it out of her hand."

Pissed off at the situation and not really at her granddaughter, Pearl lashed out.

"Must you say everything that you think child!" she yelled as she threw the rag into the bucket, causing water to go everywhere.

Startled from the outburst, Betty Jean quickly opened her eyes. She had never heard that tone of voice come from her grandmother before.

"If I don't I'll go crazy around here."

Tired, Pearl sat down on the floor, and leaned against the wall. Wiping the sweat from her forehead, she closed her eyes. Betty Jean took a deep breath and walked over to the window. Looking out at the beautiful sunny sky, she asked as if she was in a trance, "Granny...why does daddy hate mama so much?"

Pearl looked over at her grandchild and could tell that she was hurting inside. Trying to soften life difficult times she tried to explain.

"Oh baby, your daddy doesn't hate your mama. It's just that grown folks go through stuff that's all."

Growing tired of hearing her grandmother's excuses about the family problems, Betty Jean decided to test the waters of curiosity.

"Is that what happened to you and grandpa?"

Pearl immediately became defensive with the question. It's been a long time since anyone said anything about her husband. Slowly, she stood up and bent her back forward and backward to crack her aching back.

"What are you talking about?"

Betty Jean had experienced this song and dance routine from her mother and grandmother many times over. And this time she wasn't having it. Fired up with the info she just received from the two men, she had fuel for the fire and refused to back down. Looking at her grandmother with a stern look, she repeated herself.

"What happened with you and grandpa...was that grown folk stuff too?"

Pearl grabbed the bucket of dirty water and poured it down the sink.

"Now where is this going?" she asked, bracing herself for the answer.

Betty Jean went back to the table and sat down. A little nervous she started shaking her leg, when she saw that her grandmother was going to actually entertain her question.

"I don't know. I mean I just heard stuff form people."

A little light headed, Pearl took a small cup from the cabinet and filled it with cold water from the sink. She gathered her thoughts before taking a sip. Feeling a little refreshed, she rinsed the cup out and placed it back in the cabinet.

"People like who?"

"Just people," Betty Jean said nonchalantly.

Pearl walked over and stood before her.

"Well...what did you hear?"

With her grandmother towering over her, Betty Jean became scared and lost her nerve. Staring at her hands, she said nothing. And for some reason, Pearl became edgy when she didn't respond. She didn't know why, because she had never cared about what people said or thought about her or her family before.

"Child what did you hear?" she asked again only with a bit more bass in her voice.

For a split second, Betty Jean looked up at her grandmother and then quickly turned her head.

"You're going to be mad at me!"

Rolling her eyes, Pearl looked up at the ceiling, then back down at Betty Jean.

"No, I'm not."

"Yes, you are!"

"Honey, I've always told you to speak your mind no matter what; to not hold anything negative inside of you because it could cause stress. If something is bothering you, release it to whoever it involves. Now tell me what you heard that's bothering you baby."

"Mrs. Finch told Mrs. Johnson that my mama was raped by grandpa; that you caught him with his hands under her dress and that over the years, you slowly poisoned him. That's why no one knew how he really died."

Pearl became stone as a statue. This, she wasn't expecting at all. She was thinking on the lines of people talking about her husband being a womanizer and how he left them broke with nowhere to live. *For all these years, no one questioned me about his death. The police report, the doctor's report and his death certificate said, "Deceased by natural causes." Now I hear th is...from my own granddaughter...and Vivian never told us this.*

The more she thought, the more she became angry. Deep in her soul she felt the devil himself rise within. If looks could kill, Betty Jean would have been dead yesterday. Slowly, she walked back to the sink and began rinsing out the bucket.

"How long ago did you happen to hear this conversation?"

"I don't know...it was years ago when I was playing with Suzie at her house.

Mrs. Johnson had Mrs. Finch over for tea."

"So why didn't you say something back then?" she asked calmly.

"I don't know. I was scared to tell what I heard, or to even ask questions about what I heard."

Abruptly, Pearl slammed the bucket in the sink, and walked back over to Betty Jean.

"So why are you speaking of it now!"

In shock, Betty Jean eyes popped out of her head, so to speak; her heart beating a mile a minute. She had never seen her grandmother in such a negative manner before. It was as if she didn't know the woman before her. *Could the rumors I heard over the years be true...that my grandmother and mother were both snakes in the grass...that they would cut your throat and leave you for dead in a heartbeat if you crossed their path...*

Nervous, Betty Jean began to stutter.

"I...I...don't kn..."

"I'm tired of hearing you say that!" And she mimicked her, "I don't know! I don't know...! Stop saying that! Think before you speak child!"

Betty Jean closed her eyes and started to think really hard. But her thoughts weren't about what her grandmother asked; it was about how she was going to get out of the mess she got herself into. Then she thought... *I know... I'll change the subject; that's what I'll do.*

"Because daddy is always fighting mama, and you are always cleaning up the mess!"

Pearl became a little confused, because she wasn't anticipating an answer like that. She thought that she was going to hear some juicy gossip, about what people had been saying, about her and her deceased husband.

"What does one have to do with the other girl?"

Upset, Betty Jean jumped up from her chair and paced the floor.

"Granny I don't know. I just don't understand why they are always arguing and fighting. Sometimes I think they don't get along because of me. Did you and granddad fight a lot?"

Pearl ignored her question.

"Betty Jean, some things are best left alone; out of sight out of mind."

"What the hell...that don't make sense granny!"

"No it doesn't, but it sure makes life a little easier baby." "Easy for who?!"

Tired, Pearl walked around to the other side of the table and sat down. She grew tired of the conversation. Stress was upon her, and she began to rub her temple.

"It's better for everybody."

Betty Jean saw that her grandmother's energy was deflating, so she took advantage of it and escalated her demeanor with no respect toward her.

"Not for me. I mean where did you get this 'out of sight, out of mind' stuff? Was that how you were brought up?"

Pearl tried her best not to let Betty Jean's words get to her and continued to rub her temple.

"Girl, hush up."

Betty Jean was on a role. She was running her mouth so much so that she didn't hear her grandmother tell her to be quiet. She kept right on talking. With her hands on her hips, she got bold and walked up on her grandmother.

"I don't understand this family. I ask you a question about grandpa, and I get no answer. What happened to him? How did he die *anyway?*"

"Betty Jean," Pearl said softly.

Still, Betty Jean continued right on like she was grown.

"Why are there so many secrets in this *damn* house?!"

Like lighting, Pearl jumped up and slapped the holy crap out of Betty Jean; causing her to fly across the room and land in the pantry doorway. She screamed more so out of shock than pain. Her grandmother had never hit her before. Within a blink of an eye, Pearl was towering her with both hands on her hips. Her large breast and nostrils inflated and deflated with every breath she took.

"Now you listen to me! What happened between me and *my* husband is none of your got damn business! How he *died* is none of your business either! You need to learn to stay in your place and mind your own business; you hear! The only thing you have to do to maintain in this house is to do what you're told, when told to do so! No more, no less! Do you understand me?!"

Betty Jean was burning up. Hatred consumed her. The one person who she thought really truly loved her, had just smacked the dickens out of her.

"Do you understand me child?!"

If looks could kill, Pearl would have been dead last week with the way Betty Jean was staring at her. Without blinking an eye, she repeated her grandmother's words.

"Do what you're told to do, when told to do so...*no matter what it is, or who it's hurting, or whether it's right or wrong...to stay in my place and mind my own business; out of sight out of mind.* Yes ma'am, I understand alright."

Betty Jean was overwhelmed with what just happened. The realization of seeing her mother's not so loving demeanor within her grandmother was a real blower. Looking her straight in the eyes and with a monotone voice she asked, "May I be excused?"

Pearl didn't answer her right away. They just stared at each other like they didn't know one another; like two warriors who wanted to kill each other.

Pearl expected to see tears swell up in Betty Jeans' eyes, but no such thing happened. She knew that she was trying to stand her ground. So to soften the situation, she grabbed Betty Jean and hugged her. However, Betty Jean was unresponsive to her touch. It was as if her grandmother was dead to her. Of all people, she just knew that her grandmother loved her and understood her.

"Baby you'll see...it's going to get better within time. You'll see."

"No grandma...you don't understand. The only way it's going to get better for me, is when I leave this house...because if I don't leave soon, I'm going to wind up killing myself...or somebody. May
I be excused please?"

As Pearl continued to hold her, a cold chill went through her body. *Lord this child has my blood in her. So, I know she means it.*

Pearl's childhood was pretty much average, until her parents divorced for reasons unknown to her. For a while, her father still supported the household, so her mother didn't work. However, as time went on, the money came less and less. Soon it came to nothing at all. It was like her father just disappeared, thus causing them to fall upon hard times. Pearl's mother attempted to get a job. However, do to her lack of marketing skills, she was unsuccessful. This caused her to go into a depression. And to console herself, she started drinking heavily with what little money her parents gave her for food. When Pearl told her grandparents that her mother was spending most of the money on alcohol, the money slowly stopped coming in. So her mother resorted to the oldest trade in the world: Prostitution.

Her newfound job caused her to be out late at night many times. Pearl was left unattended at home without proper guidance and barely any food to eat. Being tired of her situation, Pearl decided to drop out of school to make her own money, by any means necessary. She told her mother about her decision, and her mother didn't even care. All she was concerned about was getting her drink on. At the tender age of 16, Pearl hit the streets just like her mother.

Being a virgin and new to the game, she started off with the neighborhood boys. The first guy, who was 18 years old, paid her $5.00 to pop her cherry. After that, it was on. She learned the tricks of the trade really fast, and graduated to old men who paid top dollar for her underage pleasure. It didn't matter to her if they couldn't perform sexually or not. The way she looked at it...you got to pay to play.

On the streets, word got around about her. Unlike her mother, she was in great demand. She even developed a clientele of who's who, which consisted of preachers, teachers, on up to politicians. It didn't matter to her if they were black, white, yellow or brown. All she saw was that mean green when she worked the streets.

At times when her mother was dead broke, which was often, she would ask Pearl for money. At first, she refused to help her. But then guilt was upon her, because she always heard her grandmother's voice saying, "family must help family out in times of need." So, for a minute, she did help her mother out. But that generosity was shut down like yesterday, when she realized what her mother was doing. Streetwise told her that her mother was trying to pimp her for her stash.

After about a year of working the streets, Pearl became tired of it and wanted to go back to school. She started missing all the fun she used to have like cutting class with her girls; smoking cigarettes and listening to the sounds of Motown in the bathroom. Since she had a nice stash of money, she decided to go back the following year.

Her mother had to set up a meeting with the school staff, in order for her to be admitted back to school. During the meeting, Pearl was told that she had to repeat the same grade she dropped out of. She was cool with that, because all she wanted to do was go back to school.

First day back, she went to her assigned guidance counselor to receive her homeroom and schedule. She was assigned to a fairly new faculty member, who came on board last year. His name was Mr. Eugene Badeaux. He was young, handsome and flashy, with a real down to earth attitude. He also had a touch of street swagger about himself.

Upon Pearl's entrance into her new homeroom, the teacher, who had his back to the students, was writing on the blackboard. The students were running their mouths. A girl who was voted most popular last year, saw Pearl enter the classroom. In an instant, for whatever reason, she didn't like her. Nudging one of her girlfriends, she said, "Check the new girl out." When she did, they both looked at each other and burst out laughing.

Pearl saw the girl's reaction toward her as she looked for a seat. She knew that they were laughing at her and didn't care. She told herself that they were just jealous and intimidated by her beauty. Street experience taught her that action speaks louder than words. When she found a seat, which was two rows up, to the right of them, she stuck that big ole butt of hers out at them before taking her seat. She also acted like something was irritating her cheek, and started to scratch it with just her middle finger up.

When the girls saw the 'fuck-you' finger up, they got mad as hell. One of the girls jumped up and started acting like a fool. She started selling wolf tickets big time. Pearl just started laughing to herself. At that moment, the teacher turned and addressed the classroom.

"Ok class lets simmer down. Come on simmer down."

The girl who was selling wolf tickets, girlfriend grabbed her, and told her to sit. The teacher introduced himself to the class.

"My name is Mr. Badeaux. Welcome to your new homeroom. I would like for everyone, one at a time, to stand and introduce yourself. Also, I would like to know what your plans are when you finish high school."

The first one to jump up was the girl who caused the ruckus.

"My name is Donna Lynn and I plan on going to collage to major in biology."

After Donna Lynn, only a handful of students volunteered. To move things right along, the teacher pointed to students to participate.

His first pick was Pearl. She didn't know it, but from his peripheral vision, he noticed her as soon as she entered the classroom. He thought that she was a true vision of loveliness.

"My name is Pearl Rousseau and I plan on attending…"

As she talked, Mr. Badeaux was captivated by her beauty. Whatever she was saying, he didn't hear, because the next thing he knew, another student was talking.

All that day Pearl was on his mind. He just had to find out more about her. When it was time for him to take a lunch break, he went to the main office, and looked up her personal information. He found out where she lived, her phone number, and that she had dropped out of school almost a year ago. *But why…*

That night, Mr. Badeaux started his anonymous courting by leaving letters, teddy bears and such at her door step. Her letters were always sealed in a small, beautiful colored envelope. Surprised, but yet confused, Pearl welcomed and fell in love with the indirect attention she was getting. It was totally different from what she was used to on the streets. It put her into a child's dream stage.

After a few months of courting her indirectly, he wrote…

> *My Dear Miss Pearl:*
>
> *You are the apple of my life. Everyday my eyes lay upon your beauty. I can no longer bear to see you and not be with you. My heart desires you so badly.*
> *Silently, I cry for your touch. Please be mine. Let me take care of you. I promise that you will want for nothing in life ever again.*

Pearl's heart leapt for joy after reading the letter. She too was madly in love with the anonymous man. It didn't matter who or what nor how old he was. She was in love. That night, for the first time, she left him a note on the screen door. It read…

Please knock on my door Saturday night at 11:00 My mother will be at work. She will be gone for most of the night.

On Friday night, Mr. Badeaux went to her house to leave a small bottle of perfume on her porch. As he placed the perfume in front of the door, he noticed a small piece of paper sticking out from under the doormat. He looked at his surroundings before picking it up to read it. After doing so, he became excited. That Saturday he went and got a fresh shave, nails manicured, a brand new expensive suit and some fresh Stacy Adams shoes for his first date with the love of his life.

Arriving at 10:59 p.m., he knocked on the door. Immediately, Pearl opened the door and instantly recognized him from school. Without saying a word, she flew into his arms. They hugged and kissed all over each other. He didn't know it, but she secretly adored him from day one of meeting at school. That night they made sweet love to each other like there was no tomorrow.

For months, they dated inconspicuously. Acting as her tutor, he would meet her at the public library to spend time with her. He would join her after-school activities, such as The Drama Club, The Glee Club, and Track to be near her. With him being fairly new to the school, the faculty just thought that he was very much involved with the students. On the weekends, when Pearl's mother would disappear until the wee hours of the morning, they were together at her house making love like two animals in heat.

Everything was perfect in Pearl's life, until she started getting early morning sickness on the stomach. She kept it from her new-found lover by still showing up for school on time. She also kept it from her mother for a very long time. It was easy to do because she was always wasted from drinking. Well...that's what she thought anyway.

Unbeknownst to Pearl, her mother did notice her gaining weight. She just didn't say anything.

Early one morning Pearl felt sick as a dog. Thinking that putting something on her stomach would make her feel better, she went to the kitchen and fixed a bowl of cereal. As she walked back up the steps, she saw her mother heading for the bathroom. *Wow, the dead has risen,* she thought to herself as she closed her bedroom door. After turning the television on for a little entertainment, she sat on her bed and began eating her cereal. After drinking the milk, she put the empty bowl on the floor and laid back down. However, no sooner than she did that, she regurgitated; milk was seeping between her fingers. In a panic, with both hands still over her mouth, she jumped up and ran to the bathroom. *O Lord... I hope mama isn't in there. That's the last thing I need is for her to see me like this,* she thought as she hall-tailed it to the bathroom. But to her dismay, as she burst through the door, her mother was still in there, sitting on the toilet smoking a cigarette. Pearl vomited again and this time it overflowed in her hands. She had no choice but to let it all out in the bath tub. She vomited and gagged and coughed so much, it felt like her insides were coming out. After she finished puking, with shaky hands, she turned on the water faucet and rinsed her mouth out. Afterward, she began to rinse the tub clean. As Pearl cleaned up, her mother calmly continued to smoke her cigarette, until she was done with her business. Once finished, she threw the cigarette in between her legs so the toilet water could put it out. She grabbed some tissue, wiped herself from front to back and flushed the commode. She got up, went to the sink, and started washing her hands.

"You're getting rid of that baby," she said in a calm manner.

Pearl screamed, "Mama no... I love him; he loves me. We're going to get married!"

Her mother laughed.

"Mamed... How you gonna marry a man who's already married fool?"

"No he's not! You don't even know him! He told me that he was single with no children! He's a teacher at my school Mama!"

Her mother took another cigarette out of her robe pocket and fired it up. She took a long drag and blew smoke in the air. While taking another drag she stared at her daughter.

"Is that what you believe...? That he is just a school teacher and that he ain't married. You better check around and ask somebody. Your ass is pregnant, and you know nothing about the daddy." She took another drag. "Girl, don't you know that, that's just a cover up. That man is the biggest drug pusher in the Bayou."

In shock, Pearl's mouth dropped open. She tried to speak but couldn't.

"How do you think he can afford them expensive ass clothes and shit. Can't no teacher afford that fancy shit on a school teacher's salary girl."

Pearl turned to the tub and vomited again. After she finished, she turned the faucet on to rinse her mouth out. Feeling hot, she wildly splashed water all over her face, causing some of it to get on the floor. After turning the water off, she didn't even bother to grab a towel to wipe her face off. Instead, she just used her shirt.

"How...how do you know he dresses nice? You don't know him. do you?"

Turning to the mirror on the medicine cabinet over the sink, her mother started picking at a pimple on her face.

"He was one of my tricks. That's how I know," she said in a matter of fact tone.

"Nooooooo! Pearl yelled.

"I knew you all were seeing each other on the down low. I'm your mama; I know everything that happens in my house. I read all the notes he left you too."

"But how...they were sealed."

Her mother started laughing.

"You'd be amazed at what a little steam and egg whites could do. Anyway...I read that last letter too. I hid in the bushes that night just to see who this little-fucker was. And hot damn who do I see pulling up in a money-green Cadillac with white wall tires... big time Badeaux himself. I didn't say anything to you because. well, I just didn't. Shit now here you are knocked up with his child. Matter of fact keep the damn baby, as long as y'all take care of me."

Going into one hell of a rage, Pearl jumped up and grabbed her mother by the hair and slammed her face into the medicine cabinet. Her mother screamed from the sudden impact. She tried her best to get Pearl off of her but couldn't. Pearl was furious, and her adrenaline was running overboard. She didn't feel a thing as her mother tried to beat her off of her. Blow for blow they went at each other. Her mother got loose from her grip and grabbed the toilet brush. She smacked Pearl across the face with all her might. She then took the tip of the handle and shoved it into Pearl's stomach. Pearl screamed a horrific sound and fell to the floor. She held her stomach for dear life. When her mother saw her fall in such excruciating pain, she thought that was the end of the saga. She threw the toilet brush down; spit at her daughter's feet and walked toward the door. Slowly, without her mother knowing, Pearl got up. Grabbing the toilet brush, she bum-rushed her mother; hitting her on the back of the head several times.

Ferociously, Pearl screamed, "I'm going to kill you bitch!"

When the brush broke from her hitting her mother, Pearl backed up to prepare herself for round-two. Her mother turned around and lunged at her. But as she lunged, Pearl did a little slick move that she had learned from her lover. Doing a side-step, she pushed her mother; causing her to become off balance. Trying to gain control of herself, she slipped on the small puddle of water; thus, hitting her right temple on the edge of the sink. Her mother hit the floor with a hard thump. As she laid there motionless, from her head, blood oozed out all over the black and white checkered tile. Just like that, Pearl's mother was dead. Feeling no remorse, she stared at her and thought, *After all, didn't she just try to kill my unborn child... I had to protect my baby*. To her, it was all done in self-defense. However, that's not what she told the police when she called them. She told them that she had heard her mother scream while she was eating breakfast in her room.

"When I heard my mother scream—I ran to the bathroom, and this is what I saw."

The Police believed her story like she knew they would, because after all, she was only a child for goodness sake.

And needless to say, no one knew that she lost her baby do to the traumatic jab in her stomach. After all was said and done, Pearl stopped seeing the school teacher and went to live with relatives until she met Robert Lee Page.

Taking a deep breath, Pearl released Betty Jean and told her to go upstairs and rest.

"Dinner will be ready in a few hours."

Betty Jean took off running. Mad as hell, she took two steps at a time. As she got to the top of the stairs, she noticed her mother's door slightly ajar. Quietly, she approached the door and peeped in. She observed her mother sitting at her dressing table, examining the right side of her face, which was bruised badly. As she did so, she noticed her daughter through the mirror, staring at her through the cracked door. She too was holding the right side of her face, as if she was in some kind of pain. Abruptly, Lilly Mae turned to faced her. Making eye contact, they stared at each other for what seemed like eternity. No words were said; just silent communication between mother and daughter. Finally, Lilly Mae broke eye contact and picked up her hair brush. Humming a song, she began brushing her hair as if nothing happened. Slowly, Betty Jean backed away from the door and ran down the hallway crying.

24

WHEN BETTY JEAN ran down the hall, Lilly Mae got up and closed her door to prevent anyone else from looking into her room. She laid down and started to think about what had just happened between her and her husband. But in the process of thinking, she dozed off. Now that she was awake hours later, the same questions were back in her head. *Does he really love me, or did he use me to bear his children?* Over and over she thought about this. *But we made love…so* she thought. Out of nowhere, she heard a voice from within. Normally, the voice came from her mind, but this time it was a whisper that came from her heart. *Physical love isn't the same as true love.* Shocked by what she had heard, she sat straight up and looked around the room.

"What do you mean by this?" she said out loud.

The voice responded: *To a man, respect is love. You never respected your husband. Therefore, he never loved you. It is thought; husband love your wife, and wife respect your husband. This has been known from the beginning of time. Love is not self-seeking. It is not proud. It is not easily angered. It keeps no record of wrong. Do you honor your husband? Does he honor you?*

"No."

The voice continued: *Your marriage was based on a lie from the beginning.*

Refusing to hear anymore, she put her hands over her ears and closed her eyes. She didn't want to face the truth.

"Stop it, stop it, I don't care. You hear me Lord; I don't care," she whispered.

You have a choice was the last thing she heard. Silently, she sat there with her hands over her ears for a few minutes longer. She wanted to make sure that she heard no more. Slowly, she removed her hands and vaguely heard the children down stairs talking. From the sound of the click clacking of the silverware, she knew that they were setting up the table to eat. Her mother always believed that a table should be set properly for dinner.

Lilly Mae got up from her bed and walked over to the dressing table. Looking at her face, she tried to convince herself that her bruise didn't look that bad. Satisfied with her appearance, she left her room to go have dinner with her family. As she walked down the long hallway, she thought, *dinner with my family* and let out a hearty laugh.

As she descended down the stairs, she saw her husband in his favorite room reading the newspaper. When she reached the bottom step, she saw the children, except for Betty Jean finishing up the table. As Pearl came through the kitchen door with a dish of food in her hands, she noticed her daughter standing at the bottom of the steps. They both acknowledged each other by nodding their heads.

"Betty Jean! Come on down! Dinner's ready!" Lilly Mae yelled.

She paused for an answer, but there was none.

"Betty Jean! Come on down! Your food is gonna get cold!"

As an afterthought, she said in a low voice, "Joe, come eat."

Everyone except Betty Jean was standing behind their chairs, waiting for Joe to come to the table. This rule was created by him for reasons unknown. All they knew was that he was head of household, so they never questioned it. They just did as they were told.

Joe had them standing for a few minutes before he showed up. His delay after the announcement that dinner was ready was on purpose. His belief was that it showed them that he was in control. When he walked into the dining room and saw the abundance of food and everyone standing as told, it brought a smile to his face. *See that's what I'm talking about. You got to earn your keep in my house.* When he sat, he noticed that Betty Jean wasn't in her place. But he really wasn't expecting her right away, because of what Pearl had told him earlier. However, *if she knows what's good for her, she'd better make it down to dinner real soon* he thought.

Satisfied with everything, he motioned for everyone to sit. As they sat, they kept their eyes on him and Joe kept his eyes focused on the entrance of the dining room. Two minutes later, Betty Jean came down the stairs. She knew that her father would not begin dinner unless everyone was at the table. Keeping her eyes focused on the floor, she entered the dining room and had a seat. Immediately, Johnny noticed the bruise on her face and pointed it out.

"Oh look…Mama and Betty Jean got a cherry face."

With a hateful smirk on her face, Betty Jean cut her eyes at him. Joe didn't entertain their actions.

"Let's all hold hands and bow our heads to give thinks. Heavenly father, we give thanks for the food that we are about to receive, for the nourishment of our body, through Jesus Christ our Lord and Savior, Amen."

In unity, they all responded, "Amen."

Being obedient, the children sat and waited to be served by their mother. Joe made up another rule for dinner time. He stated that he was to be served first, the boys second, then the girls.

Betty Jean and Lilly Mae really didn't have an appetite, so they ate their food slow. Everyone else ate like they had been fasting all day. What had happened between Joe and his wife earlier didn't bother his appetite not one bit.

After wiping his mouth was his tablecloth, he began a conversation with his children.

"So, are you kids ready for the summer?" he said with a smile.

The kids, except for Betty Jean of course, got excited about the question.

"Yes, no more school!" they all yelled.

"Jimmy...son, what do you want to do this summer?"

He smiled and started to say something, but his brother cut him off.

"Um, he just wants to hang out with me."

"Well, I see what you want to do for the summer," Joe said laughing.

Silently, Jimmy became angry and questioned himself...*Why do I always let him do this to me? I can speak for myself daggonit. I'm tired of him bossing me around. I don't want to hang out with his stinky butt. I don't even like him.* But he said nothing and continued to eat.

"Jimmy, is that right? You just want to hang out with your big brother?"

Here's your big chance boy, his inner voice said. *You better speak up for yourself. Do it now or forever hold your peace.*

Reluctantly he said, "Yes sir."

Jackie spoke up.

"Dad, I want to go to Bible School."

All of sudden, Jimmy stopped eating and sat at attention. He got a surge of nerve to say what he had heard from his teacher. With his heart beating fast, he took a deep breath. He said to himself, *on your mark...get set...go!* Excited, and with the speed of lighting he blurted out, "Daddy my teacher said they're having a two-week camp this summer. You get to go away for two weeks. That's what I want to do."

After he made his statement, he felt exhausted and fell back into his chair. A powerful rush of body heat was upon him. *Yes, I did it! I did it!*

"We'll see," his father said with a smile.

"Mama I want to take piano lessons this summer? I don't like tap dancing no more," Jamie said.

Lilly Mae wiped her mouth with her napkin before speaking.

"Um...ask your father dear," she said nervously.

Joe took a sip of his drink.

"I thought you loved tap dancing."

"Nope, I like piano now."

"Betty Jean, what do you want to do this summer...work? You be graduating in a few months."

Picking at her food with her fork and not giving it a second thought, she said what was on her mind.

"Work no...but to college yes." *There I said it. Now they all know. I want to get the heck away from this lunch box family,* she thought.

Stunned, Joe stopped eating. Looking at Lilly Mae and Pearl, he grabbed his napkin and wiped his mouth. Not knowing what to expect, the ladies put their heads down. He looked back at Betty Jean.

"College...? Where did you get that idea from...your mother?" In an instant, Lilly Mae looked at Joe.

"No." she said while shaking her head vigorously."

"No. I got it from James Henry. He was telling me some stuff about his school in Washington D.C. He's graduating from Howard University in May."

Joe started to eat again. Only this time he was eating with a bad attitude. He was actually stabbing his potatoes and gravy. He didn't like the subject, and was also acting like he didn't know this information already.

"Howard huh…?"

"Yes, sir."

"Well…, let's say I do *permit* you to go to college. How am I supposed to pay for it and support this family?" he asked in a sarcastic manner.

Even though her father displayed a nasty attitude, she became very happy about him just entertaining the subject.

"Well… James Henry said that with my GPA being a 3.8, I could get a scholarship, a grant or even financial aid. He said I should have been filled out the forms for that. He also said to take the SAT test…whatever that is. If I get a nice score like 1500, or being realistic, maybe 1200, I could just about get into any school a want. I know I can do it. And then after I graduate… Bam! The world of opportunity is at my door step. Success here I come," she said enthusiastically.

"What's wrong with the University here at home?" he asked a little irritated at her excitement.

At that statement, Betty Jean felt like her heart just got ripped out of her chest.

"I don't want to stay here," sadly, she responded.

Sensing her husband's disapproval, Lilly Mae intervened.

"Why not baby? This is your home. Family is here. Your church is here."

"*Church* is where your heart is Mama. Besides, I want to go see what the rest of the world looks like. I don't want to be stuck here, working at some little rink a dink job."

Joe got pissed.

"Oh, I see. You'd rather be stuck somewhere else, like up north with James Henry."

Betty Jean knew what he was insinuating and got pissed off too.

"Well it *does* beat getting *stuck* by you, *Daddy!*" sarcastically, she replied.

Totally surprised at her daughter's demeanor, Lilly Mae choked on her food. Pearl, who thought that Joe was going to jump up and help his wife, had to spring into action when she saw that he wasn't. She began smacking Lilly Mae on her back.

"Child, are you alright?"

Joe remained calm. He shook his head at Betty Jean's attitude and started eating again.

After getting Lilly Mae back under control, Pearl looked at her granddaughter and told her, "Betty Jean, you need to check your tone toward your father."

Not saying a word, they all continued to eat without looking at each other. If it wasn't for the noise of the silverware hitting the plate, you could have heard a pin drop. Tired of the silence, Pearl tried to make light of the situation.

"Come on y'all stop that. We're having a nice dinner here." Pointing at the food, she continued with a fake smile. "See we got us some, fried pork chops, mashed potatoes and gravy, corn on the cob." She looked at Betty Jean. "Come on baby pass me the pork cho…"

Abruptly cutting her grandmother off, Betty Jean stood up from the table and had her say.

"Why must you try to sugar coat everything when a problem comes up Granny? I'm tired of it. I graduate in two months, and no one's trying to help me do anything with my life!"

"Honey, that's not true," passively, her mother said.

"Yes, it is Ma! Tell me this…when were you and daddy going to sit down with me to discuss my future?"

She turned and addressed her father.

"When Daddy?"

"We still have time for that," he stated in a matter of fact tone. "I just told your mother the other…"

Tired of the lies, she boldly cut him off too.

"Stop it Daddy! If y'all were going to talk to me about my plans for the future, it should have been done like last year, or the beginning of this year! Something should have been done way before now!"

"Something still *can* be done," her mother said.

"For a loan maybe. It's too late for me to be considered for any type of scholarship or grant. You got to do that early in the school year."

Joe snickered. "Who told you that…James Jr.?"

"Yes he did. He told me a whole lot of important information."

Fed up with Betty Jean's sassiness, Joe slammed his fist on the table. The loud thump caused the other children to jump.

"Well he doesn't know what he's talking about. It's just March. You've got plenty of time to do whatever needs to be done."

"Yeah right…tell me anything."

Joe stared at her for what seemed like all eternity. Finally, he spoke very slow and deliberant.

"Maybe you need to get some information from James Henry on how to learn to keep your mouth shut, from telling me what other people are suggesting about my children's future."

Lilly Mae tried to speak up for the young man.

"Joe, I'm quite sure he's a good kid. He didn't mean any harm by telling Betty Jean…"

"Shut up! I don't want to hear no more! Now all of you listen to me! I'm the man of this household. And as long as I feed you, dress you and keep a roof over your head, I don't need outsiders telling me what I should do with my family! Now I want y'all to be quiet and eat this food that I brought with my hard-earned money!"

"Hard-earned...please...you work in a church," Betty Jean said under her breath as she sat back down.

Snickering, she made a funny face at her sisters and brothers. They all burst out laughing at her. But Joe thought that they were laughing at him. Upset, he slammed his napkin on the table and went after her.

"I done told you about your mouth girl! Come here!"

Like lighting, Betty Jean jumped up from her chair, causing it to fall on the floor. Giving herself some distance between her and her father, she backed away from the table. She began to dance around the room like she just won a championship boxing match.

"Oh, what you gonna do *Daddy?* You gonna whip me, huh? You want to whip me in front of everybody? Are you sure you don't want to take me upstairs behind closed doors to do that?"

"Girl you're going to wish you were never born!"

He lunged at her, but she was too fast and dodged out of his way. He chased her around the table. While in the Merry-Go-Round process, Betty Jean grabbed a sharp knife from the table, causing Lilly Mae and the kids to scream.

"Daddy, I'm telling you...if you don't leave me alone, I'm going to poke you; you hear...I'm not playing with you!"

"Oh you're going to poke me. Girl put that knife down right now!"

"Come on now, y'all stop it. You all are acting like pure nigga's right now. You *know* better than this. Come on sit down," Pearl pleaded.

"Granny he's the nigga! Always was one! He's just trying to prove to us what he couldn't be to his first wife. And that's being a *real* man!"

Lilly Mae was totally in shock. *Shit, she done struck a nerve now.*

And she did, because Joe screamed and used the Lords name in vain.

"Bitch, I swear to God! I'm going to kill you!"

He started throwing at her whatever he got his hands on off the table. Betty Jean didn't take his projectile's serious, because she dodged the flying objects with ease. In a panic and afraid for the rest of the children, Pearl jumped up and started clapping her hands very fast.

"Children, run upstairs now! Run upstairs right now!"

Screaming and crying, they all immediately jumped up and ran for safety. They were scared to death. They had never seen such violence before. Their father had always been such a quiet man and showed nothing but love to them. Getting out of dodge, they fell on top of each other as they ran up the steps.

Now that her siblings were out of the room, Betty Jean really started to show her true colors. Crouched, and in a defensive manner, she tossed the knife back and forth in her hands.

"Man if you touch me, I'm going to put so many holes in you, the doctor's gonna think that you're a new kind of cheese!"

When Joe saw how she was handling that knife, he slowed his role. *Where in the hell did she learn how to do that?* He thought twice about his actions. But then his pride got the best of him, and he went after her. As he charged toward her, Betty Jean side stepped him; cutting his upper arm in the process. Joe grabbed the cut as he fell over the fallen chair. Betty Jean, on the other hand, had two left feet as she tried to run and caused her own self to fall. She tried her best to get up before he did, but she wasn't fast enough. Joe pounced on her like white on rice. He started chocking her. Realizing that she still had the knife in her hand, Betty Jean began stabbing the hell out of his back. But Joe didn't feel a thing because his adrenalin was in overdrive. He squeezed her neck harder and harder. Betty Jean became light-headed and dropped the knife.

Pearl ran over to them and tried to push him off of her, but to no avail. She yelled to Lilly Mae for assistance, but Lilly Mae couldn't help. She was in a state of shock. It was as if she was frozen to her chair the whole time the madness kicked off. She saw what was happening, but really didn't believe it was happening. The sound of the commotion was distorted to her. She had gone to a place where she had gone so many times before; to her mental safe haven. She had created this place when she was a little girl. No one could do any harm to her there.

Coughing, gagging and in a struggling voice, Betty Jean yelled out to her mother.

"Mama, help me! Mama, help me please!"

From lack of oxygen, Betty Jean's face began to turn blue.

"Hold on baby girl, hold on! Joe, let her go! For God's sake let her go! You're going to kill my baby! Let her go!" Pearl yelled as she hit Joe on the back with all her strength.

In rage, he stared down at the person he was choking. At first glance, to him, he was choking his ex-wife.

"I told you not to leave me. Now look at what you're making me do. If I can't have you, no one can," he yelled.

Feeling a little light headed from the loss of blood; Joe began to feel the pain from the powerful blows to his back. He finally heard Pearl yelling, and looked back at her.

"Joe, what are you talking about?! That's not your *wife!* You're killing my baby!"

Not your wife...he thought. Looking back down at the person on the floor, he shook his head, and blinked his eyes several times to clear his mind. *Not your wife...but...this is my wife...the bitch left me for another man* he thought. He tightened his grip around her neck. In doing so he gained pleasure from the feel of life slipping from her body. Then in a quick flash, a chair crashed over his head. The blow caused him to fall on top of the person he was chocking. It also brought him back to reality. Rolling off of her, he looked at the person. In terror, he saw Betty Jean's lifeless body. Horrified, he screamed. On hands and knees, he crawled to a corner; covered his face and began to cry like a baby. Betty Jean, who was playing possum, grabbed her neck and rolled over. She began to cough something terrible. Barely catching her wind and in pain, she cried out.

"Grandma!"

"Hold on baby! You just hold on! I'm getting you some water!" Pearl went and grabbed a glass of water from off the table. Trying to sit up, Betty Jean fell back down because she was too light-headed and exhausted.

"Hold on child! I got you! I got you!"

Pearl hurried and sat down next to her. She lifted her head up to take a sip.

"Here you go baby. Drink just a little bit."

With her hands shaking badly, Betty Jean took the glass of water. She tried to drink, but it wasted all over her face and shirt. Pearl helped her steady the glass.

"Slow down now. Take it slow."

Betty Jean took a big gulp and began to choke.

"Take small sips. Come on now, small sips nice and slow. It's going to be alright."

This time she was successful with a few small sips. Pearl removed the glass from her granddaughter's hand after she had her full and began to rock her back and forth like a baby.

"Mama, why didn't you help me?! she cried out.

Pearl drew her baby close to her bosom.

"Shhh…. Baby its ok. It's over; you hear; it's over now."

"But Granny what's wrong with her?! How can she just let him do that to me?"

Pearl didn't reply, and continued to rock her.

"B…B…Betty Jean, I'm sorry. I don't know what came over me. I'll never do it again, I… I…promise."

"Like you promised not to hit mama no more! Well... I don't believe you! I hate you, and I hate this house!"

On impulse, she jumped up; swaying just a little from the sudden move and ran toward the front door.

"No, no, no more!"

Grabbing the table leg for assistance, Pearl got up and went after her.

"Betty Jean! Betty Jean!"

But she wasn't as fast as her. By the time she reached the front porch, Betty Jean was all the way down the driveway. She knew that her granddaughter couldn't hear her calling her name, but she had to try anyway.

"Betty Jean come back! Please come back!"

Betty Jean did vaguely hear her grandmother calling. However, she also heard a much stronger voice. It was telling her to run like hell from the house of pain. And as she did so, she took several looks back. It seemed like the farther she ran, the closer the house got. But she knew her mind was playing tricks on her and continued to run. She was determined to get away from that house. The voice inside her head told her to run...run like a fool...run like you never ran before; never to return to the house of hell.

As Pearl made an attempt to run after her beloved Betty Jean, sheets of rain began to pour out of the sky.

"Betty Jean! Please! Please!" in vain, she yelled.

Being on the heavy side, Pearl began to experience pain all over her body as she ran. As each foot hit the drenched, muddy ground, painful shock waves went through her body.

"Lord, why is this happening to my family?"

With shortness of breath, she called out again.

"Betty Jean, please come back! It's going to be alright!"

Soaked to the bone, she wasn't even halfway down the driveway as she saw her granddaughter disappear. Tears swelled up in her eyes.

"Baby girl come back!"

Grabbing her chest, she took a deep breath.

"Betty Je..."

Pain...so much pain Lord.

Pearl began to stagger.

"Betty J..."

She tried to continue, but was in too much pain and fell. As the watery heavens looked down upon her, a flash of light danced before her eyes. In a dream state, she saw a cute-little Betty Jean and herself, setting on the front porch enjoying the rain as it poured. They *were* singing a children's rhyme. *Rain...rain...go away. Come back another day. Rain...rain...go away. Come back another day. My roof got a hole in it, and I might drown. I say my roof got a hole in it, and I might drown.* Laughing, Pearl grabbed Betty Jean's hand, and they run into the rain singing and dancing. Little BJ hugged her grandmother.

"I love you."

Passionately, Pearl hugged her back.

"I love you more."

Ki! Ki! Boom! Went the sky, causing light to dance before Pearl's eyes again; thus, back into the now. Tears ran down her face as she remembered the good old days.

"Betty Jean..."

Faintly, she felt a slow heartbeat. *Bump, Bump... Bump, Bump... Bump...*

Back in the house, Joe remained on the floor crying. Lilly Mae, who was still glued to her chair, heard his sobbing and slowly looked over at him. Never hearing him cry before, her heart went out to him. She got up and went to comfort him. Getting on her knees, she pulled him close to her bosom and began to rock him back and forth like a child.

"Joe, it's ok. She'll be back. You'll see. Just give her some time."

Joe welcomed his wife's comfort by grabbing her waist tightly.

"I'm so sorry... I didn't mean to hurt her. I swear Lilly Mae. I didn't mean to hurt her."

She smiled at her husband's vulnerability. His heart was exposed. He was defenseless just the way she always wanted him to be. Now she felt like she was the superior one. Gently, she rubbed his head.

"It's ok. I know you didn't mean it."

Her soothing words caused him to grab tighter.

"Baby, let mama get you some water."

Not wanting his wife to move, he clung to her.

"No, please don't leave me."

A huge, menacing expression came upon her face. In a very gentle caring manner, she lifted his head up toward her.

"Let me get you a drink of water. It's right on the table," she said with a very soft voice.

Reluctantly, he released her. Smiling, she retrieved the glass of water and sat back down next to him. Giving him the water, Joe took it with shaky hands; causing the water to spill all over him.

Lilly Mae snickered under her breath and steadied his hands. With her help, he took a few sips.

"Thank you. Baby, I don't know what I would do without you."

His words were like music to her ears.

"I'm going to go get mother, so we can go look for Betty Jean, ok." Leaning against the wall, he closed his eyes.

"Ok, go ahead. I'm going to sit here for a few minutes."

Lilly Mae got up and with a little swagger in her walk, left the room. She yelled as she walked to the front door.

"Mama... Mama! I think we should go look..."

But when she got to the hallway, no one was there. Baffled, she looked at the kitchen door, and then to the study room. No one was in sight. She looked up at the staircase; nothing.

"I wonder where... Mama...! Betty Jean...!"

No answer. Not even a sound from the kids.

"Damn, the children must be scared out of their wits from Betty Jean acting like a fool."

She stood there for a few seconds longer, just to make sure she didn't hear anything. When she didn't, an eerie, uneasy feeling came over her. Deep down, she felt something wasn't right. She couldn't put her finger on it, but something felt wrong.

At that very moment, the sky flickered and lit the house up like a fire cracker. Then *Ki-Boom!* The heavens roared, causing her to jump and scream at the same time.

"Shit!"

The sky opened up, and it poured down like cats and dogs. *Bang! Bang! Bang!* She heard from behind her and froze.

"What the... Joe is that you?" she asked in a timid voice without turning around.

Bang! Bang! The noise went as if answering her. Scared to death, but knew she had to know what was going on, she slowly turned around and saw the screen door slamming against its frame. That's how powerful the wind was blowing. Rain was now all over the shiny waxed floor.

As if in a trance, she stared at the rain being blown inside. A small puddle quickly began to form in front of the door. A rhyme came to mind as she stared at it. *Puddle...tuddle...your mothers in trouble.* The rhyme repeated itself over, and over in her head.

"What the hell... Where did that shit come from?"

The thunder roared a mighty cry. *Ki, Ki, Ki Boom!* Lilly Mae screamed and ran like hell to shut the front door. However, she totally forgot about the puddle of water, and ran right into it. She slipped.

"Oh fuck!"

Trying to cushion her fall, she went for the screen door. But, that didn't do any good, because when she fell against it, her weight caused the hinges to be ripped out. She and the door hit the porch and slid down the steps into the muddy driveway. Lilly Mae laid on top of the screen with her arms, and legs spread out like a stick man.

"Unfucking believable. Gotdammit… Betty Jean where are you!"

Looking down at herself, she saw that she was a soaked, muddy mess and got pissed off.

"Shoot. Now I got to get this crap off of me."

She got up and tried to kick the hell out of the screen door, but slipped. Her legs went high to the sky. When she came back down, she landed on her booty bone with a hard thump. She grabbed her backside.

"Ouch, ouch, ouch, shit!"

The pain was so excruciating she didn't know if she wanted to laugh or cry.

Boom! Boom! Boom! The thunder went. However, what Lilly Mae heard was, *get up you fool! Look for your mother and daughter!*

"Shit!"

Discombobulated, she jumped up and ran underneath a big old, Weeping Willow tree. *What the hell… Was that the thunder or did somebody…* Looking around, she saw that no one was there and became frighten.

"Where are you guys?!" she called out in a timid voice.

There was no answer. Only the howling wind responded. Her heart began to race a mile a minute. Panic sat in. She felt as if she couldn't move.

"Ma… Joe… Somebody help!"

Look down the driveway stupid she heard a voice say. At the sound of the voice, Lilly Mae quickly turned and looked up at the house. *No dumb, dumb; down the drive way.* At that moment, as she looked down the driveway, the skies lit up something kind of crazy. That's when she saw a huge dark figure lying in the middle of the driveway. At first, she thought it was a deer, but then thought, *No that's not a deer…it's way too big.* The voice bellowed, *Go girl…* *Boom! Boom!* Immediately, as if in a trance, she obeyed the voice and started walking toward the huge figure.

Crack! Crack! Ka-Boom!

"Shit!" she yelled and hauled tailed it down the driveway.

Boom! Boom!

Go fool, hurry up! Feeling the urgency, she went even faster. *Hurry child, hurry.* As she got closer to the figure, she recognized the shape but didn't want to believe it. *No…no…no…*

Ma…? It can't be; not my mother. She became light headed. Her breathing became uneasy. Her heart was racing. Tightness was in her chest. She began to stagger. *Pain, so much pain Lord.* She grabbed her chest to ease the presser, but it did no good. The sky lit up. Clearly, she could see the figure now. Acknowledgement was upon her. She screamed a dreadful cry and fell to the ground.

"Ma!"

It seemed as if time had stopped. For a split second, she heard no rain, no wind and no thunder. Then, *Boom! Boom!* The sky lit up again.

"Lord Jesus, why is this happening to my family?!"

She tried to get up, but her body wouldn't move.

Boom! Boom! Run fool run!

She tried to move again, but couldn't. She looked to the watery heavens and pleaded.

"God have mercy on my soul! Help me! Help me!

She tried again, but couldn't move. She cried out Psalm 23 while beating her legs, in an attempt to bring them back to life. *Come on girl, move damn it!*

"The Lord is my shepherd; I shall not be in want!"

Slowly, she began to crawl.

"He makes me lie down in green pastures; he leads me beside quiet waters!" *You can do this.* "He restores my soul!"

She regained a little strength. Awkwardly, she stood up. *Yes, now run for your mother's sake. Run as if the devil himself was after you.* Obedient to the powerful voice, she started off in a trot.

"Mama! Mama!"

The more she screamed her mother's name, the stronger she became. "Mama! Mama!"

A few minutes later, she was upon her mother's motionless body and fell before her. In a panic, she shook her vigorously.

"Mama, what's wrong!"

There was no answer.

"Mama, wake up! Mama what's wrong with you!

There was still no response.

"Mama, what's wrong!"

Looking toward the house she screamed.

"Joe, something is wrong with mama!"

But Joe didn't hear her. The distance was too great, and the thunder drowned her voice out.

She cried to the heavens.

"God...somebody help!"

She raised her mother's head and placed it on her lap. She began to rock her back and forth.

She screamed to the top of her lungs.

"Help me! Please help me! Somebody...!" It all seemed surreal to her.

Boom! Boom! Boom! Ki! Ki! Ki! Boom! Boom! The thunder drowned her out. Only the ferocious storm answered her. No one saw her tears but the moon. No one felt the sorrow in her heart, but the heavens. At that moment, Lilly Mae was alone in the world.

PART EIGHT

25

*A*LOT HAD CHANGED at the Carter's residence since that dreadful, stormy night. Pearl was admitted to the hospital because of a massive heart attack and was now in a coma. And Betty Jean was still nowhere to be found. With this realization, Lilly Mae acknowledged, and accepted the continuation of her dysfunctional family. She thought Joe's money, his so called respected position in society and becoming his wife was going to change some things in her life. However, she now knows that all of that can't change who or what you are. It's your belief; what you feel inside, and what you think of yourself that change's ones being. She also acknowledged that her side of the family has some type of mental problem. She thought, *why else would I allow awful things to happen to my own daughter, and my mother permitted terrible things to happen to me. And I bet bad stuff happened to her, but she just never talked about it.*

Lilly Mae barely spoke or paid any attention to Joe. It used to be if he said jump, she would say how high, but not anymore. If she did have an ounce of respect for her husband, it was long gone for sure. Now, it's like whatever…when he brings something to her attention. She still held it down as far as her wifely duties and being a mother was concerned. However, her real focus was on finding her precious daughter and her weekly visits to see her mother in the hospital.

It's been two months, and her condition was still the same. The whole family used to visit every single day, until Joe started complaining about the visits being too long and house work not being taken care of like it used to be. But Lilly Mae thought that the real reason for the complaining was that he just didn't want to be there. She could tell, because within twenty minutes of the visit, he would be knocked out in one of the chairs snoring. And when the children saw their dad asleep, they acted like fools in hell's water.

Lilly Mae really couldn't enjoy a peaceful visit because of them. So being tired of their inconsiderate attitudes, she decided to leave them at home and visit just on Saturdays. And of course, they didn't mind her decision because actually, they didn't want to visit in the first place.

Early one beautiful, sunny Saturday morning Joe was out front watering the grass. The children were on the front also with old tin cans. They were collecting worms that crawled out from the drenched lawn. They collected them to sell to people who were always doing some kind of fishing down by the river. They really didn't need the money, but their dad wanted to show them how to be creative in starting your own business.

Johnny found a nice fat worm and instead of putting it in his can, he decided to scare Jackie with it. While she was bent over looking for her own worms, he crept up behind her and gently placed it on her neck. Snickering a little, he slowly and quietly backed away and waited for the fireworks. At first, she didn't feel a thing. But when it started to crawl, she felt something funny on her neck.

"What the…."

She thought it was a bug and smacked the crap out of her neck.

"Got you sucker!"

She looked at her hand to see what kind of bug it was, but was surprised at the slim on her hand.

"What the crap! This is nasty!"

Johnny, who was a few feet away from her, pointed his finger at her and burst out laughing. Disgusted, she looked at him and realized that he had just played a trick on her. She wiped her hand off on the grass.

"Boy I'm going to kick your butt!"

When he heard the playful threat, he dropped his can of worms, and took off running around to the back of the house. Jackie took off after him.

"Bring your butt back here boy! I'm going to kick your butt! You play too much!"

As they ran, Lilly Mae came out of the house all dressed up for her mama's visit. Joe noticed how nice she looked, but didn't give her a compliment.

"Where you going looking like that?"

Lilly Mae paid him no never mind. She didn't even look his way.

"I asked you a question."

Remembering how he used to intimidate her, she smiled to herself. *No more baby…no more.* She looked at the children playing and then up to the clear blue skies. To help keep her attitude in check, she talked to the heavens before speaking to him.

"I'm going to visit mama like I always do on a Saturday. Why. you wanna come with me?"

Without answering her, he turned his head and continued to water the grass. Lilly Mae thought as she walked down the steps to the car, *just got to have something to say; ass hole.*

The kids saw their mother getting into the car and ran over to her.

"Bye Mama! Give grandma a big kiss for us! Tell her we love her and miss her!"

"I will. Be good while I'm gone now!"

"What time will you be back? I'm not watching these kids all day!" Joe yelled as she pulled off.

Without saying a word, Lilly Mae waved him off and drove down the driveway. He stared at the car until it turned onto the main road.

26

*L*ILLY MAE ARRIVED at the hospital at her normal time, which was around 10:00am. With the bible and purse in one hand and fresh wild flowers that she picked in the other, she entered the building. From her routine visits, she became familiar with just about all the doctors and nurses. With a smile, she greeted the busy staff by their first name.

While walking to the elevator, she noticed that the small waiting room was full to its capacity. *Thank God my mother has a room* she thought as she passed the spectacle.

When she got to the elevator, she pushed the arrow button pointing up. A few seconds later the door opened. A young black couple were already on the elevator. She stepped in, and pushed the number for her floor. Being nice she gave the couple a polite smile. The man noticed how beautiful she was and smiled back. The lady looked at her up and down, in a nasty manner. The girl's action caused Lilly Mae to snicker to herself. *Lord what's wrong with these young people today? They're just not happy with themselves.*

With her peripheral vision, she noticed the young man checking out her shapely derriere. So being on get back from the girl's nasty look, Lilly Mae performed. She took her pretty, shiny, red polished nails and fingered her long beautiful hair. When she finished, on purpose, she dropped the wild flowers in front of her.

"Oh!" she said with a smile, as she looked at the man standing slightly behind her.

Instead of stooping to pick the flowers up like most people do, she slowly protruded that shapely butt of hers and bent over to pick them up. When Lilly Mae sat it out, the young man almost knocked his girl down trying to help her with the flowers. Pissed off, the girl smacked the mess out of him.

"What the hell is wrong with you? Let that chick pick up her own shit!"

Not being fazed by the smack, he smiled at her.

"Here you go Ms."

With a sexy smile, Lilly Mae said, "Thank you so much."

In the process of taking the flowers, she looked at the girl and rolled her eyes.

The elevator went "*ding*" indicating the third floor; Lilly Mae's stop. Getting off the elevator, Lilly Mae smacked one of her butt checks; causing it to jiggle. The girl was shocked at her action.

"Oh, no that bitch didn't!"

As the door began to close, Lilly Mae looked back at them and blew a Marylyn Monroe kiss at the man. But the man didn't see Lilly Mae's action because he was too busy punching the crap out of his girl for smacking him.

Laughing out loud, Lilly Mae walked down to her mother's room. She stood outside Room 373. *God's favorite numbers* she thought. Before entering the room, she smoothed her dress out and made sure her hair was in place. Gaining her composure, she took a deep breath and gently knocked on the door. *Knock-knock-knock*

No answer. Cautiously, she opened the door. The first thing she heard upon entering the room was the beep of the heart monitor.

"Mama..." she said softly, but not really expecting an answer.

Pearl was lying in the bed motionless with tubes in her arms. A short, elderly looking white nurse with bifocals on was at the foot of the bed. She was checking Pearl's medical chart. She heard Lilly Mae come in, but said nothing. After checking things off on the chart, she placed it back on its hanger at the end of the bed. The nurse went to Pearl and pulled the covers all the way up to her neck, then left the room without saying a word.

When Lilly Mae heard the door close, she went right to her mother and pulled the covers back down. She placed her bible and purse on a wooden table next to the bed. A small, clear, glass vase with some dried up wild flowers were on the table. Smelling the fresh ones in hand, she replaced the old with the new. Arranging them just so, she stepped back to admire the colorful flowers.

Throwing the old flowers in the trash can, she walked over to the window and pulled the curtains open.

"I don't know why that old lady likes to keep you in the dark Mama."

Satisfied with the light coming through the room, she went back to her mother and adjusted her pillow a little higher for today's study.

"There you go Mama. I know you like your pillow higher than how that old bat had you."

Lilly Mae knew her mother wasn't going to respond, but she talked to her just the same. Her eyes became watery as she stared at her.

"Ok that's enough of that. It's time for the good news," she said quietly as she wiped her eyes.

Walking back to the table, she sat down on a gray, hard plastic chair; she grabbed her bible.

"Let's start off our reading with the Lord's prayer. The Lord is my shepherd; I shall not be in want. He makes me lie down in green pastures...."

After reading Psalms 23, she closed the Bible and placed it back on the table. Her eyes began to water again. Taking a deep breath, she looked up to the ceiling. She had heard that if you look up while being tearful, they would go away. She took a handkerchief from her purse and wiped her eyes.

"Ever since I was a little girl; that's always been my prayer in times of need. I can remember when you and daddy first taught it to me." She laughed a little. "I think I knew that prayer before I even learned the alphabets. Time sure does fly. One minute you don't have a care in the world, then, next thing you know, you're all grown up. We had so much fun when I was little. I still remember when you and daddy were trying to teach me how to swim in the river. I was so scared of the water. But daddy held me tight. He told me to trust him, and I did. Now I can swim like a fish."

Even though she knew that there would be no two-way conversation, she smiled at Pearl and waited. Her only response was the beeping sound of the heart monitor. Another deep breath was taken.

"Mama, Betty Jean hasn't come home yet. I don't know what to do. Joe had looked and tried everything to find that girl. Vivian thought that maybe she was just hiding out. But no one, not even her friends have seen her."

Frustrated, she got up and paced the floor. She walked over to the window and stared out at the birds going about their care-free life.

"I don't know what's wrong with that girl."

"There's nothing wrong with her no more than what's wrong with me and you," said a very dry, weak voice.

Shocked, Lilly Mae abruptly turned around. Her eyes were fixated on her mother. Not being sure of what she just heard, slowly, she began to walk toward her. It was as if she was walking on egg shells.

"Mama..., did you say something?" she asked apprehensively.

"Yes I did."

Lilly Mae screamed and jumped for joy. She ran over to her mother's bed and hugged her ever so tightly.

"Mama! Mama! Oh, God thank you! Thank you, Jesus, for my mama!"

Pearl began to speak with a raspy voice.

"You need to be on your knees and ask the Lord to forgive you with the way you treated that baby. Ain't nothing wrong with her. It's you...you're what's wrong with her."

Confused, Lilly Mae stopped hugging her mother and stepped back to look at her. Trying to play her mother's comment off, she put her hands on her hips and smiled.

"What are you talking about? Look, I'm going to get the doctor, so he..." she said as she walked toward the door.

Pearl cut her off.

"I don't need no damn doctor! Now get over here and listen to what I say!"

Even with her being in a coma for so long, she still remembered that terrible day. But her daughter ignored her and continued to the door.

"Ok, I'll listen as soon as I go get...."

Irate, Pearl hit the little table hard as hell, causing the glass vase to shatter on the floor.

"Why did you let that man rape your child?!" she said as she mustered up what little strength she had to sit up in bed.

Lilly Mae stopped dead in her tracks. It was as if she hit a brick wall. She couldn't believe what her mother just asked.

Defiantly, Pearl continued.

"Yes I said it…been knew about it. Thought you were going to do something about it, but you didn't. You did nothing to help that baby. I…. It made me sick to my stomach to know that mess was going on in the house. You're her mama. You were supposed to protect her, and I'll be…."

Before Pearl could finish, in rage, Lilly Mae turned and approached her mother with her fist balled up.

"Like you protected me Mama! Like you protected me from daddy! All those nights you heard me cry for you, and you did nothing! Every time that man was drunk as a skunk, he got up the nerve to come to my room and have his way with me, and you did nothing! He talkin' bout, he was punishing me for something I had no idea of! And then the next day to appease me, he would buy me some kind of gift just because! The only reason he did that was so I wouldn't tell nobody! And you had the *nerve* to be mad at me back then! I didn't ask for that! You're my mother! I was a little girl! You did nothing! Oh, I knew you were there looking and listening. I knew you were there, and you did nothing!"

Tears began to roll down Pearls face. She had no idea Lilly Mae knew that she knew what was going on all those years.

"I did do something. Yes, I did. It might not was done fast enough, but I did do something."

Lilly Mae didn't have an ounce of sympathy for her mother's tears.

"Oh please…what did you do, huh? I mean, you didn't call the police. No cops came. He didn't get beat up by nobody. He didn't get cut up or nothing. He just up and died."

Pearl had flash backs. She remembered all the bad stuff that had happened to her and her daughter. But what could she do at that time. *I had nowhere to go. No money to take care of us.* She was totally dependent upon her husband. She remembered being hit in the face several times when trying to bring up the way he chastised

Lilly Mae physically. He would yell at her and say that she was fat, out of shape and ugly while hitting her. He told her not to ever tell him how to discipline his child. He told her that whatever he said or did was final in the household. And that was the end of that. She never brought it up again.

Crying at the terrible memories, she confessed.

"I took his life to protect us from any more harm! I took my husband's life! My God, the man I loved so dearly...I took his life to save ours! And now you done turned around and let the same thing happen to your baby!" She closed her eyes. "Lord...lord is this my punishment for my sin? How long will this go on in the family?"

Lilly Mae was mad as hell. With a nasty smirk, she got up in her mother's face and said,

"Well it looks like you're a day late and a dollar short. You should have stopped the cycle long before this situation with my daughter. You should have stopped it when I first told you about daddy putting his hands on me in a bad way. But you didn't. Because I was small, *you* told me that I was a liar. You were in denial because *you* wanted to keep your man. You didn't want to be by yourself because a man validates you."

"No, that's not the reason!"

Laughing, she backed away from her mother.

"Yes it is. Because that's why I did nothing when Betty Jean told me the same thing I told you. I didn't want to lose my man. I wanted to have a beautiful home. I choose him and a house over my own daughter. I kept telling myself that it was going to be ok. That it would be alright. Hell, I got through it, so will Betty Jean... so I thought. But now look at us Mama. Look at how messed up we are just because we didn't take a stand. You didn't care about me. All you cared about was yourself. So now the vicious cycle starts *all...over...again.* And if somebody doesn't put a stop to it... Well, no need in talking about it no more."

Turning away from her mother, she walked back over to the window and admired the birds flying freely. She analyzed her life.

"So now my baby is gone. My husband is…huh…damn. I got four brats at home. And to top it all off, my mother killed my father because of her lack of strength and protection. Wow… My family is really fucked up."

Walking back over to the bed, she grabbed the small trash can and started cleaning up the glass mess on the floor.

"You know., the only thing that's real in this world is the word of God. Other than that, nothing matters."

After she finished cleaning up the mess, she stood up and folded her arms.

"Now mother dear…tell me…. What are *we* going to do about *my* husband?"

With tears running rampant, Pearl looked away and said nothing.

PART NINE

27

MAY WAS JUST about over and Pearl was at home on bed rest. Her mind frame was shattered, causing her to talk very little. It was as if she was alive, but not living anymore. Nothing had turned out the way she wanted it to be since her husband's death. She pondered, *How could I have changed things back then?* Over and over she mentally beat herself up. *Should I have...I could have done... I would have called the....*

Lilly Mae brought food to her and checked up on her throughout the day. However, they no longer talked like they used to. She blamed her for Betty Jean's disappearance. Every time her daughter tried to read the Bible to her, she interrupted by asking if Betty Jean was home yet. The question frustrated Lilly Mae, because the only answer she could give was no. What was once a happy home, was now a living hell.

Betty Jean was gone for quite a while now. No one had neither seen nor heard from her. Her mother thought that everything was just fine in the household, until James Jr. put the idea of college into her baby girls head. She cursed the ground that young man walked on every single day. She told herself, *if I ever see that boy, I'm going to give him a piece of my mind. It's because of him my family is torn apart.*

Unbeknownst to her, he was back in the Bayou already. His graduation had come and gone. All his relatives attended the ceremony. He graduated Summa Cum Laude and received a full scholarship to Georgetown University Law Program. He also received a nice car from his family as a graduation present.

Happy that his studies were over, he was back helping his dad's business as usual. Truth be told, he was hoping to see Betty Jean for the summer. But when his father told him that she had ran away from home two months ago, he was heartbroken. For the last two months of school, she's all he thought about. He couldn't wait to get back home. He fantasized about her and him hanging out at a fish fry, going skinny-dipping in the river, listening to the bull frogs while sitting on the front porch at night, and craw fishing. Her disappearance nullified all his dreams. So, for now, he sat at the Shack, which was a pub that all the local folks hung out at. He sat there waiting to receive payment from the owner who had credit with his dad. The owner had a fish fry at his church and ran out of fish. He didn't expect to have such a large crowd.

Larry, the owner of the Shack, was a light brown, medium built, middle-aged man. He was always polite to everyone. He walked up to James Jr. from behind the bar and handed him his father's money.

"Here you go son, $25.00 paid in full. I appreciate y'all not giving me a hard time about the money I owe. I wish there were more people like you in this world."

Taking the money, James Jr. smiled at the complement.

"Man anytime. I'm just glad my dad helped you out."

Larry grabbed a tall glass and filled it was ice.

"Yes indeed, we had a nice turn out. They killed that fish man. Hell, it was gone before we even dropped it in the grease." He joked and they both laughed.

He poured the young man a nice cold Coca-Cola and James Jr. smiled at the refreshing drink.

"Well you know we folks around here believe in good eating. I'm talking about fresh catfish, crawfish, crabs, shrimp gumbo, jambalaya, and fried corn bread. Now that's good eating."

He gulped his pop down like a snow bear lost in the dessert.

"You got that right," Larry laughed.

Then with a blink of an eye, Larry got serious and changed the subject.

"Man, when you and your daddy going to come from the Bayou and move on up a bit? This here area is up and coming. You got plenty of land and job opportunities here."

Finishing off the last bit of his drink, James Jr. sat the empty glass down and belched.

"Opportunity like what…? Cleaning white folk's homes or sweating out in fields that's not even yours…no, not me. I'm going back up north to finish school and to start my own business.

Larry grabbed his pack of cigarettes off the counter and lit one up. Taking a deep drag, he blew smoke into the air.

"There're folks doing just fine here, some better than others I must say."

"Man, my dream is much bigger than this down here. I'm going to own my own business one day, and I'm going to educate my people."

Larry looked at the young man in a strange way, because he had heard that same statement before. *But who said…where was I at?* Then a light bulb went off in his head. He removed his cigarette from his mouth.

"You know…, you sound just like this girl who came through here a few months back.

"Oh yeah."

"Yeah. She was a pretty little thing. At first glance, I thought she was a white girl. But then I saw her kicking it with some of the kids who clean my tables in the evening. I overheard her telling her friends about all these big plans for herself. So out of curiosity, I walked over and asked her if she had finished school, and she told me no. I asked her how she thought she was going to do all these big things without an education, and she said that she was heading up north to attend college or something like that. Oh, that's what it was…poor girl said she was going to Howard University."

Howard, Howard… James Jr. heart started to beat fast.

"Howard… That's the University I graduated from!"

Larry took another hit from his cigarette and released the smoke into the air.

"Well, she acted like she sure knew what she was talking about. She talked about Fraternities and Sororities. She said something about joining AKA. She even said that she was going to be the first black woman to…. Now what did she say."

He thought for a few seconds but couldn't remember what she said, so he brushed it off.

"Anyway, the girl was really pretty, but she looked dirty and hungry. I asked her if she wanted something to eat and need a place to stay for a spell. You know with our kids all grown and gone, me and my wife got plenty of space. And show'nuff she said yes. So, we took her in. She ate little and slept a lot. She was no problem at all. Then one day, out of nowhere, she told us thanks for the hospitality and left. She was a nice bright girl. She told us that she was from down around your way."

James Jr. was very interested in Larry's story. As if someone was spying on him, he looked around to see if anyone was listening to their conversation. Satisfied that no one was, he leaned toward Larry.

"What was her name?" he asked quietly.

Rubbing his chin, he looked up at the ceiling and started to think.

"Now, what was that child's name? It started with a b...Billie Boo, Bobby Joe...."

James Jr. wanted to assist him. But before he said anything, he looked to the right then to the left again.

"Was it Betty Jean?" he asked shyly.

Larry snapped his finger and smiled as soon as he heard the name.

"That's it! That's it! Betty Jean!"

With excitement, James Jr. fumbling in his pants pocket and pulled out a picture. He showed it to him.

"Is this her?"

Pulling his eye glasses out of his shirt pocket for a better look, Larry took the picture.

"Yep, that's her. What.... Is she in some kind of trouble?" he asked while handing it back to him.

"No she's not in no trouble," he said as he put the picture back into his pants pocket. "She just had a fallen out with her family, and they don't know where she is."

"So how did you come to get that picture of her? Is she your girlfriend?"

He smiled at the idea.

"No. I saw her mother's friend a few days ago at the General Store. I asked her how the Carter family was doing, and that's when she told me what went down with them. I mean my dad told me that she just up and ran away. But Mrs. Vivian gave me the whole scoop."

Larry took one last hit of his cigarette then put it out in the bar sink.

"Oh, so that's the girl's last name... Carter?"

"Yeah. Mrs. Vivian said her and the girl's mother were passing out flyers with her picture on it and stuff. They're hoping that somebody might have seen her, so she gave me one. You're the first person I showed it to."

Larry took a small glass and poured himself a shot of liquor. Taking it to the head in one gulp, he squirmed a little.

"Tell me this, what is the daddy doing about her disappearance?"

"Not a damn thing, in my opinion. She's not his biological daughter, so I really don't think he cares."

"Damn, that's deep young blood!"

James Jr. sat there in deep thought. Larry didn't disturb him for a few seconds. Then *snap, snap* of the fingers. He brought the young man back to reality.

"Hey buddy don't you got somewhere to go...something to do?"

He looked at him.

"Yes, I sure do. Hey thanks for the cold one man," he said as he got up to leave.

Larry took a wet cloth out of the sink and started wiping the counter down.

"Anytime my man...anytime. I'll be praying for her, and you." James Jr. waved his hand in acknowledgement and left the Shack.

28

WITHIN ABOUT 30 minutes, James Jr. was standing at the Carter's front door. Sweat was running down his forehead from the combination of heat and nervousness. He remembered what Joe had told him about being on his property. Hesitantly, he raised his hand to knock on the door, but quickly put it down. He raised it again and then put it back down again. Before he thought about what might happen, he knocked on the screen door. A few seconds later Jackie appeared. She didn't greet him right away. She just stared at him while chewing her gum. She even had the nerve to blow a few big bubbles before addressing him. "Can I help you?" she asked with an attitude.

"Yes, is Mrs. Carter home?"

Jackie didn't answer him.

"Mama, some man at the door asking for you!" she yelled and walked away.

James Jr. shook his head, because he knew that the girl knew who he was.

"Who is it? I'm washing your sister's hair!" Lilly Mae yelled from the kitchen and waited for an answer.

When she didn't receive one, she yelled again.

"I said who it is?!"

Jackie was half-way down the hallway when she heard her mother yelling at her, but didn't respond. She knew who the man was, but didn't want to say his name. The name she had a crush on from day one of meeting him. The name who didn't know she existed. The name who seemed to be only interested in her oldest sister. Leaning against the hallway wall, she lowered herself to the floor and pondered. *Should I ask him his name? Dummy you know good and well who he is. Stop acting like a child. No, I don't want to say his name. He didn't even notice me staring at him. He was all up in Betty Jeans face. Go ahead…be a smart ass. Look dumb and ask him his name.*

"My mama wants to know who you is?!"

Hearing her voice, but not being able to see her, he leaned his head against the screen door to see if he could. But she was too far down the hallway to be seen. He cleared his throat.

"It's James Henry. Tell her James Henry Jr. is at the door?" he said with a deep masculine voice.

Immediately, he went to the top of the step and stood there. He did this to get a jump-start on getting away, just in case Joe came out acting stupid.

Jackie was about to yell to her mother, but Lilly Mae was already standing in the hallway removing her apron.

"I asked you who is it child?"

Looking at her mother, she blew a big bubble and then removed it for her mouth.

"James Henry Jr."

When she heard the name, Lilly Mae took off running for the door. When she got there, she didn't even think about giving him a piece of her mind.

"Did you…did you find out anything about my baby?!"

"Yes ma'am, I do believe so."

Lilly Mae began to weep. Finally, she heard the words that she had been praying for.

"What…what did you find out? What did you hear? Is she alright? Where is she?"

"Now Mrs. Carter, it's not a whole lot, but it's something."

"Tell me…tell me that my baby is ok!"

Now while words were being exchanged by the two of them, Jamie was still standing with her head under the running water. She became inpatient.

"Mama, is you finished with my hair! I'm tired of standing here like this!"

Joe, who was oblivious to what was going on, was in his favorite room reading the newspaper. He was trying to tolerate the girls yelling, but Jamie's big mouth was the straw that broke the camel's back.

"Look, stop that yelling in this house! I done told y'all about that!"

Jackie, who was still sitting on the floor, looked down the hallway. Lilly Mae vaguely heard her husband's voice and said nothing. Putting her finger up to her mouth, she told the young man to be quiet.

"Mrs. Carter, is everything ok?"

She didn't answer.

Joe waited for a response, but the only answer he got was the faint sound of a man's voice. Instantly, he was up and heading toward the voice. He had heard the voice earlier, but dismissed it as one of the boys playing.

"Who is that Lilly Mae?! Is that a man's voice I hear?!"

Lilly Mae remained quiet.

"Woman, do you hear me talking to you?! Who is that out there?!" As Joe's voice got closer, James Jr. slowly descended down the steps backward. He didn't want any trouble.

"Maybe I should come back another time Mrs. Carter."

Lilly Mae reached out and grabbed his arm before he could take another step down.

"No, no, please don't go. I need to know where my baby is."

Joe passed Jackie without saying a word to her.

"Who the hell...!"

When he got to the front door, he stopped dead in his tracks when he saw James Jr. Pushing the screen door open with force, he walked out onto the porch. As he did so, James Jr. quickly ran down the rest of the steps to put more distances between them. Not one to punk out from a fight, he displayed a defensive stance. But Joe didn't go after him. He stopped at the top of the steps.

"We'll look what the wind done blew in. What's going on? How's life in the city?" he asked sarcastically, and then abruptly grabbed his wife by the neck. "Go get that child now."

He pushed her toward the door, causing her to lose her balance. Grabbing the wicker chair's arm, she stopped herself from falling.

"Mr. Carter, please!" James Jr. yelled as he took a few steps forward.

After Lilly Mae regained her balance, she put her hand out to stop the young man from taking another step.

"I want to know what's happening with my baby."

Joe turned and pointed at the door.

"Your baby is in the kitchen yelling for you. Now go shut her up!"

James Henry detected that something wasn't right between the both of them. And he didn't want any part of it. He just wanted to deliver the information he got.

"I'll just come back. I see it's a bad time."

"Yeah, that's right. It *is* a bad time. Now go on about your damn business. We don't need no interference in our life from you.

As James Jr. started walking away, Lilly Mae stared at him. In a silent panic, the idea of not hearing the information he had about her daughter scared her. *If he leaves now there's no telling when he'll be back. Lord if I don't take a stand for my daughter, I'll never find her.*

She looked over at Joe, who was smiling while rocking back and forth with his hands in his pants pocket. He looked as if he was actually enjoying the situation. He was in control and loving every minute of it. Her heart told her, *Fight or flight...which one girl? You know once he gets into that car...he might not come back..., and you can kiss your little Betty Jean good-bye. Once he gets into that car...whatever courage you thought you had will be gone. It will be another opportunity to stand for what's right. gone. The strength you thought you had...gone. And he... Mr. Intimidation has won again.* She felt her blood pressure boiling. Her palms became sweaty. Her heart was beating way to fast. *If you don't say something, you will never know where your daughter is.* Tightness was in her chest. In slow motion, she visualized him getting into his car. Her mind taunted her...scaredy-cat, scaredy-cat, scaredy-cat, scaredy-cat. Louder and louder the taunting became, until she couldn't take it anymore.

"No!" she screamed as she grabbed her head.

She ran pass her husband and down the steps. Grabbing James Henry arm, she stopped him from taking another step.

"Please don't leave. Tell me...tell me where she is! Tell me what you know!"

Joe looked at her like she was crazy. He was mad as hell.

"Woman! What did I tell you to do?!" he yelled and ran after her.

Catching her off guard, he grabbed her hair from behind.

"What do you think you're doing?!"

Lilly Mae screamed to the top of her lungs. But it wasn't out of being scared of her husband; it was out of fear; fear of going through life without ever finding her daughter. It was from being pissed off from years of Joe's mental bondage. It was from not stepping up to the plate, when she had the opportunity to protect her Betty Jean. It was from the lack of protection her mother didn't give her when her father abused her.

"Damn you! Get off of me!"

Grabbing his pointy finger, she pulled it backward so far, you would have thought she broke it. In pain, he screamed and let her hair go. While cradling his hurt finger with his other hand, Lilly Mae took the opportunity of a life time. She gave him a two-piece right to the kisser. *Whop! Whop!* Her punch was so fierce; it knocked him to the ground. She busted his lip, causing blood to spatter on his shirt. He laid there for a moment spitting out blood. The more he saw his blood, the more upset he became.

"I'm going to...!"

As he attempted to get up, Lilly Mae kicked the holy mess out of his stomach.

"You bitch!" he screamed and fell back down.

She commenced to kicking the hell out of him.

"I'm sick of your shit! I'm fucking sick and tired of you!"

In trying to protect himself, he rolled away from her. But whichever way he rolled, she was right on him kicking the mess out of him. Lilly Mae was kicking him so bad James Jr. couldn't bear to watch anymore.

"Mrs. Carter, please, that's enough!" he yelled as he ran over to her and grabbed her by the waist.

"Let me go! Let me the hell go!"

He tried his best to hold her back but couldn't. Tired of tussling with her, he let her go. She ran right back over to Joe, and gave him one last powerful kick to the ribs. *Bam!*

"Now you stay down there until I hear what this young man has to say! I want to know where my baby is!"

Groaning, Joe rolled over holding his stomach from the excruciating pain. Slowly, he tried to get up again.

"Woman, I'm going to whip you're a."

Before he could finish, Lilly Mae whipped out a small, sharp, pocket knife from nowhere. With authority, she pointed it at him. Immediately, he shut up. He'd never known Lilly Mae to carry a knife before. For that matter, hit him either and with such power. He attempted to gain control of the situation.

"Woman…what the *hell* is wrong with you?!"

With piercing eyes and a deep voice, she told him real slow, "So help me God, I will cut your throat if you make one more move."

By the sound of her voice, which he'd never heard before, he knew that she was serious. He didn't move a muscle. Keeping the blade on him, she looked over at James Jr.

"Now please…, please tell me what you found out about Betty Jean."

He waited a few seconds to make sure all was calm before talking. And when he saw that it was, he took a deep breath and began.

"Earlier, I was at the Shack taken care of some business for my daddy with Larry Busha, the owner. After all business was said and done, we started drinking and talking about this and that. Well, I was drinking pop, and he was drinking liquor. Anyway, somehow some words I said to him triggered a memory of this girl who came through some time ago. He said him and his wife took the young girl in, because she didn't have a place to stay, and she looked hungry and dirty. So I asked him what the girl name was, and he said her name was Betty Jean."

"That don't mean a…!" Joe blurted out.

"Shut up Joe!" Lilly Mae yelled.

He snickered a little but shut up.

"That's what I was thinking too. I showed him a picture of her that I got from Mrs. Vivian and."

"Picture...? What are you. Why would she give you a picture of her?" Joe asked.

Pissed off with his dumb question, Lilly Mae kicked dirt at him.

"Shut up! Shut up! Shut up!"

He covered his face to prevent the dirt from getting into his eyes.

"Alright...alright stop kicking dirt at me!"

"And that's when he said that's her. She told him that she was heading up north to attend Howard University. Mrs. Carter, Howard is one of the schools I told her about. That's the school I graduated from."

Sitting up, Joe took a handkerchief out of his pants pocket to wipe his face.

"Well isn't that nice. Now the both of you can play house up there and ruin each other's life," he said sarcastically.

Pathetically, James Jr. stared at him.

"With all due respect, first of all...I'm not up there anymore; I graduated. Secondly...it seems to me that you've already done that. That's why she's not here now."

At hearing the good news, Lilly Mae put the knife back in its hiding place. She swiftly turned on her heels and headed for the house. She dashed past the kids, who were all now standing on the front porch. A few moments later, she reappeared with her pocket book in one hand and car keys in the other. Running down the steps, she made a beeline straight to the family car. Swaying a little, Joe stood up.

"Lilly Mae Carter, where in the *hell* do you think you're going?!"

Lilly Mae motioned for the young man to follow her to the car and he did so.

"I'm going to find my baby Joe! she yelled back as she looked at James Jr. "You know your way around Washington, D.C.?"

"Yes ma'am."

She opened the driver's side of the door.

"Will you come with me to help find her?"

He couldn't believe his ears.

"Excuse me...did you just ask me to help you look for Betty Jean in D.C.?"

"Yes, that's what I said. I didn't stutter. Will you, or wont'cha?"

Slowly, he smiled. The fact that he was going to find his dream girl was surreal to him.

"Yes ma'am I'll go. But we should take my car. I don't know if yours will make the trip."

"Woman you can't leave me here with these kids! I don't know what to do with them!"

Ignoring his comment, they both walked over to James Jr. car. He opened the passenger door for Lilly Mae, and she got in without even looking at her husband. Closing the door, he ran around to the driver's side and hopped in; starting the car right up. Lilly Mae popped her head out of the window and yelled bye to the children. They waved back.

"Bye Mama! See you when you get home! And bring us something good back ok! I hope you find her!"

The car took off down the road.

"Lilly Mae...what about these kids!"

Sticking her head out the window she looked back at Joe.

"Learn Negro! Learn to do something with them! And don't be bothering my mama! As a matter of fact, while I'm gone, you better get yourself some type of counseling for your problem! Because when I get back, and if my kids tell me you hurt them in any kind of way...Lord knows I'll kill you!"

Smiling, she waved to her babies again.

"Bye kids! I'll see you when I get back! Love you! Be good for grandma!"

The kids ran down the driveway after them. When the car turned on the main road, they stopped running. Laughing and playing, they all headed back up to the house. They were happy that their mother was bringing Betty Jean back home. Playfully, Johnny picked up a handful of dirt and threw it at Jamie's wet, soapy hair. Her mother totally forgot to wash it all out.

"Daddy, tell him to stop throwing dirt at me! And what about my hair...who's going to wash this stuff out?!"

She looked at Jackie, who was laughing her butt off.

"Don't look at me. I don't want to do my own hair."

Standing on the porch Joe watched the kids walk back up the driveway. Out of frustration, he took a deep breath.

"Y'all stop playing around! Come on now...get on up here! Come on get in this house!"

"Last one in the house is a rotten egg!" Johnny yelled, and they took off running.

29

*T*HE RIDE UP North was a long one. Lilly Mae had no idea that it would take about twenty hours to reach D.C. The only thing she was thinking about was getting up North to find her baby. They decided to take turns driving every three hours, to give each other a break from the wheel. It went pretty smooth, for the most part. However, there were a few times when Lilly Mae got confused with the directions James Jr. told her before he dosed off to sleep. They would be well into 45 minutes out of their way, before she decided to wake him up, to tell him that she took the wrong exit. After Lilly Mae did that for about three times, he decided to drive the rest of the way himself. He really wanted to do all the driving in the first place. The only thing he needed for the trip was a few Cokes to drink and the radio. But Lilly Mae insisted on helping with the driving since it was her daughter they were going after.

They didn't talk much on the ride there. Lilly Mae was caught up in wondering what her daughter was going through in D.C. Questions were popping up in her head every few minutes. Before she could figure out a possible answer to one, another would be standing by. The realization of the situation was that she could only speculate; she didn't have a clue as to how life in D.C. was. However, on the other hand, he knew. That's what pre-occupied his mind.

He remembered how difficult it was for him to adjust to the Washingtonians attitude. It was nothing like home. Down south when you greeted folks, they would smile and speak back. You could be passing by homes in your car or truck, and people would wave to you from their front porch, just because. The south was laid back. But, in D.C., if you spoke to people, and they didn't know you, they were ready to cut your throat, so to speak. He thought Washingtonians were mean as all got out.

Remembering one occasion, when he had a taste for some liver and onions, he caught the 92 bus up to the Florida Avenue Grill. He sat in the back of the bus minding his own business, when these young dudes got on. They all headed to the back of the bus where he was sitting. For no apparent reason, they started to mean mug him. Ignoring them, James Jr. looked out the window. Then all of a sudden they started talking about him to the max. They even started talking about his mama. To this day, he doesn't know why they picked on him. He speculated that it could have been because of the way he looked, or the way he was dressed. On the other hand, it could have been just because. On another occasion, he and some friends were out joy riding in the Adams Morgan area. When they passed a white lady riding her 10-speed bike, one of them reached out and smacked the lady's butt, as they drove by. They all died laughing.

The long ride definitely gave them plenty of time to think. And they were now in Virginia, approaching the 14th Street Bridge via 395. As they crossed the bridge, he showed Lilly Mae the Pentagon Building. She had seen pictures of the building in books and stuff, but to see it in person, and to see how huge the parking lot was fascinated her. The anticipation of arriving in D.C. increased when she saw from a distance the historical landmarks she had read about and seen on T.V. As a symbol, to her, the Monument, Jefferson Memorial and Lincoln Memorial were saying, "Welcome to the Nation's Capital."

"Oh my goodness! It's so beautiful here!" she said with excitement.

James didn't respond. He knew that on the other side of town, where they were headed, was a whole different ball game.

When they crossed over the 14th Street Bridge, he pointed out to her the Bureau of Engraving Building.

"That's where they make the money."

He also pointed out to her The Department of Agriculture Building. They continued to ride up 14th Street until they got to Thomas Circle. They went around the circle, and continued up to 14 Street; crossing over U Street. The area that they were in was considered the red-light district. Hookers and prostitutes with little to nothing on were on the strip. Pimps with stack heel shoes, and a walking cane were on the street parading around. They all were seeking that all mighty dollar; showing off their new rags; selling drugs and looking for the next female or male victim to add to their stable.

In amazement, Lilly Mae's mouth dropped open from the colorful site. However, at the same time, she was a little concerned.

"Um...why are we here in this area. You don't think my Betty Jean is somewhere around *here*...do you?"

He didn't answer. His demeanor seemed to have changed once they got into the red-light district.

"I asked you a question."

After a few minutes of looking at the people on the street, he answered her.

"This here is a very bad area. It's what you call the red-light district; the strip. You see what's going on out there...? It's Friday night and everybody, but their mama is out. Weekends are always jumping. I'mma cruise the strip to see what's going on."

Lilly Mae didn't say a word. And they continued up the street in hopes of seeing Betty Jean. Truth be told, he already knew nothing was really going on around the Howard University area. He just wanted to check the hot spots first before heading that direction.

While driving up the strip, Lilly Mae saw a huge, dark skin man decked out in a lime-green suit with lime green stack heel shoes on. He also had on a big, black hat with a lime green floppy brim. Not believing her eyes, she had to take a double look. He had this white chick pinned up against a fence. He was yelling something about getting money, and she was screaming something about don't beat me daddy. They drove by an ally and saw a man throwing up some kind of bad. When they stopped for a red light at 14th and W Street, they saw a man standing on the edge of the curve nodding out. Lilly Mae stared at him because he was nodding so close to oncoming traffic. But just as he was about to lean into traffic, he stood up and started nodding out again.

They went all the way up just pass Park Road to a place called Bob's Inn. Not seeing Betty Jean, James Jr. made a U-turn and headed back down the strip. When they got to 14th and V, the light turned red. As they waited for the light to turn green, they saw a woman who had on a long, shiny, blond wig with hardly anything on, standing on the corner. Waving to them, she ran over to the car and started rubbing her breast.

"Hey baby, what you looking for? I got what you need right here."

Lilly Mae was taken aback.

"Oh my Lord…"

"Trick, get on away from here!" James Jr. yelled.

Hearing Lilly Mae's voice the young girl bent down to look inside the car.

"I'm…I'm sorry. I didn't see the little lady. But, you know it's whatever. I can work with that too."

As soon as the light turned green, James Jr. took off. He almost ran over the girl's feet, if not for her quick reflexes.

"Hey what the. Oh, it's like that! Well fuck you nigga! Y'all probable can't handle this hot ass pussy any motherfucking way. bitch!"

After the useless yelling, she pinpointed another potential customer pulling up to the light, on the opposite side of the street. Quickly changing her attitude, she ran over to the car.

"Hey daddy."

Lilly Mae was scared to death. She had never been exposed to such street life. Looking into the rear-view mirror, she saw the girl running over to the other car.

"What in the world…?"

"She's just a hooker. Don't let any of that bother you. She's used to people talking to her that way."

Looking in the side-view mirror, she saw the girl getting into a white car.

"Well…I guess you're right. She just got into somebody's car back there."

"See, I know this city. Don't worry about a thing. We're going to get through this. We'll find Betty Jean and bring her back home."

Lilly Mae stared at all the street activity going on.

"I've *never* seen nothing like this before in my life."

"Well with the way you handled your husband, I don't know… you surprised me. Now, here in D.C., that happens all the time. Are you sure you don't have a little city life in you?"

"As God is my witness, there's no city what so ever in me. I was just fed up with my husband's way of doing things."

"I could see that, that's for sure." He laughed.

When they got to U Street, James Jr. made a left turn, and headed east. As they were going down the street, to the left of them, they heard a loud commotion. As they got closer, they saw a huge crowd in front of a night club called the Republic Gardens. That place was always packed on the weekends. They saw that the commotion was coming from two heavy set colored female's. They were fighting, and the crowd was cheering them on. The crowd was so huge, it spilled over, passing the Lincoln Theater, to a little joint called Bens Chili Bowl.

When they got to Vermont and U, he made a right turn to check that area out. He hit T Street, S Street, and R Street. He also went through a few alleys. While driving, Lilly Mae looked at the neighborhood and shook her head in shame.

"I just can't imagine my baby being here all by herself."

The young man didn't respond. He just kept driving and looking. Somehow, he already knew what was up. The dilemma for him was how to tell her. His mind was spinning. *Should I or should I not. Should I or should I not.* But his heart told him, *tell her a little bit, because Betty Jean might be ok. No need in getting the old girl all upset for nothing.*

"Mrs. Carter if I know D.C., and I do know D.C.; Betty Jean isn't out on these streets. Somebody has got a hold of that girl. And if you knew what *I* knew…well, we just got to find her like yesterday before it's too late."

Bewildered, Lilly Mae stared at him.

"Too late for what?"

He was surprised at her question. And for the first-time, he truly looked at Lilly Mae and realized that she didn't know a thing when it comes to street life.

"Ma'am, have you ever been anywhere else besides Louisiana?"
"No. For what?"

He didn't answer her.

"Let's just find your daughter."

They were now on 6 and T Street, which was a well-known drug area. It was also well known because of Howard Theater. Famous acts like Lena Horne, Pearl Bailey, Sammy Davis Jr., Duke Ellington, Ella Fitzgerald and Billie Eckstein performed there.

After looking around on that end, he decided to head on up Georgia Avenue. That's where his alma mater was located. The Wonder Bread Factory was also there. They said the smell of fresh-baked bread was heaven.

As he drove up the street, he smiled at seeing that nothing had changed. *Same old, same old* he thought. People were standing around not doing a thing. Music was blasting from cars; girls prancing around in their tight shorts and the brothers were still playing it cool when they saw a fine chick pass by.

As they approached the University, he pointed it out.

"This is Howard, the school your daughter was talking about.

"This is a huge school. All these kids out here go to this school?"

"I don't think so. Some are probably just hanging out. But some are from out of town, I'm quite sure. Mrs. Carter, let me express what I've found out from attending this school. You see it's not just about getting away from home; it's also about meeting new people; what the school can do to enhance you as a person, as well as your education. There are a lot of reasons why people rather go away to school. You don't have to stay in your home town just to get an education. You know I didn't find myself—my inner self, until I came to school here. There were so many challenges and debates of the mind at Howard. I loved it. I mean to see people from all walks of life, with different beliefs and…." He paused to reminisce. "Man it's beautiful. Having a proper education is beautiful. Knowledge is beautiful. I seek it and God's word *every* day."

Lilly Mae stared at him. Then out of guilt, she looked away. After listening to him, she now realized how she kept her daughter from expanding her mind. She had stopped her from her dreams, just like Pearl stopped her from going to Clemson University in South Caroline, to study foreign languages. When she asked her mother if she could apply, Pearl told her no; you're going to LSU. Pearl even told her what her Major was going to be: Communications. And so, that's what she did. She majored in something that she didn't have a love for. Therefore, she hadn't found a job in her field, nor was she really even looking for one. She believed that Pearl was trying to live her life through her. And here she was doing the same thing to Betty Jean.

Lilly Mae was startled out of her thoughts, when she heard a loud car horn sounding like music.

"What the…?"

She saw a psychedelic car decorated with all kinds of junk on it pass by. It had long, slim, what looked to be brass horns, along with small toys and small plastic wind mills on it. As if this was the norm, the kids outside the school yelled out his name, and the man blew his musical horn back at them.

When James Jr. saw the car, he got excited.

"Man, God is good! That's Country! And if anybody knows what's happening around here, he does."

He took off like white lighting trying to catch him. And he did as the next light turned red. He looked over at the older man and saw that he still looked crazy as ever. He blew his horn at him.

"Country! My main man! What's happening?!"

The man in the funny-looking car looked over and yelled back like he had known James Jr. for years. But in actuality, he didn't know who he was, from a hill of beans.

"Hey buddy what's going on...long time no see!

Displaying a slick smile, James Jr. looked over at Lilly Mae, winked at her, then looked back at Country.

"Nothing much man, I'm just trying to find some fresh, young skin in the area. Me and this bitch here is trying to have a little fun tonight with some young stuff; know what I'm saying!"

Excited, Country shook his head really fast.

"Oh yeah, I know just what you're saying."

He looked over at Lilly Mae and noticed how she kept her eyes straight ahead.

"Man, I've never seen that trick before. Where you cop that pretty thing from?"

Rubbing his hands together as if he just stumbled upon a gold mine, he told him, "South baby...you know all the best ones come from down south. They're fat, fresh, and pretty as they want to be. Man, now I *know* you know where that young meat is. Come on now...hook a brother up!"

"Yes sir. Yep, yep, I know... I know. I had a young girl four days ago. Suck my dick so good made me cry for my mama. Look here... you go on over to Big Moe's House. When you get there, tell the doorkeeper that I said to hook y'all up with Nice-n-Tight. I'll call to let them know that..."

Confused, he stopped in mid-sentence. He just realized that he didn't know who the hell he was talking to and tried to play it off.

"Hey my man...it's been so long, I forgot your name."

James Jr. had to think fast.

"Oh come on man...it's me...James Jr., but you called me 92 because you would always see me catching the 92 bus up to the

Grill. You used to pick me up whenever you saw me standing at the bus stop on the corner...remember?"

Country tried to jog his memory. But truth be told, that Negro couldn't remember a thing because he was a little touched in the head. People called him Country because he was a little too friendly for their blood. If he saw a person in need, he would always help them out, regardless if he knew them or not. Plus, with the way that car was looking and sounding, people just thought he was from the country.

When he heard the name, which didn't ring a bell, he acted like he remembered.

"Oh yeah, yeah, that's right. Ok I'll tellum you want the special. You're going to like that."

"Man who is this Nice-n-tight? Is that her real name?"

Country squint his face up something ugly.

"No fool! That's what she calls herself. She got a little girl's face, and her ass is soft and fat as a baby's behind. Go check her out. Sweeeeeeeet!"

"Ok, I'll do that."

The light turned green and they both pulled off going their separate ways.

"What the *hell* was that all about? I might be slow, but I'm not stuck on stupid."

While turning down an alley and heading back to 14th and U, he apologized.

"I'm sorry but if I wasn't down with the slang, I would have never gotten anything out of Country. That brother knows all and tells nothing unless you're cool with the game...sex game that is."

"What the heck is a sex game?"

"There are a lot of older dudes up here who love young girls... real young. They would give their last dime just to have pleasure with them, if you know what I mean. What I'm thinking is this.

Betty Jean probably didn't have any money for a place to stay or food to eat on her way up here. So she probably did what she had to do to survive. Get what I'm saying."

She got it alright and burst out crying. She shook her head in denial. She didn't want to believe all that was taking place. She prayed out loud.

"Lord Jesus, please God, give me the strength to get through this. Please forgive me Lord for not protecting your child. I'm sorry Lord. I'm so sorry. Please forgive me. Help me find your child Lord. Help me find her in good health."

Pulling a white handkerchief from her pocketbook, she wiped the tears from her eyes. James Jr. didn't say a thing. He continued down more dark alleys until he reached 14th Street again. He made a left turn back onto the street and headed for U Street. When he got there, he made a left turn and immediately got into the right-hand lane. Further up the street, he saw a car pull out, that was parked right across the street from the club.

"Hot dog, the Lord must be with us!"

He eased right on in that parking space and turned the car off. Scoping the activities up and down the street, he noticed the large crowd had disbursed. Small groups of people were now hanging out in front of the club. He had also noticed that there were men going in and out of the alley between the Lincoln Theater and Bens Chili Bowel.

Curiosity got the best of him.

"Sit here for a minute."

Before Lilly Mae could respond, he was running across the street to Bens Chile Bowl. Through a nice size window on the front, she watched as he started talking to a dude sitting at the counter. She also saw him repeatedly looking out at her while pointing at the car. Suddenly, with a big ole smile, the dude stood up and waved to Lilly Mae. And doing what comes natural, she smiled and waved back. At her response, both men burst out laughing. As they continued to talk, the guy turned and pointed to the back of the store. More words and laughter were exchanged by both men, as one of the attendants gave James Jr. a brown bag. In return, he gave the attendant some money. Within a few minutes, he was running back to the car. Lilly Mae saw him coming and unlocked the door. He got in.

"Why did you lock the doors and roll up the windows?"

"Why you think…? I don't know nothing about this place. I don't know who is who, or what is what."

He smiled at her, because she was thinking outside the box. He would have done the same thing if he was in her shoes.

He opened the brown bag and pulled out two sandwiches.

"Are you hungry? I got two hot half-smokes with chili."

Lilly Mae took the half-smoke and opened the foil. The wonderful smell lit the car up. After taking a big bite of the sandwich, her eyes went up in her head and her taste buds done went to heaven.

"This is really good. I wish we had this back home." She took another big bite.

Smiling, he bit into his. "Um…um, one of D.C.'s finest eating spots.

While looking at the action across the street, he took another bite and wiped his mouth with his napkin. He continued to eat while talking.

"Now look here. We're going to have to do some roll playing to get up in Big Moe's House."

"That sign says The Republic Gardens, not Big Moe's House."

"Right, that's the Club."

He pointed to the alley between the Lincoln Theater and Bens Chili Bowel.

"Big Moe's House is down there around the corner.

"How do you know that?"

"Mrs. Carter, book studying ain't the only thing I was studying up here. Anyway, you see all those people in front of the club?"

"Yes."

"Notice anything about them?"

She looked and looked, but didn't notice a thing.

"I don't see nothing but people all dressed up going in and out of the place."

"Right. Now look down that dark alley. What do you see?"

She stared for a few minutes, but still didn't notice a thing.

"I don't see…"

"Look harder."

Lilly Mae literally squint her eyes, but still didn't notice anything.

"I don't notice a darn thing. All I see is a hand full of men getting in and out of their cars."

"Bingo! Look, most of those men have suits on. And they are getting in and out of nice cars *and* limos. That's where I do believe your daughter is right now. Don't ask me why, but something is telling me that she's there."

"But that's an alley."

"Yes I know, but the house is down that way. You have to make a right, and pass some garages where mechanics are working on cars. The house is located on V Street. I knew of Big Moe's House, but never knew exactly where it was. So, the guy you saw me talking to, told me what was what after I broke him off a little something. He told me that there's a special entrance for customers in the back. And depending on how fat your pockets are…you either go through the front door or the back; back being better. He said that most of the high-profile folks went in that way."

"High profile. What do you mean by that?"

"Well, you got your doctors, lawyers, the mayor, congressmen, big-business owners, artists and what-not. They might want to cut loose and get buck wild for a minute. But they don't want anyone to know their business. So they call the house and speak directly to the Madam who runs the place."

"Madam…?"

"She's the one that runs the joint. You know., like scheduling the girls and sometimes guys with clients. But an old dude name Moe owns the house.

"Guys…! What the…"

"Yes guys, Mrs. Carter. All men don't want to be with women you know. And they sure don't want their significant others or the public, to know that, for real, for real…*men* are their preference. The Madam makes sure that all these high-profile people needs are met no matter how freaky their sexual desires are."

"Are you serious?!"

"Well you never know what a person's preference is."

"Well, I don't care about the people you're talking about. I'm just shocked that my little baby might be in an environment like that. If she is in there, we have *got* to get her out."

"That's why I have a plan."

"Let's hear it," she said as she finished her food.

He also finished off his and then pulled out another one. He bit into it.

"Um…um… This is *so* good. Now here's the plan. I'm going to act like I'm your pimp, and you're going to act like you're my whore. I'm going to be really pissed off at you and cussing you out, because you came up short with my money for tonight. I'm going to literally drag you down the alley. While I'm doing that, I'm going to be yelling that I owe Moe some money, and that you're going to work that ass off until the debt is paid in full. This is just to get pass those folks in the alley. For all I know, they could be look-out boys for the house."

Lilly Mae understood the plan, but didn't appreciate his language usage.

"My goodness, do you have to be so vulgar with...."

He cut her off because he knew the clock was ticking. The more time that passed the worse it could be for the girl of his dreams.

"Look...do you want to find her or not?!"

"Yes," she said with a high pitch voice.

"Then follow my lead; ok!"

As soon as his words were out of his mouth, he started readjusting his clothes to not look so neat in appearance.

"Pull your skirt up to your thighs."

"Excuse you?!"

Finishing off his sandwich, he pulled his shirt out of his pants and opened a few bottoms on his shirt.

"You heard me. Pull your skirt up to your thighs. And open your blouse some. You look too proper to be a prostitute."

Lilly Mae just sat there staring out the window. This was too much for her. Shaking her head, she didn't want to believe what she was about to do.

"Come on now, get a move on. We don't have time to waste." Reluctantly, she got in gear.

"You got any makeup?"

"No."

When James Jr. reached over to open his glove compartment, he accidentally brushed her leg. A little surprised, she waited for an apology, but received none. He reached into the compartment and took out a thin black magic marker.

"Here, put this on, over your eye lids."

She took the marker and with the help of the side-view mirror, applied it like it was eyeliner. From the arm rest, he pulled out a small jar of Vaseline and handed it to her.

"Put some of this on your lips."

"Huh?"

"No wait. Take this first."

He reached into his pants pocket and pulled out a cherry Now and Later candy. He opened half of it and gave it to her.

"Suck on this for a minute. After it melts down, rub it on your lips. Then take the Vaseline and rub over it. It will make you look like you have on red lip stick. And while you're at it, let your hair down."

Taking a deep breath, she did as she was told.

When everything was all said, and done, Lilly Mae fit right in with the crowd. As long as she didn't speak, you would have thought that she was from D.C. Getting out the car, they ran across the street, into the dark alley.

30

OVER AT BIG Moe's House, things were going pretty smooth as usual. A lot of high rollers were in the house. That's how it always was on the weekends. The bartender had the guest preference of drinks abundantly available. Men socialized personally and professionally while smoking Cuban cigars, supplied by the Madam of course. Some of the little ladies of the night were displaying their goodies in fine lingerie, while lounging around on a red velvet couch and matching love seat. Other's periodically walked down a long hallway to a door that had a red light blinking above it. That door lead to the front of the house where irregular costumers waited.

A house attendant, who was stationed at the front door, would ask the men what their pleasure was; which was a wham, bam, thank you ma'am, most of the time. And in return, the attendant would collect the price for such pleasure. Then with a push of a white button on the wall, a red light would blink on the other side of the door. This would summon the girls to come up front to take care of the customers.

The Madam developed this system to keep up with all money earned in the house. Plus, the system was developed to keep up with the whereabouts' of all her workers. When a girl was summoned for the front business, she would first report to the Madams office, which was located in the back of the house. The Madam would check the girl Out of Commission (OOC) on her chart of employees before going to the front. After the girl finished off her customer, she would report back to the Madam. She then would put her Back in Commission (BIC). This way if a high roller with an appointment came in, and didn't see his regular girl already waiting for him, she would tell him that his special lady of the night was preparing herself for him.

For the front business, the price was always the same, so it was just a matter of keeping up with the number of times the ladies were in and out up there. However, for the distinguished, regular high-paying guest list, that was a horse of another color. What they desired sexually was coded along with the price, in the Madams little leather black book of names. That price was charged to their credit card, which she obtained from them in advance. That way when the men came to enjoy themselves, they didn't have to worry about paying the girls directly. She thought that it was tacky in doing so. Upon the arrival of her guest, all they had to do was check in with her, and she did the rest.

The Madam was always in her office, unless there was a serious problem, which was very rare. She would be seated behind her mahogany desk, dressed in business attire. Her preferred apparel made her stand out from the rest of her employees. It also reminded the ladies of who the boss was. Her suits were always by a name-brand designer and her shoes were top of the line stilettos. And unlike the little ladies of the night, she never wore four or five different gold bracelets and necklaces at one time. One of the young employees noticed it and questioned her about that.

"Madam, how come you don't wear a lot of jewelry like we do? We make good money, and our jewelry represents it."

The Madam gave her an Appearance 101 Class.

"How much jewelry you wear doesn't represent success. It's *how* you wear it that does. You and your jewelry look really cheap when you wear four or five bracelets and necklaces at the same time. To *me*, that represents confusion of the mind. Plus, how can you appreciate the beauty of your jewelry, if you have a lot going on, in the area you're wearing it. Jewelry is supposed to enhance you, not make you look like a slave. You see, the jewelry that I wear is very simple yet expensive. I have on a pair of five carat, diamond earrings. And the one ring I have on is a five carat, pear shape diamond. When you keep it sweet and classy, men will look at you in a different manner. They won't look at you like some dope head hooker off the street, looking to just get paid to get another hit. They can get that kind of action anywhere. That's why they come to Big Moe's house. Here, they come to enjoy the finest, cleanest, dope-free ladies of the night."

After the pep talk, the girls learned that simplicity was the best thing when it comes to accessorizing the body.

The Madam knew everything about the girls that worked for her. Believe it or not, most of them were professionals with degrees. Why they were in the business of catering to men, she never asked. She really saw it as none of her business. She just knew that as long as men and women have needs that were not being met at home; she would always be in the business of making people happy. That is until the law shuts her down. But even if that was to happen, the law would never know who she was. That's because no one really knew. It was as if she didn't exist. The only thing people knew or speculated about her, was that she was in her early 40's; that she arrived in the D.C. area via Miami; and that she was tight with Big

Moe, the owner of the house and the dude that had all of D.C., Maryland and VA locked down, when it came to the drug game.

Back in the day while attending college in Miami, the Madam met Moe at a pool party given by a very well off mutual college friend. The friend introduced them, and the two hit it off right from the start. They have been friends ever since. No one really knew how deep their relationship was. But what they did know was that if you messed with the Madam, you're messing with Moe. And with his rep…you don't want to be on his bad side. That's the reason his house had never been raided, nor shut down. And judging from his cliental, who would want to. The place was a haven for VIPs. It was as if the men were members of an exclusive yacht club or something.

On this particular night, the Madam was sitting at her desk going over the appointment book, when a VIP walked into her office. He was about 6'5", black as the night and weighting about 310. Even though he was a huge brother, the Madam knew that he was a gentle giant by nature.

"Look here beautiful, can a grown man get some kind of service around here?"

The Madam looked up and smiled as if she was seeing an old friend. She got up to great him.

"Darling, how are you? You're late. I was wondering if you were coming at all."

When they hugged each other, he whispered in her ear.

"Big Teddy…please," she said giggling.

"Say it again for me baby."

"Big Teddy," she whispered softly into his ear.

Her voice was angelic to him.

"Say it again," he asked smiling.

"Big Teddy," she repeated very soft and slow.

He got excited and started doing some kind of playful, crazy dance. He always acted that way when she called him that. That was her own personal nickname she gave him.

Smiling at his little jig, she told him to calm down. He did so, but was still excited by the anticipation of tonight's festivities. He clapped his hands together and started to rub them over and over.

"O.K. where're my little darlings at... I've had a long hard week, and I've been looking forward to this."

The Madam stepped back and clapped her hands twice; fast and hard. And in an instant, two Asian girl's dress in a traditional geisha outfit appeared out of nowhere. Giggling, they each took his arm and escorted him out of the Madams office.

When the Madam found out that this particular VIP loved very young Asian girls, she personally went out and recruited the two young ladies. Unbeknownst to him, the girls were actually Grad students at Georgetown University.

"Enjoy!" she yelled to the happy party.

31

A S THE CLIENTELE at Big Moe's House settled in for their night of pleasure, James Jr. and Lilly Mae were making their way down the long, dark alley. He was yelling up a storm; something about messing up his money. Poor Lilly Mae was going along with everything, but was looking at him like he was crazy for talking to her in such a nasty manner.

"I told you bitch to stay where you were until all them motherfuckers got served!"

"Don't beat me daddy. I'm sorry. I thought you said something else."

One of the men walking down the alley heard the commotion. "Man, smack that trick!" he yelled with excitement.

Ignoring the man, James Jr. grabbed Lilly Mae by the neck. "See, there you go thinking again! Who told you to think?" Putting on a good act, Lilly Mae began to stutter.

"I....I...."

Noticing the men watching him to see what he was going to do; he slapped the back of Lilly Mae's head and kicked her in the butt. He started mocking her.

"I.... I...what...? You no thinking, country talking son of a bitch! Girl I should take my belt off and beat that ass!"

He pulled on his belt buckle, acting like he was about to take it off. Raising her arms, Lilly Mae acted like she was protecting her face.

"No daddy, no...don't beat me!" she yelled sounding like a little girl.

Not believing what came out of her mouth, she snickered at what she said and how she said it. For the life of her, she just couldn't understand why grown men loved to be called daddy by women. *Half you don't even want to be bothered with your own damn kids, more less being called daddy by them*, she thought for a split second.

Grabbing her arm, James Jr. violently pulled her down the rest of the alleyway. Lilly Mae resisted big time. When they turned the corner, they saw several small garages with lights on. Men were setting on milk crates and standing around shooting the breeze. Some of the men had on dark blue, dirty overalls working under the hood of cars. As they heard the commotion coming their way, they all stopped doing whatever they were doing to check out the action. What they saw was a sight for sore eyes. They all started laughing.

"That's right, beat that ass baby! Show that bitch who the *got* damn man is!" yelled a man while holding his private part.

A drunk who was sitting on the ground just outside the door of another garage was taking his Wild Irish Rose wine to the head.

"She ain't acting right...put that coat hanger to her ass. I bet'cha she'll straighten up quicker then hell freezes over!" said the drunk man.

They continued on without responding to them.

At the end of the dark alley, you could see street lights and traffic. To the left of the alley was another alleyway. Only this one wasn't lined with garages. It was lined with the backyard of people's houses.

A huge green trash compactor piled up with junk was in front of the second backyard from the main alley. James Jr. continued to yell as he pushed Lilly Mae behind the compactor.

"Girl...I told you...!"

For good measures, they continued their little charade a few more minutes. During the commotion, he peeped around the compactor to see if anyone was looking. Satisfied that no one was, he looked at Lilly Mae, and they both burst out laughing at the same time. Playfully mimicking Lilly Mae's voice, he put his arms up to shield his face.

"No daddy, no. Don't beat me. Mrs. Carter, I wanted to die. Where in the *hell* did you get that from?!"

Lilly Mae was bent over laughing her butt off.

"From the white girl I saw with the dude on the street. Oh, my lord, that was too funny. Did you hear what that man back there *said*...he said to take a coat hanger and beat me with it. What in the world..."

"Man, I don't know...but we should be getting a move on."

Remembering what the guy at Bens Chile Bowl said, they started walking toward the fourth house from the main alley. As they did so, James Jr. noticed that the row houses were not connected to each other, like the ones he had seen in other neighborhoods.

When they reach the fourth house, he was surprised to see how well kept it was compared to the others. The first three houses looked like they needed some serious home improvement. Screens on the back windows either had holes in them or were missing. Some of the opened porches didn't even have doors. Paint was peeling off the houses, and some of the windows up top were busted. But the most important thing that was noticeable about the fourth house was the single red light above the closed-in back porch door. He looked up and down the row houses to see if they had a light fixture above their door, and they didn't. Before entering the yard, he stared at it.

"What's the problem…? Let's go in." Lilly Mae said as she went toward the gate.

He immediately stopped her by pulling on her arm.

"The guy said depending on how fat your pockets are determines the back or front door."

"What difference does it make? I want to get my daughter." Starting for the gate again, he pulled her back.

"What is your problem?" she asked as she yanked her arm away from him.

"Don't you get it? Country didn't tell me which customer he was." This bit of info caused Lilly Mae to ponder.

"Tell me what he said."

"He said to tell the doorkeeper that Country said to hook y'all up with Nice-n-Tight, and that he was going to call to let them know that we were coming."

"You also said that the dude in the food place said to either enter the back or front of the house; back being better right?"

"Right"

"Well I'll go to the front door and see what's what. You just stay out of sight."

"What! You can't go up there; you're a girl!"

"Well you *did* say that you never know what a person's *real* preference is right?"

"Ok, you got me on that one."

"Look, don't worry. I got this. Just leave it to me."

In silence, they walked back down the alley. He stopped and leaned against the fence of the first house. Lilly Mae went around to the front and walked down to the fourth house. There, she saw a blue light on just above the front door of the house. Looking at the other houses, she noticed that they didn't even have a light fixture next to their door. *Well, I guess this is the one.* Taking a deep breath, she slowly walked up the steps. She had told James Jr. not to worry, and that she had it. But for real, for real, she didn't have a clue as to what she was going to do or say.

Standing before the door, she took another deep breath. *Here goes nothing.*

Bang! Bang! Bang!

A few seconds later, a tall, heavy-set person wearing jeans and a white tee shirt answered the door. The person's hair cut was very short. She was taken aback with the way the person looked. *Damn... is this, a man or a woman.* She cleared her throat.

"Is Country here?"

The big individual looked Lilly Mae up and down and gave a huge smile at seeing how short her skirt was.

"Where you from baby? It sounds like you from way down south somewhere."

Lilly Mae was shocked. Judging by the tone of voice, she knew it was a female, but she looked like a man. *Crap... What the hell....* She had to put on a facade like she was tough to cover up her nervousness.

"Where I'm from is none of your bees wax. Is Country in there or not?"

The he be/she be, saw right through her fakeness and laughed. But more so she laughed at her deep southern accent.

"Baby you got the wrong address. Don't no Country live here."
"Thank you very much," she said as she turned to leave.

As she went down the stairs, the big woman stepped out onto the porch.

"I can be your Country if you want me to be baby."

"No thank you," Lilly Mae said without turning around.

"Yeah..., well after I eat that pretty pussy of yours out, you won't be saying that; trust me baby!"

Laughing, the girl went back inside the house.

Keeping her head down, she walked right pass James Jr. without saying a word. He got up and followed her. When he reached her behind the big dumpster, he saw that she was hyperventilating.

"What happened?"

After taking several deep breaths she began to laugh.

"I thought a man answered the door, but when he started talking, it was a woman's voice. She tried to hit on me!"

"What!"

"Yes, and she didn't know who the hell Country was. It's *your* turn now. I can't take another one of those. Oh, and you know what, the house had a *blue* light on over the front door."

"Blue light, what the…?"

"I don't know but…"

With that being done, they went back to the back of the house with the red light. As they walked down the concrete walkway with several cracks in it, James Jr. gave the backyard and house a quick look over. He noticed how well kept the grass was, compared to the other trashed filled yards. He also noticed that the house had a fire escape, but the others didn't. When they got to the end of the walkway, they descended down two steps, into a very small flat concrete area. In front of them were a set of black cast iron steps. Before going any further, James Jr. cautioned Lilly Mae.

"Now Mrs. Carter, I'm not saying that your daughter is in there. All I'm saying is that it's a great possibility that she is. If she's not, then we'll just keep looking, Ok?"

"Ok."

Slowly, they walked up the steps. You could tell by looking at the door that it wasn't your regular house door. It was just too thick compared to the other cheesy looking back doors. Plus, there were no small square windows in it like the others. However, what it did have and they both thought that it was odd, were two closed brass looking slots. One slot was eye level and the other one was hip level. They looked at each other, but said nothing.

James Jr. knocked on the door. *Knock-knock-knock* They stood there and waited for a few minutes. Nothing happened. A little nervous, Lilly Mae looked to see if anyone was coming from either end of the alley. When she saw the area clear, she told him to bang on the door. *Bang! Bang! Bang! Bang! Bang!* A few seconds later the small, top slider opened up. The only thing they saw were a pair of eyes staring at them.

"Can I help you?" a falsetto voice asked.

"Yes. My name is James Jr. Country told me and my lady friend to come on down."

"Name..."

Confused, he looked at Lilly Mae then to the pair of eyes. He didn't understand what was being asked.

"Huh?"

"Name..."

He looked at Lilly Mae again for answers, but she shrugged her shoulders.

"Name... I don't...?"

Impatient the doorkeeper took a deep breath.

"Look, you must have the wrong house. This here is a shelter for battered women. Anybody that comes *here* must have made contact with one of the girls who live here. So...whoever the girls made *contact* with would know their *name*."

When the doorkeeper put emphasis on the word *contact* and *name*, a light went off in his head.

"Oh...oh yeah... Nice-n-Tight; she told me to come by and see her. You know...she wanted me to make sure that everything was alright with her and everything."

"Um...everybody wants to check-up on her high yellow ass." the doorkeeper responded with an attitude.

When the bottom slot opened up and a hand appeared, he and Lilly Mae look at it, and then to each other. By the expression on their face, you could tell that they were confused as hell. The hand shook vigorously.

"Look, I ain't got all day!"

Lilly Mae quickly caught on and hit the young man's arm. She made a head motion toward his pants pockets. That's when he caught on.

"Oh...ok...my bad."

He pulled out a $20.00 and slapped it into the doorkeeper's hand; which disappeared. Not even a second later the hand reappeared throwing the money back out.

"Hey what the." James Jr. yelled as he caught the money.

"And you said *Country* sent you? Baby you must have gotten this house mixed up with some other house. Good-bye." The slot closed.

In a panic, they immediately started banging the hell out of that door.

Bang! Bang! Bang! Bang!

"Hey! Hey come back! Come back!" they yelled.

The doorkeeper opened the slot and spoke as if nothing happened.

"Can I help you?"

"My fault baby...my fault," James Jr. said as he reached back into his pants pocket and pulled out a $50. 00.

The doorkeeper opened the lower slot again, and the hand reappeared. He slapped the money into the waiting hand. The hand disappeared. And this time, within seconds, several latches were heard being unlocked and the heavy door opened. The doorkeeper, who they now saw was a man, stood about 5'11", dark skin, slim built and dressed in a long dashiki dress with a blond wig on.

"Welcome to Big Moe's house where every fantasy comes true. We ask you to wipe the bottom of your shoes here on this brown rug, because we don't want any dirt on our beautiful, *gorgeous*, thick red carpet. After doing so, *please* step over to the bartender and order your favorite drink. Once you have been served *please proceed* over to the lovely waiting area with the beaded doorway. The Madam will be assisting you with your *naughty* heart's desire," he said gleefully.

After the announcement, he sat down at a beautiful oriental design desk and began to file his long, red nails; blowing them a few times after each brush, while chewing gum.

As they wiped the bottom of their shoes off on the rug, they looked over to where the bar was. There, they saw several men in business suits standing around drinking and smoking. As they walked to the bar, they noticed how huge the inside of the house was. From the outside, you couldn't tell that it was spacious.

Looking around, they saw a door at the end of the hallway with a red light over top of it. At the other end of the hall was a small room with red and gold beads hanging down as a door. There was a kitchen full of women just off to the right side of the bar. It looked like they were making a fuss over several trays of food. As one of the girls prepared a tray, another one came by and smacked her on her rear. The one who got smacked acted as if nothing happened. With one hand, she grabbed her tray and put it high in the air, as she walked out into the crowd of men. Feeling out of place, they made their way over to the bar.

"What will it be?" asked the bartender, who was an older gentleman with salt and pepper hair.

"Can I get a Southern Comfort and a Gin and Tonic? How much is that, my man?" James Jr. asked as he pulled out a few bills.

Surprised, the bartender stopped him from trying to give him money.

"Oh, you must be new, because everybody here *knows* that money is *never* presented in this house."

"Damn that's right… I forgot. It's been so long since I've been here."

The bartender prepared their drinks and gave it to them. As they stood at the bar with drinks in hand, the bartender snickered to himself. He knew that they were green as a cow's pasture. He also knew that he was perpetrating big time about being at Big Moe's before. Because once you got a taste of Moe's house, you simple don't forget anything that you experience while there.

As Lilly Mae stirred her drink, she watched James Jr. gulped his down. After he finished and shivered from the strong drink, he noticed that she was still stirring hers.

"What's the matter, you don't like your drink?"

"I don't drink," she said with a frown.

Before speaking, he looked at all the different characters in the room.

"Hell... I don't drink either, but by the time you get through the night you will be. Go head now take a sip. We got to play the part and people are looking."

First, Lilly Mae smelt the strong drink and frowned. Then reluctantly, she took a sip and immediately gagged from the taste.

"Hey take it easy."

"What? I told you I don't drink," she said as she coughed up a storm.

"Ok, will...just act like you're sipping it."

"Next please..." They heard a soft female voice say.

Looking in the direction of the voice, they saw two distinguished looking white-men disappear beyond the beaded doorway.

"Come on, that must be the Madam."

They went to the waiting area and sat down in two chairs, closes to the beaded doorway. They vaguely heard what the Madam was saying to the two men.

The Madam stood up from her big beautiful mahogany desk to greet the two men.

"Gentlemen please have a seat. We missed you last week. We had everything ready for you. What happened?"

"Oh we are so sorry, but my man was sick, and I just *couldn't* have fun without him."

"I understand. And how are we feeling today?"

"*We* are much better and thank you for asking."

"Good. So, shall we have fun gentlemen?"

"Oh yes, yes *indeed*. We are ready to boogie with our big, beautiful, African *gorilla* honey."

The Madam gracefully escorted the two men out of her office. As they made a right turn to go down a small hallway, Lilly Mae caught a glimpse of one of the men squeezing his lover's butt-cheek. Playfully, his partner pushed him away.

"Stop that, you know what that does to me."

"What the hell." in shock, she whispered.

Not believing what she just saw, she turned to the side, and took a big gulp of her drink. She had heard about gay men, but had never seen them in action.

After a few short minutes, the Madam reappeared. Entering her office, she sat back down and began making notes in her black book.

"Next please."

They got up and were about to enter the office, when suddenly James Jr. stopped. He couldn't help but notice that no one moved. He addressed no one in particular.

"Say, I'm sorry. Are any of you next?"

One of the men spoke up.

"No. We are waiting for a particular. Please go ahead."

"Damn, is she worth the wait?"

"Yes she is. She is very special," said an elder looking white man.

"She can make you feel like you are the only man in her life," said a man who looks like he was from the Middle East.

"Next please."

They heard again and went in. The Madam stood up to greet them.

"Good evening. Welcome to Big Moe's house. How can we help you tonight?"

With nervousness and not really knowing what to say, James Jr. spoke up.

"Well me and my friend here are…well you see we're from out of town, and I wanted to… Um put it this way, Country told me about…."

When the Madam heard Country's name she instantly smiled and put her hand up.

"Say no more. We know Country *very, very* well here. We know just what he likes. Would you like the same?"

Even though he wasn't really clear on what she was talking about, he went along with what she was offering.

"Yes I would. But I would like to include my lady friend."

His suggestion caught the Madam by surprise.

"Oh…did you let Brenda know at the door? She didn't inform me of this."

"Brenda…" Lilly Mae said with a high pitch voice. "Lady, I don't know if you've noticed or not, but there's a man dressed up as a woman, at your back door."

The Madam laughed at her.

"Yes, I know. That's Ms. Brenda. She takes excellent care of us here.

She's been with us for years."

Baffled by what she said, the two just stared at her like a deer in head lights. Seeing that they were confused, the Madam brushed them off.

"Oh never mind. I understand that this is your first time. Don't worry about it. Tell me…who do you have in mind to see?"

"Country told me to ask for Nice-n-Tight."

The Madam's expression changed when she heard that particular name. Concerned, she went to her desk and flipped through several pages.

"She's a very popular girl, and she is with a client right now. And there *are* others before you as well. However, you *are* out of town friends of Country."

Having made a decision, she closed the black book.

"Tell you what…let me see what I can do. If she's not available how about, I send you someone who closely fits her description. Will that be ok?"

"That's fine with me. How much?"

The Madam shook her head.

"Sir, no money is allowed in this house. Besides, Country paid in advance already."

"How could he., why would., I just talk to him."

In understanding, the Madam put both hands up.

"I know… I know. This isn't the first-time Country has done this. The man just has a kind heart *and* a lot of money. So, when he calls we simple accept. Now, let me show you to your room for the evening."

She led then in the same direction the other two gentlemen went. As they walked, she began to explain the rules of the house.

"You have one hour for playing and 10 minutes to freshen up afterward. We like for our guest to go out the same way as they came in; nice and fresh."

When they turned the corner, they went down a very short hallway that led to the stairs. Walking up the steps, they saw that the second floor was just as big as the main floor. This area had five rooms, each one probably being occupied by guest of the night, no doubt. The Madam escorted them to the very end of the hallway. They stopped in front of a door that had a yellow star hanging on it.

"Are we ready?"

The Madam took a key out of her suit pocket and unlocked the door. Slowly, she pushed the door open. When they walk in, Lilly Mae gasped at the beautiful enormous room. Its decor was red and black. The walls were painted a deep, rich, beautiful red. The curtains were black velvet and thick. There was a king-size bed in the middle of the room that had a black and red silk comforter on it. Gold-colored, silk pillows were placed precisely on the bed. The headboard, nightstand and chest of draws were of black lacquer trimmed in gold. Lilly Mae walked over to a slim mirrored door. Grabbing the gold-colored door knob, she pushed then pulled to open it, but it didn't budge. Smiling, the Madam went over and slid the door to the left. To Lilly Mae's delight, it was a walk-in closet, with decorated cloth hangers hanging from a long pole.

"This is…man this is nice. This is top flight here," James Jr. said as he looked around the room.

"Well, I'm quite sure you know how Country rolls; only the best for our top guest. Enjoy."

She exited the room.

Lilly Mae carefully sat on the bed. With it being so beautiful, she didn't want to mess it up. James Jr. walked over to the thick, black curtain and looked out of the window. The fire escape was right at the window. He then walked over to the walk-in closet.

"Man I tell you. Some people have the good life."

"You got that right. My goodness, is this how all the rooms look?"

"Who knows, maybe…"

Walking over to the door, he cracked it open just a little to see what was going on in the hallway, which was nothing. Closing the door back, he looked at Lilly Mae.

"What's wrong with you?" she asked.

"Man it's a lot of rooms in this house."

Lilly Mae started walking toward the door.

"Let's knock on all the doors to see if she's in one of them." "We can't do that! It's paying customers in those rooms." The realization of what he just said made her slow her role.

"What are we going to do? I don't want to sit here all night. We need a plan before Ms. Hooker comes in."

Suddenly, there was a soft knock at the door. *Knock-Knock-Knock* Caught off guard they looked at each other. *Knock-Knock-Knock* James Jr. motioned for Lilly Mae to hide in the closet. She hurried in and closed the door. He sat on the bed. *Knock-Knock-Knock*

As he sat there he had butterflies all up in his stomach. No one, not even his father knew that when he first laid eyes on Betty Jean, he fell in love with her. He never said anything to anyone about her because she was still in high school. He decided to lay low until she graduated. Then, he was going to make his move on her. Well...that idea went out the window when he found out that she ran away.

Now, of all places, he was back in D.C., sitting in a whorehouse hoping to see his first love; hoping to save her and to bring her back home with him. His plan was that after she graduate from high school, he would take her far away from the Bayou; just the two of them against the world.

"Come in."

Slowly, the door opened. Afraid that the girl entering the room wasn't his beloved, he kept his eyes on the floor. He was also fearful that if it was his beloved, she might look terrible because of drug usage and the street life.

The hooker entered the room and closed the door; locking it behind her.

"What's your pleasure, sir?" she asked as she slowly walked toward him.

As she came into view, his eyes came upon a pair of open toed, bright-red stilettos. The girl's toes were painted a pretty red to match. She also had a milky, white complexion, the same as Betty

Jean. But her voice…her voice was too hard. It wasn't the same high pitch girly voice like Betty Jean. His eyes slowly moved up her slim body; taking in all the small curves in detail. With one hand on her hip, she swung the other back and forth. He saw that her nail color was a perfect match with her toes. The girl had on a beautiful sheer red and black two-piece teddy, exposing her small breast just enough. When his eyes reach her face, he didn't recognize it. She had on a lot of make-up. Her lips were like red cherries, and her hair and eye lashes mimic the actress Betty Davis. You could tell that she was very beautiful at one time. You could also tell that something wasn't right with her.

Chewing gum the way a cow chews grass; she stood before him.

"What's your pleasure?"

Looking at her, he wasn't too sure if it was Betty Jean or not; the girl looked so much older.

"Betty Jean…is that you?" he asked with hesitation.

She started to scratch her neck as if she had a rash or something.

"Mister, you got one hour."

He stood up and grabbed the girl's face, forcing her to look into his eyes.

"Betty Jean…. Is your name Betty Jean Carter?"

Taking a few steps back, she began scratching her arm, while nodding out. Then, within a matter of seconds, she straighten back up.

"Look here, I don't know no Betty Jean. Now you got one hour. I ain't telling you no more."

Reaching into her top, she pulled out a stub of cigarette and lighter. As she walked to the head board, she lit it and started to smoke.

"I know it's your dime, but it's my time. I got some shit that needs to be taken care of before the Madam finds out that…. Look what's up…what'cha going to do…"

As he continued to look at her, she began to nod out again. Not wanting her to hurt herself, he made an attempt to catch her, but she pulled herself back up. Amazed by her timely action, he stopped in his tracks. *No...this isn't my Betty Jean, no way Jose* he thought.

"Ms. please. I'm looking for a friend of mine. Her name is Betty Jean. And I do believe that...."

Pissed off, the hooker lunged at him; pushing him out of her way.

"I done told you already... I don't know no got damn Betty Jean! Now you're wasting my time! I need a fix like yesterday, and you holding me up!"

Reaching into his pants pocket, he pulled out some money and extended it to her.

"Please...if you could just tell me where she is, or if you know of anyone who."

"What the fuck! You trying to get me caught up?! You know ain't no money allowed in this fucking house! I'm out of here! You ain't trying to fuck! Madam!"

Abruptly, she grabbed her stomach and bent over in excruciating pain.

"Oh my goodness, help me. I need a fix."

Her eyes rolled to the back of her head, and she fell hard to the floor.

"Oh shit. Hold on Ms., just hold on. I got you!"

James Jr. grabbed a pillow from off the bed and ran to her. Getting on his knees, he attempted to place the pillow under her head. But as he lift her head, all of her hair shifted a few inches forward.

"What the..." *That's odd* he thought.

And before he could ask if she was alright, the girl leaned her head to the side and threw up. That's when he noticed several long, soft, sandy brown strings of hair coming from the nape of her neck.

"Hold the fuck up."

Feeling like he was moving in slow motion, he looked closer. As she was vomiting, he pushed the black hair a little further to the side. *Sandy brown hair...? Is she wearing a...? This is...* He yanked it off.

"This is a wig!"

In shock, he saw that it was his beloved and screamed.

"Betty Jean! Oh, Lord! Betty Jean! What have they done to you?!"

Shaking uncontrollably, he held her tight. Looking up at him, she pleaded.

"I...help me. I... I need some dope. It feels like I'm about to die."

She threw up again.

"Mrs. Carter! It's her! It's Betty Jean and she's sick!"

Lilly Mae burst out the closet screaming and crying.

"Betty Jean! Oh, my baby!"

Running over to her she dropped down to her knees, and grabbed her out of his arms. Holding her tight, she began to rock her back and forth.

"Baby...baby its mama.... I'm here. I'm.... We're going to take you home."

Noticing that the girl had patches of make-up on one or her arms, he took the bottom of his shirt and wiped it off.

"Track marks...they got her on dope...look!"

Lilly Mae looked at the horrible dark marks and screamed.

"Oh my God what have they done to my baby?!"

She started brushing her daughter's hair from her face with her hand. But with every stroke, Betty Jean remembered the pain and hurt her mother caused her. She remembered the burning smell of her hair, as she sat on the kitchen floor, in between her mother's legs, as she attempted to press her hair with a hot comb like her sisters. She tried to tell her mother that her hair was to fine for the heat. But her mother thought that she was trying to act like she was better than the rest of her sisters; trying to act like she was too good for a hot comb. In an attempt to get away from having her hair burned out, she remembered being clunked on the head several times with the hot comb to sit still. She remembered the times when she wanted to go to the movies…times she wanted to go to the after-school dance… times she wanted to go to the Ice Cream Parlor with her friends on Saturdays. But her mother made her stay home to babysit or to do chores. Remembering times when she cried out to her, because she knew what her stepfather was sexually doing to her was wrong. She would never forget when her stepfather tried to beat her in front of the whole family and she didn't come to her rescue. So many bad memories clouded her head. The flash backs over whelmed her. The sound of her mother's voice stung her heart. Her mother's touch burned her flesh. Refusing to take it anymore she screamed.

"No! Get your hands off me! Get off me!"

Hitting her mother several times, she tried to get away from her. But her mother held her tight, because she knew where all of her daughter's anger stemmed from. In an attempt to stop the physical attack, James Jr. grabbed her hands.

"Please stop it! That's your mother!"

Betty Jean's eyes bulge out of her head.

"She ain't no mother of mine! I hate her! Look at what she made me become! I'm a hooker on dope because of her!"

"No you're not! Don't say that!"

"Yes I am! And it's because of her and that man of hers!"

A flash back of him and Mr. Carter's conversation played in his head. *Are you trying to get my Betty Jean up north so you can have your way with her…?* Looking confused, he stared at her. Betty Jean noticed his perplexed look and stopped struggling. He let her hands go.

"What are you talking about…? He's your father."

Lilly Mae was hurt by her words.

"Baby please, don't say that. I'm your mother."

Because of the pain, Betty Jean laughed what little she could at her mother's words. Starring at them both, James Jr. realized that he really didn't know anything about the Carter family. But still.

he knew what he felt in his heart for Betty Jean. And he wanted her with him.

"Betty Jean, please," he begged.

"Oh…you don't know do you? she asked looking serious.

In amazement, she looked at her mother.

"You didn't tell him…did you Mama. Tell him Mama…tell him what y'all done to me. Tell him how my *stepfather* been sneaking into my room late at night, having his way with me since I was little and you did nothing!"

"What!" James Jr jumped up as if he was stung by a bee. Pacing the floor, his mind was on fire. He looked at Mrs. Carter, who was now crying. "Are you serious…?!"

"Please stop it Betty Jean." Her mother begged but to avail.

Betty Jean continued. She longed for this day to come; to finally tell her mother that she knew exactly what was going on.

"He didn't want you anymore after you gave birth to his children! He hated you, and you knew it! That's why you didn't want me to go away to school! You wanted me to stay home to take up the slack in what you fell short of as a woman, and that was keeping your man happy!"

Just then a terrible pain shot through her body from in need of a fix.

"Oh God help me!"

Unbeknownst to them, out in the hallway there was a loud commotion. Guests were yelling for the Madam, because of the noise coming from the room. The Madam heard pandemonium from her office, but didn't go to see what was going on. She simple picked up her phone and called security. The waiting guest, saw two big dudes name Anthony and Carl, in all black fatigues, run by. Showing concern, one of the guests jumped up.

"Madam, is everything all right? Will I get to see mother tonight? I must see her."

The Madam came to the doorway and assured that everything was alright.

When security got to the top of the stairs, they saw the guest standing in the hallway half naked or with a sheet wrapped around then.

"What's going on up her? Get back in your rooms!" they yelled to regain order as they walked down the hallway.

"We would if the motherfucker's down the hall stop all that got damn noise! The one night I get a chance to hang out, and this shit happens!" yelled a short, colored, skinny man, with a heavyset white woman hanging all over him.

Betty Jean screamed from the pain again, and the two men took off running to the last door.

"What's going on in there…?!" yelled the men, while banging on the door.

No answer.

One of the men pulled on the door knob, but it was locked.

"Unlock this door right now!"

Still, no answer.

"Man, use your keys!" Anthony yelled.

"Keys…man I thought you had the keys!" Carl yelled back.

"Gotdammit, run down stairs and get Brenda! Hurry up!"

Running back down the hallway, Carl pushed the guest out of his way.

"Move! Make a hole! Make it wide! Get out of my way damn it!"

Taking two steps at a time, he descended the stairs.

"Brenda! Brenda! We need you upstairs…some shit is popping off girl!"

Anthony continued to bang on the door.

"I'm warning you…open this door!"

Hearing the noise outside the door, James Jr. went into action.

"Y'all come on…get up; we got to get out of here!"

Betty Jean didn't want to move because she was in too much pain.

"No! I need a fix damn it!"

"Honey, mama will get you whatever you need. But first we got to get out of here before those fools break down the door."

"No! I'm not going anywhere with you!"

"Come on now. My car is right outside. We can be home within 15-20 hours. You can go back to school and…."

Betty Jean looked at him like he was out of his freaking mind.

"School…? Fool is you crazy. Look at me. I'm a junky. This here is my life now. I don't need *no* education. I just want my shit. Now get away from me!"

Pushing her mother away, she struggled to get to her feet. Staggering, she headed for the door. But to prevent her from leaving the room, Lilly Mae ran past her and spread eagle in front of the door.

"Betty Jean Carter… I forbid you from going out this here door."

She ignored her mother and pulled on the door knob. Her mother smacked her hand as if she was a bad little girl.

"Now I done told you no. You are going home with us."

Laughing at her mother's reaction, Betty Jean stumbled backward. "Oh see…now that's funny…real funny. Don't do that shit again." Making another attempt for the knob, her mother slapped her hand again. Only this time it was much harder.

"Betty Jean, I done told you now! You're not going out there!" Rubbing her nose, Betty Jean stumbled backward again.

"See man…didn't I tell you…."

Out of nowhere and with swiftness, Betty Jean pulled out a small knife and cut her mother's cheek. Lilly Mae didn't even see it coming. Grabbing her face, she screamed. Blood was all over her hands. Betty Jean laughed at her.

"I done told your ass, I need my shit!"

What just happened to Lilly Mae was surreal to her. Her mind was spinning. *Did she just cut me? No...she didn't cut me.* She touched the gash across her face again. *My face...it's....* She looked at the blood on her hands again. *But my hands, my hands are....* Realization kicked in. *She cut me. That heifer done cut me.* Like a mad, crazy woman, she screamed.

"Bitch I'll kill you! Look what you did to me!"

In a blind rage, she rushed toward Betty Jean. But like a pro fighter, Betty Jean side stepped her. And with the quickness of hands, she took her knife and stabbed her in her side and back several times. *Whop! Whop! Whop!* It happened so fast James Jr. couldn't react in time to stop her. Screaming like hell, Lilly Mae fell on the bed and then tumbled to the floor.

"Look what you've done to me. I'm your mother!" she yelled in shock as she coughed up blood.

Her daughter laughed at her.

"I love you Betty Jean. Please forgive me," her mother said with her last breath.

Betty Jean didn't hear a word she said. She walked over to the dead body and stood before it.

"I didn't ask you to come here. Now look what you made me do. I told your dumb ass that I needed my shit!"

By this time, Brenda was at the door yelling and fumbling for the master key.

"Y'all bitches bet not be fucking up the room!"

He finally got the door open.

"What the hell is going on in...oh my Lord...!"

His mouth dropped open from the site of Lilly Mae lying on the floor in a pool of blood. He looked at Betty Jean, who was still standing over her mother with the knife in hand. James Jr. was standing in the middle of the room. *This can't be happenings...this can't be happening*, he repeated over and over.

People in the hallway were running their mouth and trying their best to peep into the room to see what was going on. But Carl and Anthony blocked their view. And of all people…. Big Moe's, mole; a short, stocky, manly looking lady bogarted her way through.

"Move…let me see. I can't see."

With force, she pushed Carl out of the way.

"Move damn it; shit…what the hell is going on up in here?"

When she got through and saw the mess, she yelled, "What the fuck! Oh hell no, this can't be happening in Moe's House! That motherfucker is going to be pissed off!"

From her outburst, everyone got quiet. The eerie silence and people staring overwhelmed Betty Jean. Like a scared child, she looked around at the strangers, then back down at her mother's lifeless body. Tears began to fill her eyes. Because for a second, just for a split second, she realized what she had done. Leaning her head back she let out a horrific scream.

"Mama!"

Dropping to her knees the knife fell out of her hand. Crying like a lost child, she shook her mother.

"Mama…mama…wake up!"

Her screams brought James Jr. back to reality. He ran over to Lilly Mae and checked her pulse. There was none.

"Somebody call an ambulance! Somebody go get some help!"

But the crowd didn't move. They just stood there looking. The bloody situation didn't even faze them. They were used to seeing fatality scenes, just not at Big Moe's.

"Ok shows over! Go back to your business! Come on move it people!" Carl and Anthony yelled to disperse the crowd.

Slowly, the people turned and walk away.

"Well at least they ain't making no damn noise no more," said one lady laughing as she walked away.

As they cleared the hallway, the Madam appeared before the door. Expressionless, she entered the room. She didn't even look at the situation at hand. She didn't care.

"Brenda, can you please escort this gentleman and his two lady friends out of the house. As far as I'm concerned…nothing happened *here* in *this* house…understood," she said in a calm voice.

"Yes, I understand."

Brenda grabbed Betty Jean by the arm, and Carl grabbed Lilly Mae's body. But before he could pick her up, James Jr. reached over and grabbed his arm.

"What are you doing?"

Like the speed of lighting, Anthony pulled out a gun and pointed it at his forehead. Scared shitless, he released Carl's arm.

"I… I…."

Looking at him like he was a fool, simultaneously, Brenda pointed his finger, stomped his foot and rolled his head in a circular motion

"Oh no honey… I don't *think* you want to go there…or do you?"

The Madam slowly walked over to Anthony and lowered his gun. He returned it back to his backside.

"Mr. Country's friend, we are in the business of making people happy. No more…no less. We don't make our girls do this line of work. They do it because they want to. We didn't ask you to come here to our establishment. You came because you wanted to. Now if you will excuse me, I have a business to run."

She turned her attention back to Brenda.

"Please, be so kind and take out the trash…*immediately.*"

Not waiting for an answer, she turned and walked away.

Brenda let go of Betty Jean's arm and picked up the dead body. He threw it over his shoulder like it was a rag doll. Walking over to the window, he pulled the curtain back, lifted up the window and stepped out onto the fire escape.

"What are you doing?!" James Jr. yelled.

Not liking his attitude, Carl hauled off and hit him in the face.

"Now that's the second time you done said that. I don't want to hear it no more. And for your information, he's taking the trash out. Now shut the hell up and move."

Carl grabbed him by the collar and pushed him toward the fire escape. He stepped out as Brenda descend. Carl was right behind him. Anthony grabbed Betty Jean up off the floor by her hair. Being resistant, she grabbed his hand and screamed.

"Stop! What are you doing! Let go of my hair!"

He slapped the crap out of her face.

"Shut the fuck up bitch. Your time is up. I've been sick and tired of you and that nasty attitude of yours for a long ass time."

"No! Stop! Wait!"

He shoved her toward the fire escape.

"I'm going to Howard University." He mocked her with a dainty voice. "Get your ass down them steps."

Brenda jumped down to the ground from the last step. Looking up, he saw the two men.

"Come on now...hurry up."

James Jr. jumped down to the ground, then Carl. Stepping back, they looked up to see if Anthony and Betty Jean were right behind them...they weren't.

"Anthony where you at dog...Anthony..." Carl yelled lightly.

Finally, Anthony emerged from the window with a hand full of Betty Jean's hair.

"Man this dope-head, ass bitch is putting up a damn fight; can you believe this shit?" he yelled to Carl.

Putting her foot on the window seal, Betty Jean tried her best to prevent Anthony from pulling her out onto the fire escape. She didn't want to leave because she knew she could get a fix from her customers anytime. Plus, she knew that as long as she was in the house she had steady money coming in for her drug habit.

"Please! Let me go! I don't want to leave! I'll do anything! I'll suck your dick!"

"Hey! Shut that bitch up! She's making too much fucking noise!" Brenda yelled lightly.

With one foot on the first step, Anthony yanked Betty Jean out onto the platform.

"Get the fuck out here!"

Face first, she fell and cut her lip. Licking the warm blood, she became outraged and tried to kick him.

"Motherfucker, you done messed my face up! How the hell am I..."

Anthony took his fist and cold cocked her. *Whop*! Blood flew out of her mouth.

"Now shut the fuck up bitch!"

He got her up to her feet and pushed her down the fire escape. Holding onto the railing for dear life, she broke her fall. Seeing that she didn't have a choice, she went down the steps with Anthony right behind her. When she got to the last step, he pushed her down to the ground. Brenda and Carl burst out laughing. Betty Jean laid there moaning and groining.

"Man why you so hard on that trick?" Carl asked.

Anthony jumped down to the ground.

"Man I can't stand this fake ass, white wannabe; I'm going to Howard U bitch."

James Jr. attempted to assist Betty Jean, but Anthony wasn't having it.

"Man, don't do it. I'm telling you...don't do it."

He noticed Anthony had one hand behind his back; no doubt on his gun. So, he stopped dead in his tracks.

"Man, why you tripping on this trick for? She's used to this kind of treatment," Carl said laughing.

"Man she's just a child. She's just a confused little girl."

Anthony stepped to him.

"We didn't ask this country trick bitch to come here. She came to us. Now get to steppin'."

Brenda started walking up the walkway to the gate. Blood was all over his pretty dashiki dress. And amazingly, he didn't miss a beat with his stilettos on. Not once did he complain about the mess that unfolded in Big Moe's house. All he knew was to take the trash out and get back to work.

Leading out to the dumpster in the alley, they all followed him. However, Betty Jean was having trouble walking. Reason being, she had a monkey on her back. She fell repeatedly, causing everyone, except for Anthony, to be several feet ahead of her. Anthony stayed behind her like white on rice.

"Look bitch...if you don't stop falling, I'm going to bust a cap in that pale ass of yours. Now get up!"

Kicking her several times, she staggered to her feet and continued down the alley. Once Brenda got to the dumpster, with little effort, he lifted the dead body high above his head and threw it in like a trash bag. Stepping back, he finally took a good look at his bloody outfit.

"Oh good grief, look at me... I'm a mess."

James Jr. became deranged at what he just did.

"Hey! Come on! You can't do that! You just can't throw her in there like that! You can't leave her like that! She's a human being!"

Being tired of his mouth, Carl grabbed him by his shirt and hit him in the stomach. The punch was so hard, James Jr. threw up and fell to his knees.

Brenda smiled and blew Carl a big kiss.

"Thank you daddy."

"No problem sweet cheeks."

Betty Jean and Anthony finally reach the rest of them.

Betty Jean was out of it. Her mind was gone. She was in so much pain. She didn't care what they did to her, so as long as she got her fix. It no longer registered that her mother was dead anymore. She didn't even notice James Jr. on the ground in pain.

"Can you help me…can you help a sister out…. I'll do anything. I'll even let y'all fuck me in my ass."

Brenda looked at her and laughed.

"Hello…excuse you honey…first of all, you are *not a* sister. And secondly, I'm strictly dickey; ok…*don't* get it twisted sugar."

At that moment, Betty Jean bent over and upchuck something terrible. Brenda stared at her. With a little sympathy, he reached into his bra and pulled out a small plastic bag. He tossed it at her.

"Here bitch take this. And don't bring your ass around here no more."

Betty Jean tried to catch the bag of dope, but it landed on the ground. As she was about to pick it up, Carl ran over and snatched it. Tossing it from hand to hand, he threw it up the alley toward the garages. In a panic, Betty Jean ran after it while falling several times. Anthony took off running after her. When he reached her, he pushed her down, to prevent her from getting the bag of dope first. When he got to the bag, he picked it up and threw it even farther up the alley. Except for James Jr., they all laughed.

Betty Jean saw their reaction, but dare not move a muscle. She laid there on the ground, but like a hawk, saw where the dope landed and kept her eyes on the prize. She cut her eyes over at Anthony as he walked passed her. Not sure of what they would do next, she just laid there.

"What the hell are you waiting for…go get the bag bitch!" Brenda yelled.

The men laughed their butts off. While they were laughing, Betty Jean got up and ran for the dope. When she reached it, she didn't pick it up immediately. First, she looked down at it then back to Brenda and his crew. She looked at them with sad puppy-dog eyes. It was as if she was waiting for permission to pick up her food. When she saw them surrounding James Jr., she grabbed the dope. Without looking back, she laughed and skipped up the alley into the dark. In vain, James Jr. called her, but she didn't hear him. She didn't hear his cry as the men beat the hell out of him. She didn't hear the sound of a firecracker going off. She didn't see the flash of light for a split second. Betty Jean disappeared into the heat of the night.

PART TEN

32

OWN IN THE Bayou colored folk could only afford but so much, let alone a nice funeral. Still, when they heard that the good Lord had called one of his children home, they came to pay their respect. More so it was like an event. And that's the way Joe Carter treated it. He did what any good husband would have done: gave his wife a very nice funeral. She went out in style. Lilly Mae will be laid to rest in a beautiful, white casket. Pink Roses and white Lillie's adorn it. Huge bouquets of flowers were placed all around the church. Family members and friends cried and comfort each other.

The Carter family sat on the front row quietly as people paid their respects. After hearing the news about her daughter and granddaughter, Pearl suffered a massive heart attack again. She was placed back into the hospital. James Jr., who was left for dead by a single gunshot wound to the back of the head, was wheeled up to the casket by his father. It was obvious that God wasn't finished with him yet, because out of nowhere, some old drunk dude (no doubt an angel in disguise) found him in a pool of blood. Next thing you knew, the police and fire department arrived upon the scene.

As he paid his respects, he heard a girl's voice that almost sounded like Betty Jean.

"Daddy, who's going to take care of us and grandma now that mama, is gone?"

Slowly, he turned his head and saw the Carter family sitting on the front row. Staring, he saw Joe patting Jackie's leg and moving his hand up and down her thigh.

"I am baby-girl. I'm going to take care of you all. And *you* are going to take care of daddy," he said without looking at her.

Jackie smiled at her father.

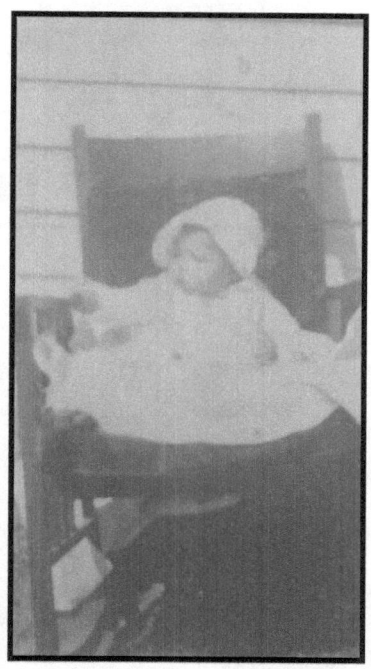

Betty Jean (2 years old with her mother)

Betty Jean -aka- Cotton-top (6 months old)

Betty Jean (18 months old

Betty Jean (2 years old with her mother)

Betty Jean (3 years old with an authentic
Charlie McCarthy Doll)

Betty Jean (7 years old)

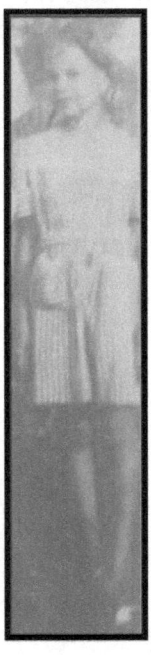

Betty Jean (8 years old)

Betty Jean (16 years old)

Betty Jean (age 18)

Betty Jean (age 56)

www.ingramcontent.com/pod-product-compliance
Lightning Source LLC
Chambersburg PA
CBHW021212130626
46554CB00004B/1195